Invitation to Law & Society

The Chicago Series in Law and Society
Edited by John M. Conley and Lynn Mather

KITTY CALAVITA

Invitation to Law & Society

An Introduction to the Study of Real Law

SECOND EDITION

The University of Chicago Press Chicago and London

KITTY CALAVITA is chancellor's professor emerita in the Departments of Criminology, Law and Society, and Sociology at the University of California, Irvine. She is the author, most recently, of *Appealing to Justice: Prisoner Grievances, Rights, and Carceral Logic.*

The University of Chicago Press, Chicago 60637
The University of Chicago Press, Ltd., London
© 2010, 2016 by The University of Chicago
All rights reserved. Published 2016.
Printed in the United States of America

25 24 23 22 21 20 19 18 17 16
1 2 3 4 5

ISBN-13: 978-0-226-29644-9 (cloth)
ISBN-13: 978-0-226-29658-6 (paper)
ISBN-13: 978-0-226-29661-6 (e-book)

DOI: 10.7208/chicago/
9780226296616.001.0001

Library of Congress Cataloging-in-Publication Data

Calavita, Kitty, author.
 Invitation to law & society : an introduction to the study of real law / Kitty Calavita. — Second edition.
  pages cm — (The Chicago series in law and society)
  ISBN 978-0-226-29644-9 (cloth : alk. paper) —
ISBN 978-0-226-29658-6 (pbk. : alk. paper) —
ISBN 978-0-226-29661-6 (ebook) 1. Sociological jurisprudence. 2. Law—Social aspects—United States. I. Title. II.Title: Invitation to law and society. III. Series: Chicago series in law and society.
  K370.C35 2016
  340′.115—dc23
                                        2015018041

♾ This paper meets the requirements of ANSI/NISO Z39.48-1992 (Permanence of Paper).

For Zellie and Luca

Contents

Preface to the Second Edition

The first edition of this book was published in 2010, just as I retired from full-time teaching and moved to Berkeley, California. Among the many changes this brought, I became directly involved in my local community in ways I never had before. The consequence is that I have met people I never would have encountered, have had experiences unlike any in my academic life, and have sometimes undergone dramatic shifts in my social location.

Among the most powerful of these experiences, in 2012, I became a Court Appointed Special Advocate (CASA) for a young girl, Akira (pseudonym), who—together with her sister—had recently been reunited with her birth mother after years in foster care. I figured that being a CASA would draw from my knowledge of law and sociology, and it was consistent with my concerns for social justice and child welfare. What I hadn't figured on was how powerfully the experience would affect me, both intellectually and personally. My CASA assignment has ended, but I remain close to the family and continue to see them regularly. This friendship has exposed me directly to the chaotic life experiences and daily challenges of those who live in poverty, as this mom and her two daughters move from unaffordable apartment to unaffordable apartment, to motels, to SROs, and—periodically—to the street.

At the same time, I was given the opportunity to teach sociology at San Quentin State Prison through the Prison University Project. This program offers the only in-class, accredited college courses in California prisons, and it provides those who complete the course sequence with a degree equivalent to that of a two-year community college. My three semesters of teaching San Quentin prisoners have been some of the most rewarding teaching I have ever done. Not only are the students excited to learn and hardworking, but they bring unique perspectives because of their life experiences. I will never forget one older African American prisoner who, at our last class, said how much he had enjoyed sociology, especially the concept of social structure and its links to race and class inequality. But he added, "When I get out of here, I'm going to have to act as if it doesn't apply to me."

These friendships and interactions with people who are in my community, but who are in so many ways socially and physically removed from it, have given me a new and deeper appreciation of how real law works. They have brought me into the machinery of poverty law, housing discrimination, welfare accounting, and traffic warrants, teaching me their Kafkaesque particularities. More broadly, they have viscerally brought home for me the dominant force of law in the lives not just of the prisoners I teach, but also of Akira and her family and millions more like them. In this second edition, I have included illustrations of this profound penetration of law into the lives of the poor, for example in my discussion in chapter 2 of the St. Vincent de Paul Homeless and Caring Court.

I have made a few other changes as well, more directly related to advances in the scholarship. Since I wrote the first edition of this book, the law and society field has continued to expand and diversify. It is more than ever true that diversity and innovation are among our field's great strengths. It would be impossible to capture all the law and society developments over the past five years in this slim volume, and I have not attempted to do so. This book is meant to be not an overview of the field, but rather a sampling of some of the questions posed by law and society scholars, a taste of some of the ways we think about law, and an invitation to join us in conversation. What I have also done in this new edition is update the many illustrations and anecdotes that I use to clarify concepts and theories, so they may more directly resonate with the contemporary reader.

I have added a new chapter too—"Reflecting on Law's Image: An Inward Turn?"—in which I introduce the reader to the law and cultural studies movement. Some of the themes discussed there will be familiar, as they make brief appearances throughout the book. Others will be new, some radically so. Many scholars in this movement identify more with the humanities than with social science, and their methods and foci reflect this. Here, I provide you with a few examples of this broad movement and question the suggestion that it represents, as some have argued, a turning away from the kind of political engagement that inspired so many early law and society scholars.

A number of people have read and provided feedback on this new material. I especially want to thank my friend and sometimes coauthor Val Jenness, who has read it all more than once and has provided her input throughout. In addition to her keen insights, she is far more up on popular culture than I, and I rely on her to keep me up to speed. My former University of California, Irvine, colleagues and friends Susan Coutin and Sora Han read the new chapter 8, and I am grateful to them for their suggestions for additional scholarship and illustrations. As always, I continue to benefit from the scholarship of colleagues both near and far. I hope I have adequately captured the scholarly contributions of those I have included here and apologize in advance for errors of omission or commission—the former being a particular hazard in such a brief work as this. Finally, I thank Akira and her family and the many San Quentin prisoners who have allowed me into their lives and have taught me so much these past few years.

Acknowledgments

I could not have written this book without the encouragement, friendship, and feedback of many people. While my debts over the years are too many to name all of them here, several deserve special mention. Lynn Mather and John Conley, editors of the University of Chicago Press's Chicago Series in Law and Society, encouraged me in the project from the beginning, and I have counted on their support and insightful suggestions all along the way. John Tryneski, social science editor at the Press, has been everything an author could wish for, and more. Not only did he support me at every turn; he also spurred me on to write this second edition.

The Department of Criminology, Law and Society at University of California, Irvine, and the School of Social Ecology generously facilitated my scholarship over the years. Colleagues and friends have also been important to me in the course of conceptualizing this project. My colleagues at Irvine are that rare breed: intellectually stimulating, generous with their time, and—here's the clincher—*fun*. Henry Pontell and I go way back, we wrote together on the savings and loan crisis (harbinger of the more recent financial meltdown), and I have benefited from his friendship, smarts, and biting wit. Susan Coutin's work on Central American immigration to the United States and, earlier, on the sanctuary movement continues to be an inspiration, as she herself is to her many admirers. Carroll Seron has been an esteemed friend and colleague for decades, and she is one of the most formidable members of our department. Carroll read and provided me with predictably incisive feedback on the first edition of this book. Val Jenness, close friend and departmental colleague, also read large sections of the book and as usual gave me invaluable suggestions. Her knowledge of the literature is broad ranging and profound, and I can depend on her to tell me of that central piece I missed or that analysis that was just a little off. I would be remiss, though, if I didn't mention another of Val's key contributions. She tries her best to make up for my appalling deficit of pop culture knowledge and has offered me entertaining tidbits and racy examples for which the reader will no doubt be especially grateful.

Peggy Nelson, sociologist at Middlebury College, has the gift of C. Wright Mills's "sociological imagination" to an uncanny degree, and she has shared her many insights with me over the course of our thirty-year friendship. Our fields of specialization don't overlap, but no matter. She is always there in the background of my life, making a difference.

Of course I could not have written this book without the prolific efforts of hundreds of law and society scholars over the past several decades. Some I have included in these chapters, but there are many others, too numerous to cite. It is the dynamism and energetic intellectual exchange of the field that inspired me to write this short invitation. I can only hope I do that dynamism and excitement justice in the pages that follow.

Bill Chambliss died in early 2014. He was my dissertation chair more years ago than I'd like to admit. His cut-to-the-chase intellect and keen eye for the contradictions of the political economy, and of the human condition itself, influenced me profoundly way back then and still do. His influence can be found throughout this book, although I can't pretend to have captured that unique mix of eloquence and creativity that was his alone. Over the years, Bill represented a model of scholarship to which I aspire. He was a dear friend, and I miss him more than words can say.

The greatest indulgence of all at a time like this is that authors get to express their gratitude to partners, children, and other loved ones. I dedicate this edition as I did the first one, to my precious grandchildren, Zellie and Luca. They bring me unbelievable joy. My two sons, Joe and Marco, and their partners, Jill and Michelle, are also a source of joy—and I have to say it, pride—and a kind of faith that social justice may yet prevail. Finally, my husband, Nico, deserves a medal for his patience and forbearance during the writing of this book, but also for the times he made me stop writing and go with him for a walk by the shore.

CHAPTER ONE Introduction

Everyone has some idea what lawyers do. And most people have at least heard of criminologists. But who knows what "law and society" is? A lawyer friend of mine, a really smart guy, asks me regularly, "What exactly do you people *do*?" Once when I was at the annual meeting of the Law and Society Association, my taxi driver was making the usual idle conversation and inquired what I was in town for. I told him I was attending the Law and Society Association's annual meeting. His interest suddenly aroused, he turned to face me and asked with some urgency, "I've been wondering, when is the best time to plant a lawn?"

I write this book as an invitation to a field that should be a household word but obviously isn't. Peter Berger's (1963) *Invitation to Sociology* is one of my favorite books, and I have shamelessly copycatted it for my title and for the concept of this book. I want to offer, like Berger, an open invitation to those who do not know this territory, by mapping out its main boundary lines and contours and explaining some of its local customs and ways of thinking. This mapping and explaining is more difficult in law and society than in some other academic territories, because its boundaries are not well marked and because it encourages immigration, drawing in people from many other realms. The population includes sociologists, historians, political scientists, anthropologists, psychologists, economists, lawyers, and criminologists, among others. Like the pluralistic legal cultures we sometimes study, our diversity is both a challenge and enriching.

First, a disclaimer. This is not meant to be a comprehensive overview or textbook introduction to law and society. I am bound to antagonize some of my colleagues in this selective sketch of the field, as I speak in the language I know best—sociology—and inevitably favor some approaches and just as inevitably neglect others. In addition to mostly "speaking" sociology, my primary language is English. This means that besides slighting much that is of interest in political science, economics, and other fields, I include here only a tiny fraction of the excellent works written in languages other than English. I cannot possibly do justice to the whole rich terrain of our field in this small volume, and I do not intend it to be an overview of law and society's many theories and methodologies. Instead, I hope that this book's limitation will be its strength, as an accessible and concise presentation of a way of thinking about law. It is meant for undergraduate and graduate students and their professors, but it is also written for my lawyer friend who can't figure us out, for my taxi driver, and even for an occasional colleague, because it is always entertaining to see others attempt to describe what we do.

In the pages that follow, I will try to construct a picture of (some of) our ways of thinking by presenting a few of law and society's overarching themes, arranged roughly as chapters. There is some slippage and overlap among the chapters, and the divisions should not be taken too seriously. What I am after here is a composite picture, a gestalt of a way of thinking, not a comprehensive inventory. I am treating this as a conversation—albeit a one-sided one—and will keep you, the reader, in my mind's eye at all times. Partly in the interests of accessibility and a free-flowing conversation, I have sacrificed theoretical inclusiveness and instead provide many concrete examples and anecdotes from everyday life.

Peter Berger (1963, 1) started his *Invitation to Sociology* by lamenting that there are plenty of jokes about psychologists but none about sociologists—not because there is nothing funny about them but because sociology is not part of the "popular imagination." Well, law and society faces a double difficulty. When people don't confuse us with experts in the care and maintenance of grass, they are likely to think we are practicing lawyers, which is—judging from the number of lawyer jokes in circulation—the world's funniest profession. Complicating matters, some of us are *in fact* lawyers, but not the funny kind.

The law and society mentality is broader than the specific themes I introduce here. And some of these themes are mutually contradictory and represent conflicting visions of the field. But just as all creatures are greater than the sum of their parts, there is a law and society perspective that transcends its sometimes self-contradictory themes.

One way to get at this perspective is to contrast it with how people ordinarily think about law. I do not want to oversimplify here because people have many different views of law. As we will see later, the same people think of law differently according to whether they are getting a parking ticket, suing a neighbor, negotiating a divorce, or being sworn in as a witness to a crime. But most people tend to hold up some idealized version of law as the general principle, and individual experiences that deviate from that version are thought of as, well, deviations. Law in the abstract somehow manages to remain above the fray, while concrete, everyday experiences with law—either our own or those of others we might hear about—are local perversions chalked up to human fallibilities and foibles. This view of law was brought home to me powerfully when I saw a bumper sticker on a pickup truck that read, "Obey gravity. It's the law." I cannot be sure, but I think the point was to underscore the inevitability and black-and-white nature of law, in a sarcastic jab at moral relativists. Like gravity, law is *Law*.

Even when we are cynical about the law, this cynicism seems not to tarnish the abstract ideal of Law—the magisterial, unperverted, gravity-like sort. Consider jury service. If you have ever served in a jury pool or on a jury, you might have been aghast at the shortcomings of some of your peers, who might, in your view, have been less than intellectually equipped to wrestle with the complex issues being presented (and they no doubt were at the same time scrutinizing you). But, if you are like me, it is hard not to feel a certain awe for the majesty of the process and the aura it projects. The Law—with a capital "L"—in this idealized version resides in a realm beyond the failings of its human participants and survives all manner of contaminating experiences.

Law and society turns this conventional view on its head. For all law is a social product, and the abstract ideal is itself an artifact of society. Many interesting questions follow: How does real law actually operate? How are law and everyday life intertwined? Where does law as abstraction come from, and what purposes does it serve? What can we learn from the disparity between abstract law and real law? And why is the idealized version of law so resilient even in the face of extensive contrary experience?

Law and society also turns on its head the jurisprudential view of law usually associated with jurists and often taught in law school. This view approaches law as a more or less coherent set of principles and rules that relate to each other according to a particular logic or dynamic. The object of study in jurisprudence is this internal logic and the rules and principles that circulate within it. According to this approach, law comprises a self-contained system that, with some notable exceptions, works like a syllogism, with abstract principles and legal precedents combined with the concrete facts of the issue at hand leading deductively to legal outcomes. While this model has been updated to allow for the intervention of practical considerations in judicial decision making and some concessions to social context, this lawyerly view of law still dominates law school training and jurisprudential thought. That's why U.S. Supreme Court Chief Justice John Roberts (2005, A10) could say at his Senate confirmation hearing: "Judges are like umpires. Umpires don't make the rules, they apply them. . . . If I am confirmed . . . I will fully and fairly analyze the legal arguments that are presented." Despite the famous quote long ago by one of America's most noted jurists, Oliver Wendell Holmes Jr. (1881, 1), that "the life of the law has not been logic: it has been experience," the view of law as a closed system of rules and principles that fit together logically has proved just as resilient in many legal circles as the layperson's idealization.

So, jurisprudence is mostly devoted to examining what takes place inside the box of legal logic. Law and society takes exactly the opposite approach—it examines the influence on law of forces *outside* the box. If the issue is free speech rights in the United States, jurisprudence might catalog judicial decisions pertaining to the First Amendment and trace the logical relationship between these precedents and some present case. Instead, a law and society scholar might probe the historical origins of the American notion of free speech and expose the political (i.e., extralegal, "outside the box") nature of First Amendment judicial decision making. David Kairys (1998), for example, shows us that the common assumption that a free speech right emerged full blown from the First Amendment is a myth; that the right we associate with the First Amendment today was the product of political activism in the first part of the twentieth century, especially by labor unions; that since then it has been alternately expanded and retrenched according to political pressure and ideological climate;

and, last but by no means least, that Americans' myths about the origins and scope of our free speech right have powerful impacts on our assumptions about the exceptional quality of American democracy. So, judicial decision making on issues of free speech—in fact, the very concept of free speech—is the product of social and political context. And our entrenched mythical abstractions about free speech, while factually inaccurate, have profound sociopolitical effects. The broader law and society point here is that law, far from a closed system of logic, is tightly interconnected with society.

But we can go farther. Because not only are law and society interconnected; they are not really separate entities at all. From the law and society perspective, law is everywhere, not just in Supreme Court pronouncements and congressional statutes. Every aspect of our lives is permeated with law, from the moment we rise in the morning from our certified mattresses (mine newly purchased, under a ten-year warranty, and certified by the U.S. Consumer Product Safety Commission, the U.S. Fire Administration, and the Sleep Products Safety Council, and accompanied by stern warnings not to remove the label "under penalty of law") to our fair-trade coffee and NAFTA (North American Free Trade Agreement) grapefruit, to our ride to school in the car-pool lane on state-regulated highways, to our copyrighted textbooks, and so on, for the rest of the day. But in the form of legal consciousness, law is also found in less obvious places, like the mental reasoning we engage in when we are pondering what to do about our neighbor's noisy dog. Law so infuses daily life, is so much part of the mundane machinery that makes social life possible, that "law" and "society" are almost redundant. Far from magisterial or above the fray, law is marked by all the frailties and hubris of humankind.

Not long ago, I read a book about the imperfect nature of medical science. Surgeon and author Dr. Atul Gawande introduces this provocative volume with a personal anecdote that I quote at some length because it is both powerful and pertinent to our study of law. He writes:

> I was once on trauma duty when a young man about twenty years old was rolled in, shot in the buttock. His pulse, blood pressure, and breathing were all normal. . . . I found the entrance wound in his right cheek, a neat, red, half-inch hole. I could find no exit

wound. No other injuries were evident. . . . [But] when I threaded a urinary catheter into him, bright red blood flowed from his bladder. . . . The conclusion was obvious. The blood meant that the bullet had gone inside him, through his rectum and his bladder. . . . Major blood vessels, his kidney, other sections of bowel may have been hit as well. He needed surgery, I said, and we had to go now. He saw the look in my eyes, the nurses already packing him up to move, and he nodded[,] . . . putting himself in our hands. . . .

In the operating room, the anesthesiologist put him under. We made a fast, deep slash down the middle of his abdomen, from his rib cage to his pubis. We grabbed retractors and pulled him open. And what we found inside was . . . nothing. No blood. No hole in the bladder. No hole in the rectum. No bullet. We peeked under the drapes at the urine coming out of the catheter. It was normal now, clear yellow. It didn't have even a tinge of blood anymore. . . . All of this was odd, to say the least. After almost an hour more of fruitless searching, however, there seemed nothing to do for him but sew him up. A couple days later we got yet another abdominal X ray. This one revealed a bullet lodged inside the right upper quadrant of his abdomen. We had no explanation for any of this—how a half-inch-long lead bullet had gotten from his buttock to his upper belly without injuring anything, why it hadn't appeared on the previous X rays, or where the blood we had seen had come from. Having already done more harm than the bullet had, however, we finally left it and the young man alone. . . . Except for our gash, he turned out fine.

Medicine is, I have found, a strange and in many ways disturbing business. The stakes are high, the liberties taken tremendous. We drug people, put needles and tubes into them, manipulate their chemistry, biology, and physics, lay them unconscious and open their bodies up to the world. We do so out of an abiding confidence in our know-how as a profession. What you find when you get in close, however—close enough to see the furrowed brows, the doubts and missteps, the failures as well as the successes—is how messy, uncertain, and also surprising medicine turns out to be.

The thing that still startles me is how fundamentally human an endeavor it is. Usually, when we think about medicine and its remarkable abilities, what comes to mind is the science and all it has given us to fight sickness and misery: the tests, the machines, the drugs, the procedures. And without question, these are at the center of virtually everything medicine achieves. But we rarely see how it all actually works. You have a cough that won't go away—and then? It's not science you call upon but a doctor. A doctor with good days and bad days. A doctor with a weird laugh and a bad haircut. A doctor with three other patients to see and, inevitably, gaps in what he knows and skills he's still trying to learn. (Gawande 2002, 3–5)

A Supreme Court intern told a colleague of mine that once he had been "behind the scenes" at the Court, he "could never teach constitutional law with a 'straight face' again. This insider argued that the reality of the Chief Justice wearing his slippers inside the Court demystified the Constitution" (Brigham 1987, 4). A little like Dr. Gawande, who routinely sees the weird laughs and bad haircuts of the real doctors who put flesh and blood on the abstraction of "medicine," this budding law and society scholar had peered behind the curtains and seen the Wizard of Law at the controls in his slippers.

At some level, law and medicine are fundamentally different. After all, medicine has provided us with "ways to fight sickness and misery." To cite just one example, over the past four decades enormous strides have been made in curing cancer; many of those afflicted with the disease now live healthy lives when they once would have died of it. In contrast, we have arguably made little progress in fighting crime and are no closer to a cure for the injustices of the legal system than we were four decades ago. Medicine—its theory and its practice—is affected and shaped by sociocultural forces and human fallibility, but at its core it is oriented toward physiological realities. Instead, law is a social construction through and through. This means that its limitations are the mirror image of society itself and are not only—or even mainly—about missing knowledge or skills not yet learned.

In other ways, though, Dr. Gawande's depiction of medicine applies to law as well. Both law and medicine enjoy almost mythic status. Like the confidence that doctors have in their own know-how and that patients bestow on them as they allow themselves to be drugged, intubated, and sliced open, law too benefits from and demands complete authority. The police officer who stops me for speeding is likely to find that I am as compliant and submissive as a patient awaiting surgery. And there is an eerie, graphic similarity between the patient strapped to a gurney for an operation meant to save her life and the death row prisoner in the execution chamber ready for his lethal injection. In both cases, we tend to put blind faith in the fundamental legitimacy of the enterprise.

The aura of infallibility and authority that surrounds both medicine and law survives compelling evidence to the contrary and even blistering critique. There are probably no two professions that can elicit more passionate attacks than that of lawyer and doctor. At your next social gathering, tell a story about some incompetent doctor, miscarriage of justice, or greedy lawyer, and you are bound to hear a chorus of amens, followed by more stories. But the myths and auras of law and medicine mysteriously endure. And for all the horror stories we share with each other, we rarely examine in any systematic way what those stories add up to, what their common elements are, or why they persist. The field of law and society is exciting precisely because it does this and more, probing "how it all actually works."

Here is a brief preview of what follows. The next chapter provides a glimpse of research about the links between the kinds of law in a society and the social, economic, and cultural contours of that society. There is disagreement among scholars about what those links consist of and how definitive they are. But the broader, formative idea in law and society scholarship is that law—far from an autonomous entity residing somewhere above the fray of society—coincides with the shape of society and is part and parcel of its fray. Chapter 3 takes up the related idea that law is not just shaped to the everyday life of a society but also permeates it, even at times and in places where it may not at first glance appear to be. As we'll see, the probing law and society scholar turns up law in some unlikely places, such as in our speech patterns and, even more unlikely, in a squirrel in a chimney in small-town Nebraska. Chapter 4 describes research that documents one important aspect of this interpenetration of law and society, having to do with race. Providing a brief synopsis of what is called critical race theory, this chapter traces the kaleidoscopic color of law across many venues, from early pseudoscientific theories of immigrant inferiority to contemporary criminal justice profiling. After that, chapter 5 turns to a discussion of legal pluralism, which focuses on the fact that in any given social location there are almost always multiple legal systems operating simultaneously. Sometimes they nest comfortably inside each other like those Russian dolls of decreasing size that stack neatly together; sometimes, they are an awkward fit; and in a few rare cases, cracks are exposed between the layers so that some groups and institutions fall out of accountability altogether. In chapter 6, I engage a canonical concern for law and society scholarship: the gap between the law-on-the-books and the law-in-action. Noting that the law as it is written and advertised to the public is often quite different from the way it looks in practice, law and society scholars have long had an interest in studying that gap. It is not only a powerful lens for understanding the various dimensions and stages of law; like a broken promise, it reveals a lot too about the institutions or other social entities that made the promise and cannot or will not deliver on it. Chapter 7 wrestles with the question of law's role in social change. There we will encounter scholarship that interrogates the limits of law to advance real change, as well as works that highlight law's progressive potential. Returning to the theme of chapter 2 that societies get the types of legal forms and laws that they "deserve" (and vice versa), we will see the challenges of trying to upend entrenched social arrangements using the lever of law. The final substantive chapter, chapter 8, segues from this focus on the possibilities for progressive social change and sociolegal scholars' increasing recognition of the stubborn challenges facing reform efforts to examine the "cultural turn." Some have said this turn represents an inward focus in the face of political disillusionments, but as we will see, the reality is more complicated, for the cultural turn is every bit as variegated as the rest of the field.

One final disclaimer before I begin. When I talk about *real* law in this book's subtitle, I clearly do not have in mind laws relating to real estate or other property. Less obviously, I do not intend to confine my discussion to the actual practice or enforcement of law as opposed to its texts or written dictates (the topic of chapter 6), as some of my colleagues might surmise. The gap implied by my reference to *real* law is far broader than this. It is the gap between the popular and jurisprudential version of law as reified and gravity-like and the actual life of the law (on the books or in action), which is wholly social. The *reality of law* is that it is a sociocultural product, whether that product is formal legal texts or police tactics, images of law in popular culture, or the shouted rules of a pickup basketball game. It is this social reality that I have in mind when I talk about real law.

Peter Berger (1963) wrote that if you are the kind of person who likes to look behind closed doors and, by implication, cannot resist snooping into your friend's personal effects while house-sitting, then you have the right aptitude for sociology. People who are drawn to law and society might also be curious about their friends' hidden lives and what they might find by snooping around their houses. But our curiosity is aroused even further by questions like why snooping is considered wrong in the first place, and which unwritten code it violates in our society and why. And if snooping in a friend's house might reveal some dicey secrets about his or her personal life, snooping around a society's written and unwritten laws to expose the secrets behind their public mythology reaps rewards that are in equal measure subversive and thrilling.

CHAPTER TWO Types of Society, Types of Law

Two middle-aged friends of mine are deeply in love and want to get married. But there is one issue that has caused tears and recriminations, and that is the dreaded prenuptial contract. Their love is blinding in its intensity, but now they have to imagine what happens in case they get divorced; they feel their love in their very souls and in the chemistry between them, but now they must enter into a business contract. Their intellect tells them a prenup is a reasonable thing to do. The angst it produces underscores the tension between romance and the ultimately more seductive reason.

Public television pundit and *New York Times* op-ed writer David Brooks (2015) recently wrote a column about online dating sites and the clash between self-interested rationality and falling in love. He argued that while these sites result in much dating, they rarely result in lasting relationships. "Online dating," he said, "is fascinating because it is more or less the opposite of its object: love." To fall in love, Brooks argued, people must move from a rational mind-set that calculates the other's physical and social assets to an open mind-set that takes "the enchantment leap." He continued, "The people involved move from selfishness to service, from prudent thinking to poetic thinking, from a state of selection to a state of need, from relying on conscious thinking to relying on their own brilliant emotions" (A25).

The prenup and the stress it is causing my friends, and the contradictions of looking for poetic love through calculated selection, remind me of Max Weber's (1954) theory that in modern capitalist societies, rationality permeates all realms of human activity, including those that were once the province of other motivations. Rationality, Weber wrote, increasingly displaces tradition, religion, emotion, and other such forces as a primary motivator for human behavior. It's the clash between romance and rationality that makes the prenup so stressful and that limits the romantic potential of online dating services, with their photo galleries of available mates.

For Weber, as reason and calculation increasingly motivate all human activity with the advent of modern society, law too becomes more rational. What he meant by this is that modern law is driven by logic and calculation rather than by irrational forces like oracles, tradition, or emotion. In the process of rationalization, law also becomes more functionally insulated from other institutions, such as religion or politics, and is therefore more "autonomous."

None of this is a coincidence. Instead, for Weber (1958), rationalization emerged with Calvinism—specifically, the Calvinist principle of predestination. Imagine for a moment that you are a Calvinist who believes you are predestined by God from before birth to be a chosen one or to be damned for eternity. If chosen, you will spend your life on Earth blessed and live an afterlife at the hand of God; if not, you will have a miserable life and, worse, a miserable eternity. In Weber's view, this late sixteenth- and early seventeenth-century Calvinist idea of predestination produced an intolerable level of anxiety. In part to alleviate that anxiety, Calvinists searched for signs of being chosen. In looking for signs, they produced the very signs of the chosen life—hard work and the accumulation of wealth—they were looking for. This hard work, accumulation of wealth, and frugal lifestyle that were taken as signs (presumably subliminally, since God kept his decisions to himself) were compatible with the emergence of capitalism, and all of the above were accompanied and facilitated by a calculating, reasoning mentality. So, there is an "elective affinity," to use Weber's term, between Calvinism, capitalism, and rationality. As rationality became the organizing principle of modern society, law too was rationalized. The broader point is that, for Weber, the nature of law and the nature of society evolve in tandem through elective affinity.

The idea that different types of society produce, or at least coincide with, different types of law is a foundational element of the law and society framework but is at odds with commonly held notions of law's transcendence. Modern Western views of law as transcendent can be traced back to Plato and Aristotle, and to St. Thomas Aquinas, who, despite their considerable differences and the fourteen centuries separating Aquinas from the Greek philosophers, all argued that law ideally reflects some universal morality, some divine natural order.

Hence, the concept of natural law, and, as on the bumper sticker I mentioned a few pages ago, law's kinship with other natural phenomena like gravity. In book 3 of *Politics* Aristotle wrote, "He who bids the law rule may be deemed to bid God and reason." For both Aristotle and Plato, since law is ideally the tangible expression of morality arrived at through reason, the whole ensemble is God-given, universal, and natural. Obedience to just law is the highest virtue and is indispensable to a just social order. St. Thomas Aquinas also believed that law—to the extent that it is law and not simply an unjust command—is a creation of God. Later surfacing in John Locke's influential ideas about inalienable human rights, the natural law approach is hard-pressed to explain the enormous variation in legal systems historically and cross-culturally—unless we're willing to take the convenient but dubious position that the Western legal system is natural and all others are arbitrary cultural constructions.

While the a priori, natural appearance of law may be central to its legitimacy, sociolegal scholars have long theorized that legal systems are no less social (that is, human) products than the economic systems they are often linked to. Evolutionary social theorists such as Henry Maine, Émile Durkheim, Karl Marx, and Max Weber posited that legal systems develop in concert with socioeconomic systems, changing form and becoming more complex over time. According to this thinking, the modern Western legal system represents the current stage in a linear evolution and corresponds precisely to the social and economic forms that emerged with it.

Henry Maine (1861/2008), writing a generation before Weber, had the idea that legal systems go through definitive stages, from status to contract. He reasoned that the primary unit of social organization in ancient societies was the clan or extended family, while in modern societies the individual is the primary unit. In the feudal period, when landed gentry ruled the countryside of England and serfs toiled on the gentry's land, both statuses (gentry and serf) were inherited. In this social system, people saw themselves as, and were treated as, members of a social class and parts of a family, but rarely as separate, independent individuals. As the social order evolved, the free association of individuals and free agreements among them became primary, with the family relegated to a supporting role.

Coinciding with this development in social organization, law shifted away from dealing with people as members of specific clans and with particular *statuses* to dealing with individuals with certain rights, obligations, and *contracts*. In fact, Maine thought this was the defining quality of modern ("progressive") civilization. In *Ancient Law* he wrote, "We may say that the movement of the progressive societies has hitherto been a movement *from Status to Contract*" (Maine 1861/2008, 86, emphasis in original). Maine was short on empirical data, and at least one sociolegal scholar has dismissed him as an "armchair scholar" who was "factually wrong" (Sutton 2001, 30).

Not the least of Maine's problems was a kind of naive optimism about modern law, stripped of any status biases, such as those based on race, class, or gender. I read in the newspaper that in central Florida they arrest (mostly African American) children as young as six years old for disruptive behavior in the classroom, handcuffing them and booking them for a felony. In Mississippi, a twelve-year-old boy was arrested for disturbing the peace in a school hallway after a brief shoving match (Fields and Emshwiller 2014). In Texas, a fourteen-year-old girl received a prison sentence of up to seven years for pushing a hall monitor at her high school (Herbert 2007a, 2007b). Another newspaper article reports that a seventeen-year-old boy in Georgia was sentenced to ten years in prison for consensual oral sex with a fifteen-year-old girl at a New Year's Eve party (Goodman 2007). A front-page story in the same newspaper revealed that employers who subject their workers to unsafe conditions resulting in accident and injury are not being prosecuted (Labaton 2007). And a 2013 PBS *Frontline* program titled "The Untouchables" noted that "Wall Street's leaders escaped prosecution for fraud" that brought the world financial system to the brink of collapse in 2008. Discrepancies like these, between African American children arrested at school and financial titans who appear to be immune to prosecution, have led most contemporary sociolegal scholars to conclude that status—or something like it—still matters.

But Maine had his fans. Émile Durkheim (1893/1964) borrowed some of his ideas when, writing in France at the turn of the twentieth century, he argued that homogeneous societies of the past, which were based on "mechanical solidarity," had evolved into more complex, heterogeneous societies bound together by "organic solidarity." Durkheim maintained that in premodern societies like tribal groups of hunter-gatherers, where solidarity was based on the fundamental similarity in people's daily material lives, consensus over moral values was strong and deep. For Durkheim, this strong moral consensus reflects the fact that values are rooted in material conditions, and where people's material conditions are similar, their values are likely to be shared as well. He called this deep well of shared values the "collective conscience" (or, the *conscience collective*, in the French original).

When a strong collective conscience is violated—as it is when someone commits a crime—people react with shock and outrage at the almost unthinkable offense. That is why, according to Durkheim, ancient societies had passionate "repressive law," by which he meant they emphasized punishment for punishment's sake. Don't get the wrong idea from the sound of this word "repressive." Durkheim used the term analytically, not normatively or judgmentally. He believed that repressive sanctions served the important function of shoring up the collective conscience and reestablishing the boundaries of acceptable behavior. A public hanging, for example, has the potential to bond upstanding citizens together in their outrage and in the social quality of the occasion, and to spell out once again the unacceptability of the offense.

Durkheim theorized that in modern societies with a lot of division of labor and occupational diversity, it is our *differences* that bring us together. The division of labor makes us literally dependent on each other for survival. I, for one, can do research, teach, write, and sometimes cook a good meal, but without other people to plant and harvest crops—not to speak of slaughtering animals—and to manufacture and periodically service my car, produce the garb that passes for fashion in my circles, and otherwise do almost everything required for my material sustenance, life as I know it would fall apart. And so it is for you and most likely everyone you know. In this context, said Durkheim, the nature of law shifts from repressive to "restitutive." Since it is important to restore the balance in complex, interdependent societies, when an offense is committed, the emphasis in restitutive law is on quickly returning things to the way they were before the status quo was disrupted. And because the collective conscience is not so strong (given our diversity and differences in our material existence), the response to an offense is not one of moral outrage or passion of the type that drives repressive sanctions.

Suppose I do not pay my income taxes. If I'm caught, the penalty is I have to pay. I might have to pay some interest, but only in extreme cases would I be sent to prison or otherwise punished. Partly because it's so important to restore harmony in this interdependent society and partly because our diversity has diminished the collective conscience, sanctions are less passionate and do not come from a deep moral anger. This is not to say that the collective conscience has completely dissipated. Instead, according to Durkheim, there is a moral value placed on fulfilling our obligations to each other and performing our social roles (as in tax law, family law, or commercial law), since our very survival depends on reciprocity. Once again, for Durkheim our values follow our material conditions and survival needs.

When Durkheim (1893/1964, 228) said, "Every society is a moral society," he did not mean that every society is morally good. Instead, he was saying that every society—if it is a society and not just a collection of individuals—is bound together by moral values. This is so, he said, even in modern societies based on organic solidarity. Consider the case of "Octomom." As the first edition of this book went to press, Nadya Suleman, the woman who gave birth to octuplets on January 26, 2009, was being skewered in the court of public opinion. Fifty discussion groups formed on Facebook in one week alone, with headers like "What Nadya Suleman Did Was Totally Wrong." Suleman's former publicist, who quit after receiving death threats, is quoted on the website Dvorak's Cage Match as saying, "In terms of reaction to her, I would say not in my experience have I ever seen anything like it. And I would add that I was involved in public relations for Three Mile Island after the [1979 nuclear power plant reactor meltdown]."

The response to this octuplet phenomenon changed dramatically over the course of the first few days. When the births were initially reported, people were fascinated with the rare event and Suleman was "The Miracle Mom." But once it was known that she had six other small children and was single, unemployed, and receiving food stamps, the miracle woman quickly became a mercenary out to rob already-strapped taxpayers. One of the most watched YouTube videos on the topic featured the "Octo-Mom Song," where a popular parody singer played Suleman giving birth, with a doctor wearing a baseball glove catching babies as they flew out and the sounds of a cash register in the background. The Suleman case probably made people angry for a variety of reasons, and not everyone was equally obsessed with her single-mom-on-welfare status. But one thing is sure: even in this otherwise fragmented, diverse society where a Durkheimian consensus seems elusive, the Octomom episode galvanized us in agreement that "what Nadya Suleman did was totally wrong." As Durkheim would have predicted (although he might have been surprised by the passion and intensity of the response), our organic society is still capable of moral union. Also predictably, calls went out to impose legal sanctions on Suleman's fertility doctor and to establish a regulatory regime to prevent the birth of any more "Franken-babies," as one faith-based radio show mercilessly called the octuplets.

But our moral consensus is often fleeting. The battle surrounding the right for same-sex couples to marry is a case in point. Consider the debate that raged around Proposition 8 in California. California voters passed this proposition in November 2008, changing the state's constitution to prohibit same-sex marriage. Opponents immediately appealed the validity of the proposition on the grounds that it would substantially revise the constitution, not just amend it, and therefore required legislative action and a two-thirds majority vote. In May 2009, the California Supreme Court upheld the contentious proposition, effectively banning same-sex marriage in the state. A year later, a U.S. district court found the measure unconstitutional, and in 2013 the U.S. Supreme Court ruled that its proponents lacked legal standing to appeal. The issue has continued to stir powerful passions, but a decided shift has taken place. As I write this, thirty-seven states now allow same-sex marriage—as a result of legislation, court action, or popular vote. By the time this goes to press, there will be more, and a pending U.S. Supreme Court decision may effectively declare state bans unconstitutional. In a rapid reversal from just two decades ago, most Americans now support the right of same-sex couples to marry. This evolution of the culture war over same-sex marriage suggests that whatever moral cohesion there is, is sometimes ephemeral.

The very concept of culture war speaks to a profound problem in Durkheim's theory: true consensus may be lacking on many issues of profound moral meaning in contemporary society. In her award-winning book *Free to Believe: Rethinking Freedom of Conscience and Religion in Canada*, Mary Anne Waldron (2013) discusses the ways Canadian courts have interpreted Canada's Charter of Rights and Freedoms and makes a case for more expansive judicial interpretations of religious freedom. In the process, Waldron examines landmark cases that deal with controversies about same-sex marriage, abortion, and the religious practices of certain minority groups. *Free to Believe* makes it clear that there are profound moral schisms in contemporary Western societies, and that they are of a magnitude and force that is inconsistent with Durkheim's consensus theory.

Despite these problems with Durkheim's theory, his concepts of mechanical and organic solidarity and repressive and restitutive law, and his emphasis on the functions of law in providing social equilibrium, are ingenious and have inspired important elaborations over the decades. I should add here, though, that in at least one more respect, Durkheim got his facts wrong. Anthropological evidence suggests that premodern societies used primarily *restitutive* law, and more complex modern societies emphasize *repressive* sanctions, not vice versa (Sheleff 1975). This makes a certain sense from the point of view of Durkheim's own theory, since the collective conscience is weaker in modern societies and the need for repressive sanctions to help reinforce it is greater. This is no small matter for Durkheim's legacy. It would be like having the genius to discover gravity, but then theorizing that the gravitational force is *away* from the earth rather than toward it.

Despite Maine's dearth of data and Durkheim's fatal sequencing problem, they were on to something: the form of law roughly coincides with the form of society. You could say that the legal order and the social order are fashioned from the same cloth. For Weber, the main thread of the modern cloth was rationalization; for Maine, it was contract; and for Durkheim, it was organic solidarity and division of labor.

For many other law and society scholars, economics are paramount. Macaulay, Friedman, and Stookey (1995, 7) have said that "sooner or later, [legal systems'] shape gets bent in the direction of their society. . . . *Medieval law looked, smelled, and acted medieval.*" Following the same logic, capitalist law looks, smells, and acts capitalist. Civil law provides the legal infrastructure for manufacturing, the execution of contracts, investments, and financial transactions of all kinds. And it codifies social relations grounded in the capitalist economic structure, such as those based on individual rights and the nuclear family as opposed to caste and kinship networks. In criminal law, it coins new legal concepts like theft and larceny that protect private property; and it bestows the mantle of normalcy on capitalist coercion—specifically, the coercion associated with the capitalist workplace.

Jeffrey Reiman (1984) discusses this normalization of coercion in explaining why things like workplace hazards and air pollution are not criminalized in the same way street crime is. He says that "the current division between criminal and noncriminal is built into [the capitalist] structure" and in that sense is "'read off' the face of capitalism" (135–36). Under capitalism, the vast majority of people are required to work for an employer and have little say about their working conditions, since the workplace is owned by others. Drawing from Karl Marx, Reiman argues that there is coercion involved here—most people either work in the capitalist workplace or lack the basic necessities of life. This arrangement is rarely recognized as coercive but is seen instead as contractual, and the dangerous conditions a worker may be subject to are recognized not as violence but rather as risks the worker assumes as part of his or her contract. Reiman uses an analogy to clarify: "Imagine . . . a society where there were only a few sources of oxygen owned by a small number of people and that others in the society had to work for the oxygen-owners in order to get a chance to breathe. Even if no overt force were used in arranging the 'labor-for-breath' exchanges, it would be quite clear that the workers were slaves to the oxygen-owners" (139). Just so, he says, capitalist labor contracts are coercive and labor conditions not freely chosen. But capitalist law does not treat unsafe working conditions as violent crimes because our understanding of the concepts of violence and crime are, as Reiman put it, "'read off' the face of capitalism."

Law not only follows the contours of society and its economic base; it is implicated in shaping those contours. Michael Tigar and Madeline Levy, in their 1977 book *Law and the Rise of Capitalism*, show that the economics-law symmetry is no coincidence. They argue that feudal law was transformed into capitalist law in England and France during the period from 1100 to 1800, through strategic alliances between the new commercial bourgeoisie, monarchs who benefited from tax revenues on the budding commerce, and lawyers who for a price provided both the technical expertise and the philosophical justification for legal change. The legal ideology of free contract advanced by lawyers in this alliance was central because it supplied a normative justification for the dismantling of the hereditary bonds and forced servitude of feudal relations. In this rendition, in contrast to Maine, whom they cite with some derision, the principles of private property and free contract did not emerge spontaneously out of the new social form. Instead, as a new class began to gain economic power through long-distance trade, it used that power to advance legal principles that accelerated the socioeconomic transformation and further elevated its position. Once entrenched, capitalist law—with its principles of private property, free contract, and individual rights—came to be seen as part of the natural order of things.

This pattern repeats itself today as we witness the contemporary equivalent of those early alliances among merchants, monarchs, and lawyers. The unfettered finance capitalism that became the dominant global economic form in the late twentieth century flourished on the support it received from political leaders of all stripes, and from the lobbyists and lawyers who secured a favorable legal and regulatory climate. Beginning in the 1980s, the banking industry—or, more precisely, its lobbyists, finance experts, and legal professionals—mobilized a deregulation movement that paved the way for new investment options. They were wildly successful, in 1999 achieving a repeal of the 1933 Banking Act that had been passed at the height of the Great Depression and had restricted the risks that banks could take with other people's money. One of the new investment instruments to flourish in this environment was the so-called credit derivative, a key factor in the collapse of financial markets in 2008. It is too complicated to go into how it works here, but its importance to the ballooning finance economy can be grasped by a single figure: by the early 2000s, credit derivatives had become a $58 trillion market worldwide. The larger point is that the elite in the prevailing economic form—or in an emerging one—can use their considerable resources to advance their position and bolster the dominance of that economic form (despite its risks) through legal interventions facilitated by alliances with political leaders, lawyers, and a stable of experts. The result over time is a convergence between the legal form and the economic form.

Half a century ago, James Willard Hurst (1964) produced the iconic law and society work that, among other things, traced this convergence in one industry. Hurst outlined in meticulous detail the legal history of the lumber industry in Wisconsin in the late nineteenth and early twentieth century. Presenting data from statutes, official reports, court proceedings, and a host of other sources in this masterwork that runs almost a thousand pages, Hurst drew a complex picture of the interactive effect of law and industry. He was careful not to over-generalize or sensationalize, and his findings were many, from the dominance of legislation in this arena, rather than judicial action or regulation, to the inefficiencies of the market and the relative ineffi-cacy of police powers. Most relevant for us, Hurst made it clear that law—particularly legislation—was "an important economic asset" and that it worked primarily "to create facilities that might multiply private production" (20).

Another nuanced version of this convergence between law and the economy is evident in Amanda Perry-Kessaris's (2008) study of law and global capitalism in the city of Bengaluru (previously Bangalore) in southern India (colloquially referred to as the Silicon Valley of In-dia). Perry-Kessaris starts from the premise that a primary function of law in Bengaluru is to build and sustain trust among three relevant groups—government, foreign business interests, and civil society. The legal system does so, she says, by coordinating the activities and mediating differences among these diverse actors, and by encourag-ing and facilitating their participation in the process. But in the end a familiar pattern emerges—the dovetailing of economic interests, ideology, and law. Over time, Perry-Kessaris reports, there has been less and less room at the table for civil society organizations and a corresponding ascendance of World Bank "investment climate" dis-course and the foreign investors it privileges. Toward the end of the book, she quotes the Indian finance minister, who quipped that India "is willing to tolerate debate and perhaps even dissent, as long as it does not come in the way of eight percent growth" (119).

Several explicitly materialist analyses trace the historical pattern in broader sweeps. William Chambliss's (1964) analysis of the invention of vagrancy as a legal concept is an excellent example of this stream-lined materialist approach. Chambliss shows us that the first vagrancy law, passed in feudal England in 1349, was designed to deal with a scarcity of workers and skyrocketing wages. After the bubonic plague had killed off half the English population in 1348 and caused a spike in wages, the vagrancy law made it illegal to refuse work, put a ceiling on wages, and outlawed the giving of alms (which were thought to allow the lower classes to shirk work). The fact that the ban on alms was a direct violation of the principle of Christian charity prevalent at the time, at least at the level of lip service, underscores the power of economic imperatives to trump other considerations.

Georg Rusche and Otto Kirchheimer (1939) provided another historical study of this convergence of law and economics. They focused less on the individual agents of change and more on the structural congruence between law and the nature of the economy it is embedded in. Rusche and Kirchheimer noticed that human societies across time and place have punished their members for violations of law in all sorts of ways. It is hard to conjure up a form of punishment that hasn't been used at some point. Branding, mutilation, humiliation, exile, dismemberment, beheading, fines, forced labor, indentured servitude, imprisonment, electrocution, whipping—they're all there in the historical record. But they noticed a pattern: in any given historical period, only one or two forms of punishment predominate. During the reign of Henry VIII in early sixteenth-century England, death by hanging was so prevalent it was used against seventy-two thousand petty thieves. In seventeenth- and eighteenth-century England, public whippings were a favored punishment. In the United States today, punishment is less public, with millions of convicts warehoused in prisons.

So, Rusche and Kirchheimer asked, what drives the pattern? Their answer was that the form of punishment depends on the type of economic production system (for example, whether it is feudal, slave, mercantilist, or capitalist), the population size relative to the need for labor, and the type of labor required. The lords on feudal estates were unlikely to impose the death penalty, since executing a serf would have meant destroying one's own assets. Instead, corporal punishment was used, with the henchman taking care not to cause permanent injury. During the heady mercantilist period of colonial expansion, English convicts were put to use through indentured servitude in the colonies, galley slavery, the military, and—in those days of labor shortages and an embryonic factory system—"houses of correction." These were based on the convenient premise that criminals could be morally "corrected" through hard factory labor. The full-blown Industrial Revolution in England brought continued mechanization and, with it, increased unemployment. The surplus population was crowded into prisons, but instead of the prison labor of the late mercantilist period—irrelevant at a time of mass unemployment and plentiful labor reserves—the treadmill and other forms of prison torture were invented to ensure that going to prison was not a tempting alternative to the homeless and starving masses on the streets.

In the realm of theory, as in most human endeavors, nothing is new under the sun. Rusche and Kirchheimer, Chambliss, and Tigar and Levy were following in the dialectical-materialist tradition of Karl Marx. According to Marx (1906), the way production and the creation of wealth are organized in a society shapes most other aspects of that society, including law. Further, in all economic forms, those who own the wealth and those who work to produce it are locked in a conflict of interest, the playing out of which produces social conflict and change. That mattress I woke up on this morning, with all its tags and dire warnings of legal liability, was no doubt produced in a privately owned factory by workers toiling at some bare minimum wage and sold by the owners of the factory for a profit. In its simplest form, this is the logic of industrial capitalist production. The production and economic relations in feudal societies are instead organized around agriculture and large landholdings and function according to their own distinct logics, with their own specific consequences for social relations, conflict, and law. In each economic form, according to this argument, laws are tailored to the needs of the prevailing production system—ensuring an adequate supply of workers, setting up the ground rules, providing the infrastructure, and handling the inevitable social disorder and conflict.

FRENCH PHILOSOPHER and social theorist Michel Foucault had a somewhat different take on all this. A "poststructuralist," Foucault was convinced that economic structure does not inexorably determine power relations or the exact form of law and social control. Instead, he argued, power is decentralized, dispersed, and fragmented, constituted as it is of actual social practice and the discourse (or talk) that is a key element of practice. Power is not an entity that is imposed top-down as in Marxist structuralism, but an emergent relation emanating from local social practices and the discourses that permeate them. Law and legal systems from this perspective shift with changes in discourse and "knowledge" (what we think to be true at any given time), which are embedded in specific social contexts.

In *Discipline and Punish: The Birth of the Prison* (1977), Foucault traces the shift from the gory public executions and torture of convicted criminals in eighteenth-century France to the use of regimented and largely bloodless prisons less than a century later. For Foucault, this shift coincides with and is emblematic of the emergence of modernity, with its emphasis on predictability, rationality, the dispersion of "power/knowledge" throughout society, and the internalization of discipline by society's members. Foucault coins the term "panopticism" in this context. The panopticon was a circular prison designed by Jeremy Bentham in 1787 that was never actually built but that provided a loose model for some modern prisons. The panopticon design would allow prison authorities to keep inmates under constant observation. Foucault used it as a metaphor for modern society, with its ever-widening capacity for scrutiny of the individual. What matters in the panopticon is not that prisoners actually *be* under surveillance at all times, which would consume unnecessary resources; rather, it is the *potential* of being watched at any given moment—and prisoners' uncertainty about when that potential is being realized—that produces conformity. According to Foucault, the intense surveillance of modern society in the long run produces an internalization of discipline that reduces the need for external restraints.

The creation of advanced technology that facilitates surveillance has opened up a debate among parents about the appropriate use of these seductive devises for the monitoring of their children. Drug testing, GPS for the car, and other such gadgets potentially let parents keep an ever-watchful eye on their children. An opinion article in the *New York Times* entitled "The Undercover Parent" points out that computer spyware can help parents monitor who their children are chatting with and which websites their children access (Coben 2008). The author writes that, for the children to self-regulate (at least on that computer), it may be sufficient for parents to warn their children that they have installed the spyware. He concludes, "Do you tell your children that the spyware is on the computer? I side with yes, but it might be enough to show them this article, have a discussion about your concerns and let them know the possibility is there" (14). We can see parallels here to Foucault's prison: as middle-class parents eschew corporal punishment, they increasingly employ disciplinary surveillance, including the intimidating uncertainty associated with it.

Unlike Rusche and Kirchheimer's structural and materialist analysis of punishment systems, Foucauldian poststructuralism highlights the microprocesses of power and the discourses and knowledges that constitute them. Economic structure is not unimportant for Foucault, who frequently cites Marx, but his poststructuralism incorporates the contingent and unpredictable in the messy world of social interaction, knowledge construction, and practice.

In *The Culture of Control* (2001), David Garland takes from Foucault this idea that punishment and social control policies are organically linked to sociocultural forces in ways that can be explained after the fact but that are often unpredictable. Garland notes the abrupt rise in punitive responses to crime in the United States and England over the past several decades, including among other things massive increases in incarceration and a rejection of rehabilitation. He wonders why we made this sudden turn to punitiveness that seems "oddly archaic and downright anti-modern" (3) and that veers away from the "rationalization" that Weber argued characterizes modern society, since it does not seem important whether or not the tough policies actually *work*.

In a far-ranging analysis, Garland argues that rising crime rates in the 1960s, suburbanization, the fragmentation of families, increased economic uncertainties, and the dismantling of welfare protections have produced a "late modernity" that is fraught with chronic insecurities. These social, economic, and demographic shifts, and their accompanying anxieties, reverberate in formal and informal systems of control that are meant first and foremost to contain danger. Garland was writing before the terrorist attacks on the United States in September 2001, events that significantly heightened people's anxieties and tightened the culture of control. Government surveillance by the National Security Agency, not only of suspected terrorists but also of ordinary citizens, now takes the form of wiretapping telephones, intercepting mail and email, and searching through business records and bank accounts. The scope of the surveillance network is enormous, as revealed by whistle-blower Edward Snowden, a former contract employee of the National Security Agency and the focus of the widely released documentary *Citizenfour*. Notice two points here. First, this surveillance appears to go beyond anything in recent U.S. history and is a dramatic illustration of the intensification of control that Garland wrote about. Second, the relative lack of collective pushback to these unprecedented measures suggests that this cultural field of anxiety and control is potent indeed.

Its potency is also evident in the incarceration boom that began in the late 1970s. With safety resonating as a strong cultural value in what were perceived to be unusually dangerous times, and with rehabilitative policies debunked as weak-willed, state after state passed get-tough policies. In this context, more people were sent to prison, sentences were longer, and furloughs were curtailed or eliminated. While some of these policies have recently been reconsidered— primarily on the fiscal grounds that they cost too much—the mass incarceration they triggered goes on mostly unabated. As Garland (2001, 178) said more than a decade ago, "The prison is used today as a kind of reservation, a quarantine zone in which purportedly dangerous individuals are segregated in the name of public safety."

The targeting of some types of people in the name of safety is not confined to imprisonment in this cultural field of control. As Sean Hier (2010) shows in *Panoptic Dreams: Streetscape Video Surveillance in Canada*, the closed-circuit television cameras on streets throughout Canadian cities capture all who pass by, but suspicion is focused on racial/ethnic minorities, lower-income people, and the homeless. Hier is careful not to homogenize or reify "they" who are watching "us" as he delineates an array of interests promoting such security measures as well as privacy advocates who are pushing back. Nonetheless, he makes clear that the expansion of closed-circuit surveillance throughout Canada (and, I would add, across the United States and elsewhere) is one more "panoptic dream" in this age of control.

This culture of control extends also to a broad range of civil and criminal law enforcement practices, and to a creeping overlap between the two. Issa Kohler-Hausmann (2014) did an empirical analysis of the rapidly increasing arrests for misdemeanor offenses in New York City, noting that the current era is characterized not only by mass incarceration but also by "mass misdemeanors." Whereas before 1994 felony arrests in New York outpaced misdemeanor arrests, between 1993 and 2010 misdemeanor arrests doubled and now are far higher than arrests for felonies.

Kohler-Hausmann's data show that the dismissal rate for these low-level offenses (such as marijuana possession, assault, trespassing, turnstile jumping, disorderly conduct, petit larceny, prostitution, and unlicensed street vending) is high and the conviction rate low. This high misdemeanor arrest rate, combined with relatively few convictions, suggests that the system is designed not to penalize specific behaviors so much as to "manag[e] people through engagement with the criminal justice system" (611). More precisely, it manages specific kinds of people, targeting blacks and Hispanics. While the rate for misdemeanor arrests of whites increased by 35 percent between 1990 and 2010, the rates for blacks and Hispanics increased by 105 percent and 158 percent, respectively (633). This New York system marks violators for future targeting, whether or not they are convicted. The proactive use of the criminal justice system to manage populations perceived to be risky—such as the poor and people of color—is a common feature of the current culture of control.

The sorting and managing of the poor extends far beyond New York City. In their book *Banished: The New Social Control in Urban America* (2010), Katherine Beckett and Steve Herbert demonstrate how a host of new policies in Seattle bans certain people from public spaces and gives the police broad powers to arrest those who don't comply. These policies include anti-loitering ordinances, youth curfews, gang injunctions, park exclusion orders, and public-housing trespass measures, to name a few. They are officially rationalized on the same grounds that gave momentum to "broken windows" policing and "zero tolerance"—that social disorder must be nipped in the bud, lest it lead to more serious crime. But Beckett and Herbert show that these policies emerged at a time of rising urban poverty and homelessness, side by side with increasingly gentrified urban centers and associated concerns for property values. The result in Seattle has been not reduced crime or improved public safety, as proponents of zero tolerance would have it, but the criminalization of poverty. This criminalization is part and parcel of the culture of control, as it allows the police and other enforcement officials to monitor and control populations perceived to be potentially dangerous or undesirable.

In the wake of the 2014 police shooting of Michael Brown in Ferguson, Missouri (which we will talk about again in chapter 4), it was reported that this town of twenty-one thousand people had issued twenty-five thousand arrest warrants in 2013—or an average of three per household. Most of the warrants in Ferguson, where more than two-thirds of the residents are African American and 20 percent of people live beneath the poverty line, were for failure to pay fines for what defense lawyers call "poverty violations"—for example, driving without insurance. So the cycle goes: the inability to purchase car insurance results in a fine that compounds over time (one Ferguson resident told a reporter that his traffic fine rose to $2,000 when the court did not allow him to pay his original fine in $50 installments), and the failure to appear in court to pay those fines leads to arrest warrants, suspended licenses, potential jail time, and exclusions from decent housing and jobs.

This debtor's prison redux operates in cities and towns across America. I recently accompanied a friend to an orientation at the Homeless and Caring Court run by the Society of St. Vincent de Paul in Oakland, California. This well-meaning program allows poor people to meet with a public defender and potentially waive and expunge certain tickets and fines from their records. Orientation occurs weekly and always draws a full house. The day I was there, the presenter informed the overflow crowd that because of the huge demand, it takes a year to get an interview to start the process. Upon hearing that she had to wait a year for any hope of reprieve from the exclusionary consequences of tickets that had gone into collection, the distraught woman in front of me said to no one in particular, "So, how am I supposed to get housing for me and my kids? Use a fake name?" In this cascading chain of events, poverty is criminalized first through unaffordable fines and arrest warrants, and then through a woman's last-ditch efforts to escape their dire consequences.

Clearly, the effects of the culture of control that David Garland (2001) so aptly described go far beyond the "quarantine zone" of the prison. They permeate the everyday lives of us all in one way or another, from airport security protocols to surveillance cameras in public places to metal detectors in schools. This is what Jonathan Simon (2007) means when he talks about "governing through crime," as social institutions from the family to schools to neighborhoods adopt the policies and metaphors of the war on crime. In the process, the very rationale of governance has shifted from the distributive justice discourse of the 1960s to today's rhetoric of danger containment. But enhanced engagement with the criminal justice system at all levels is the special preserve of the poor, and it is there that the effects of the culture of control and the new governance are most deeply felt.

In this day of Internet blogs and chat rooms, we hear loud and clear the anger that animates this shift. In these voices, anxieties about safety translate into support for zero tolerance, long prison terms, and the death penalty. One blogger asked his discussion group what they thought of the Federal Death Penalty Abolition Act originally introduced in 2007. The responses varied, but the visceral anger of the majority who opposed the abolition was palpable. One virtually shouted into his keyboard, "Why should we waste taxpayer dollars supporting this garbage in prison for the rest of their lives, or worse yet, release them back into society where they can do someone else harm?" Another response included echoes of Garland's "quarantine" theme: "the only way I would agree to ending the death penalty is if every criminal convicted of a capital crime was moved to a remote island and left to fight for his or her life."

The online *Orange County Register* has a crime blog that once featured the column Stupid Criminals. One issue told the true story of a man who was suspected of murdering his girlfriend and was overheard on a police microphone discussing a cover-up with his father. In an earlier lead-in story, readers learned that the girlfriend was pregnant at the time, had other children, and had used fraud to enter people's homes. Many bloggers ridiculed the man's "stupid gene" for speaking to his father about the crime inside a police car. Others simply wanted him "to fry." Another blasted the accused for what he had done and then for how "hateful and mean" he made her feel. The punitive impulse was not confined to the accused. Several found the victim equally repugnant: "Why was she homeless looking for kind Irvine [Orange County] strangers to take advantage of?" These are real-life expressions of Garland's "cultural field," permeated as it is with safety anxieties, economic uncertainties, taxpayer hostilities, and anger toward those who embody society's myriad "blights." In this sociocultural landscape, it's not just criminals but sometimes their victims too who make people feel "hateful and mean."

A few law and society scholars have found the "mirror paradigm"— in which types of law and types of society reflect each other— altogether too tidy and have tried to unsettle it. Brian Tamanaha (2001) points to the transplantation of U.S. law in Micronesia to make his point that sometimes the form of law can be completely out of sync with social organization, values, and customs. "To cite a few examples," he says, in the islands of Yap "they had a thriving caste system, yet the [imported] law prohibited discrimination; their culture was consensual in orientation, but the law was based upon the adversarial model; their understanding of criminal offences required a response by the community itself . . . , but the state insisted that it had a monopoly on the application of force" (xi). Tamanaha makes an eloquent case (and we will take up this topic of the transplantation of legal systems again in chapter 5), but for now the reigning mirror paradigm has not been dislodged.

SO FAR, I have talked about law without defining it. Defining law is surprisingly tricky business. Most people probably assume that when we speak of law we are referring to a set of written rules governing the conduct of society's members, rules that are propagated, interpreted, and enforced by agents of the state or local authorities. One problem with this definition is that it is culturally biased, fitting modern Western societies best. In fact, if this is our operative definition, then many societies have no law at all.

When anthropologist Bronisław Malinowski (1926/1982) studied the Trobriand Islanders off the New Guinea coast in the early 1920s, he found a preliterate society without formal law. This is not to say there was no social control or rules governing social conduct. It's just that they were not written down, and they were not enacted and implemented by state officials (there were none). Instead, the islanders had informal rules for behavior, including specific rights and obligations for all members of society and sanctions for infringement. These rules were every bit as binding as formal law is in modern Western societies.

A familiar example from the United States might help underscore the potency of such informal rules, even in a society with a codified legal system. I went to a restaurant with European houseguests who were visiting the United States for the first time. As is customary in some circles, our guests wanted to treat us to a restaurant meal. When the bill arrived, I could see they were pleasantly surprised it was not more expensive. But their faces fell when we told them about tipping customs in the United States and that we were expected to leave at least a 15 percent tip for the waitstaff. They were so dismayed by this unexpected requirement that they asked if it was a law. Their dismay turned to shock when we explained it is not a written law but that it may as well be, given how strongly normative it is and how strictly obeyed. In fact, other guests from Italy had once been chased down on their way out of a restaurant after failing to leave a tip. It strikes me that this tipping norm—which for all intents and purposes is a "law"—is a lot like some of the Micronesian obligations and sanctions that Malinowski wrote about, none of which is codified.

The absence of formal legal structures is not unique to preliterate societies; although admittedly rare, communities with and without formal law may sit side by side. Richard Schwartz (1954) did a study of social control in two Israeli communities, a moshav (a cooperative) and a kvutza (a socialist settlement). The first was based on private property and the family as the primary social unit, while the latter adhered to egalitarianism and collectivist principles, such as sharing all meals and property and raising children communally. Schwartz found that in the kvutza, where interaction was intense and face-to-face and where communal principles were passionately adhered to, public opinion was more than enough to keep people in line, and there was no need for formal legal institutions. In this tight-knit community where even showers were public gatherings, people were highly attuned to informal controls, with tone of voice, gestures, gossip, and other tools of social disapproval performing the role of law. Instead, in the moshav, where work, meals, and presumably showers were private affairs, people were less concerned with their neighbors' opinions of them. One moshav member, speaking of the referral to the justice system of a group of boys who had stolen some melons, explained to Schwartz that if all the community did was "scold" them, "they [would] laugh at you" (490). Schwartz distinguished between law and informal controls and concluded that law emerges only in communities where informal controls are weak and that once formal legal institutions are established, the power of informal controls atrophies even further, to the point of being laughable.

Not to get too far off the track, but it has come to my notice that even in its more formal state, law may be considered a laughing matter by some. The *New York Times* reported in 2008 that a group of high school boys in Vermont vandalized the farm home and museum of the late poet Robert Frost (Barry 2008). Breaking windows and furniture, writing on walls, urinating and vomiting from an excess of beer and other liquor, the boys partied late into the night. When the state police caught up with them, they were arrested and prosecuted for trespassing. The sergeant in charge was struck by the irreverence of one boy, who asked if he could post his mug shot on Facebook. Not even formal sanctions were enough to make this American youth take his transgression seriously. What would be even more shocking to members of Schwartz's kvutza is that this young man, far from fearing communal shame, wanted to advertise his transgression to his whole Facebook community.

WE HAVE SEEN that social form and legal form tend to converge, with types of law corresponding to the societies they are embedded in. There is another tradition in law and society that links not just the contours of law but also the shape and practices of the legal profession to social, cultural, and economic conditions. Richard Abel and Philip Lewis's (1988–89) three-volume *Lawyers in Society* provides information about legal practice in nineteen different countries and anchors the sometimes dramatic differences to the distinctive socioeconomic forces that the legal profession is part of and contributes to.

These links can be seen too in shifts in the profession in the United States in the last half of the twentieth century. Some of the earliest works in law and society revealed a highly stratified legal profession in the post–World War II period. Jerome Carlin's (1962) study of solo lawyers of the 1950s depicted these lone practitioners as isolated, competitive, and struggling to meet the demands of their mostly individual clients while also warding off encroachment by their competitors. At the other end of the status hierarchy, Erwin Smigel (1960) showed us the professional life of the Wall Street lawyer in firms that serviced corporations. Reflecting the status of their clients, Carlin's solo practitioners were more likely to be ethnically diverse and enjoy little occupational security; in contrast, the corporate lawyers described by Smigel were almost all white Anglo-Saxon Protestant—with the exception of the white "ethnics" who often handled the litigation end of things for corporations—and had much higher incomes and job security.

The highly stratified quality of the legal profession was under-scored again by Heinz and Laumann (1982) in their landmark work, *Chicago Lawyers*. They interviewed 777 lawyers in Chicago and con-cluded that the profession was bifurcated according to whether one's clients were individuals or institutional entities, such as corporations, and that professional status was dependent on the prestige of one's clients. The most prestigious corporate law firms comprised almost exclusively men who had gone to the top law schools and who were, not coincidentally, white Anglo-Saxon Protestants. Those who had less prestigious solo practices servicing individuals or small busi-nesses usually had gone to regional law schools and were more often Jews or Catholics. This "elitist tendency" (83) of the legal profession paralleled exactly, and arguably helped reproduce, the prevailing in-equalities of midcentury American society.

As social and economic conditions in the United States shifted in the last decades of the twentieth century, so did the contours and practices of the legal profession. The number of lawyers increased significantly, from just over 355,000 in 1971 to more than double that in 1995; law firms grew larger, with more of them practicing corpo-rate law; and there was a proportionate decrease of solo practitioners and small firms (Halliday 1986; Abel 1989; Seron 1996, 2007). More striking was the entrance of previously excluded groups into the pro-fession. During the first half of the twentieth century, the American Bar Association had barred African Americans from membership, and women were denied entry to most law schools. But by the end of the century, almost half of law students were women, and the proportion of minority law students had risen to 20 percent.

In their sweeping documentation and analysis of these changes, Heinz, Nelson, Sandefur, and Laumann (2005) reveal that the legal profession is really two distinct professions, with those specializing in services to corporate clients a world apart from the mostly solo practitioners and small firms serving individuals with injury claims and divorce proceedings. In fact, the profession is even more stratified than it used to be, with specialization and income inequality among lawyers greater than ever. While it is true that more women and mi-norities now practice law, they are rarely partners in large firms and on average have lower incomes (Epstein, Sauté, Oglensky, and Gever 1995; Chambliss 2004; Heinz et al. 2005). The processes that produce this glass ceiling are less explicit than the outright exclusions of the past and often take the form of sexual harassment and/or stereotyping (Epstein et al. 1995). What remains of the notion that law resides above the fray is put to rest by this extensive body of literature tracking the zigs and zags of the legal profession as its structures and inequalities parallel those of society.

The global economy has triggered changes in legal practice too. In a book about transnational commercial arbitration called *Dealing in Virtue*, Yves Dezalay and Bryant Garth (1996) describe how disputes between international parties in business transactions are handled through a private justice system. Most important for us here, the authors trace transformations in this arbitration that closely shadow broader economic and political changes. The cadre of elite lawyers who serve on panels of highly paid arbitrators in these business disputes was likened to a "mafia" by one insider. As he put it, "It's a mafia because people appoint one another. You always appoint your friends—people you know" (10). Like the conventional legal profession, this club has diversified somewhat with the times, admitting a handful of women and minorities. More fundamentally, Dezalay and Garth tell a story of institutional change, as U.S. business interests have refashioned an informal means for handling disputes into a more formal, technocratic one with a greater resemblance to U.S. litigation practices. Adopting Weber's model of increasing rationalization in modern society, Dezalay and Garth argue that the charisma and elite credentials of the "grand old men" who traditionally made up this transnational arbitration club continue to provide it with an aura of genteel legitimacy, but that its actual operation has been rendered highly technocratic and rational.

This internationalization of legal practice parallels the globalization of the economy and its legal culture, and it can be found from Taiwan (Winn and Yeh 2011) to countries across Latin America (Dezalay and Garth 2002). It also has been institutionalized in the form of subtle and not-so-subtle changes in legal education in even the most entrenched systems. In Latin America, for example, although the curriculum in most law schools has not dramatically changed in the contemporary period, reforms in teaching methods and courses on human rights, and law and economics, have crept in even against resistance (Pérez-Perdomo 2011). As Pérez-Perdomo puts it, "Legal education has been affected by social change and . . . the dynamic of reform, driven out through the door, has timidly returned through the window" (63).

We find another example of the close relationship between legal practice and economic form in California's Silicon Valley. This time the emphasis is on transformations in the legal profession in response to the demands of one industry. Lawrence Friedman, Robert Gordon, Sophie Pirie, and Edwin Whatley (1989) began to study high-tech industries in Silicon Valley just as the region took off as the American epicenter of high-tech start-ups. Friedman and colleagues reject the broad notion that lawyers are "either indispensable to entrepreneurship or a wasteful drag on it" (566–67), preferring a more data-driven, industry-specific approach. But while they are unwilling to commit to the theory that legal practices advance (or retard) economic growth, they make it crystal clear that the converse is true: the contours of the economy shape legal practice. This is no doubt in part because, as the authors say of partners in law firms, they "dance to the tune of their clients" (566).

Another study of the legal profession takes us far afield from the globe-trotting arbitrators described by Dezalay and Garth and the high-tech legal consultants in Silicon Valley studied by Friedman and colleagues. In their book on local divorce lawyers in Maine and New Hampshire, Mather, McEwen, and Maiman (2001) introduce the concept of communities of practice as a way to think about the links between socioeconomic forces, professional norms, and personal values. They find that the conduct and communication of these lawyers, mediated by personal factors and constrained by economic incentives, reproduce powerful professional norms among these solo and small-firm practitioners.

Two cumulative points emerge from these studies, despite their many theoretical and methodological differences. The first is that, as Carroll Seron recently told me, "It is in some ways misleading to talk about 'the legal profession,'" given the dramatic professional differences among types of lawyers. The second broad point is that the legal profession(s) and legal practice, like law itself, are both constituted by and in turn help constitute the surrounding social, political, and economic landscape.

AS THIS CHAPTER comes to a close, I return to the question of how to define law. Whether we should make "law" synonymous with rules for social behavior and mechanisms of control—however informal—as it was for Malinowski, or reserve the word to refer to specialized and formal legal institutions as Schwartz did, is open to debate. The Central Alaskan Yupik language apparently has over a dozen words for "snow," which suggests that when precision is important, we can maximize it by using different words (in our case, "law," "norms," "social mores") for variations on a similar phenomenon. But what we gain in precision by limiting what counts as "law" we might lose in analysis if it inhibits us from seeing beyond differences in social control practices to their functional similarities. Snow in all its many forms is cold and wet; the task, then, is to decipher under which atmospheric conditions one form or the other will fall. Terminological disputes aside, Malinowski and Schwartz show us that the very presence or absence of a formal legal system depends on social context.

So, law in both its particulars and its generalities is contoured to society—a law and society insight that shakes to its very foundations the myth of law as transcendent, natural, or divinely inspired. Who knows, maybe our *faith* in this myth does have its roots in biology or divine intervention—not so far-fetched an idea since belief in the sanctity of one's own legal system seems to be a constant across societies. But myth it is, and law and society scholarship that highlights the variability of law according to social structure and social relations goes a long way toward debunking it.

Oh, and in case you are wondering, we paid the tip.

CHAPTER THREE

Law in the Everyday, Everywhere

Law and its evil twin, crime, permeate the cultural vernacular in the contemporary United States. Arguably, no other institution gets so much press. The economy is relegated to its own section of the newspaper, "Business," for those who want to know about such arcane affairs or whose job it is to know (at least until the latest financial collapse forced economic news onto the front page). Education is something everyone says they care about, but it draws yawns if you go on for too long about it. Politics gets a lot of media attention during election cycles, but even then most people probably don't know or care much about, say, what the Electoral College actually does. And some people are still undecided about which candidate they prefer for president of the United States right up to Election Day (these are the much-courted "undecideds" who decide election outcomes). But when it comes to law, people's passions stir, and few are undecided about things like the death penalty, Megan's Law, three strikes, or the guilt or innocence of O. J. Simpson. The very fact that we call these laws by their nicknames—"Megan's Law" and "three strikes"—suggests an easy familiarity.

No wonder. We are introduced to law over and over again in so many personas, often sexy and usually sensational. When Paris Hilton was sent to jail in June 2007, the media were on high alert for days, keeping us apprised of her status, whether or not people with DUIs go to jail and for how long, the whereabouts of health care for those in her jail, exactly what the terms of her probation were, and other enticing details. Michael Jackson's 2005 trial on child molestation charges was such a media draw that a reenactment of the day's events was broadcast nightly on Court TV. O. J. Simpson's fame as Heisman Trophy winner and one of football's greatest running backs was dwarfed by the infamy of his trial for the 1994 murder of his wife,

Nicole Brown Simpson, and her friend Ronald Goldman. His not-guilty verdict in October 1995 was watched on live television by more than half the American population. By then, virtually every adult in the United States could tell you the most obscure details about the case and the trial, and we all had become instant pundits, second-guessing the jury decision with the confidence of experts and the passion of a populace aroused. Neither the passion nor attention to detail faded with time. In early 2008, I asked my undergraduate research assistant (who was seven years old during Simpson's murder trial) to read this chapter and give me her feedback. She noted in the margins here, "Don't forget O.J.'s recent armed robbery charges!" Even before his conviction for this latter offense and the wide press it received, she was fully apprised.

The O.J. trial has been called "the trial of the century," but every season brings its own galvanizing legal spectacle. In 2011, the assistant football coach at Pennsylvania State University, Jerry Sandusky, was indicted for sexually assaulting underage boys, and in 2012 he was sentenced to a minimum of thirty years in prison. If you did not follow every detail of Sandusky's indictment, his trial, and the reported attempts at cover-up, you no doubt know someone who kept you informed. Two years later in 2014, the trial of South African sprinter Oscar Pistorius, accused of fatally shooting his girlfriend through the bathroom door, was the headline grabber.

It's not just celebrities who get celebrity coverage. Think of Laci Peterson's disappearance in December 2002 and the subsequent arrest and conviction of her husband, Scott Peterson. Even people like myself who do not buy the tabloids or watch much commercial television somehow knew of Scott's fishing trip, Laci's late-term pregnancy, the sensational arrest despite Scott's amateurish efforts to disguise himself, and the risqué audiotapes of Scott and his masseuse girlfriend. These spectacles draw audiences not just for the material's salacious nature but also for the apparent "news" value and the psychic satisfaction we get from our moral outrage, even if that outrage seems to be—as in the Simpson case—alternately directed at the alleged perpetrator and at the legal system itself.

Coverage of such cases shares a lot with crime shows on reality TV. *America's Most Wanted, Unsolved Mysteries, World's Wildest Police Videos, Cops,* and *Dog the Bounty Hunter* were so popular they launched spin-offs of the spin-offs. Duane "Dog" Chapman (the bounty hunter) has written a best-selling memoir available in airport bookstores, where other offerings are paltry. *You Can Run, but You Can't Hide* chronicles Dog's exploits, first as a gang member and drug dealer and later as "the world's most famous bounty hunter." His website gushes that Chapman "went from ex-con to American icon." The sensationalism and gritty realism of these shows no doubt provide much of their appeal, but it seems hard to go wrong when peddling anything relating to law and crime. According to my cable guide, truTV (originally called Court TV) allows people to watch legal trivia around the clock.

One aside here. This media coverage of real legal cases may be pervasive, but the "reality" the media present is often misleading. In *Distorting the Law*, William Haltom and Michael McCann (2004, 33) expose the many fallacies in the media coverage of "pop torts" like the McDonald's coffee burn case. As Haltom and McCann reveal, contrary to sensational reports of a multimillion-dollar windfall for an opportunistic victim in the McDonald's case, the claimant was left with permanent injuries from third-degree burns and a final payment that was not even one-fifth of what the jury had awarded her. Clearly, the media saturation of true-crime stories does not ensure the truth of their portrayal.

The same could be said of the ever-present fictional crime genre, which now dominates more than half of my television channels. The *Dragnet* and *Perry Mason* of my childhood have given way to a crowded field. *Law and Order* and its many knock-offs, *CSI* (and now *CSI: Miami* and *CSI: New York*), and a whole crop of shows about the legal profession are among the most prized products of the entertainment industry. Many—like *The Practice, LA Law, Boston Legal, Ally McBeal,* and *The Good Wife*—achieve immortality as reruns, "on demand," or on old-fashioned DVDs. *CSI* has become such a part of the cultural lexicon that *Time* magazine ran a cover story on "the CSI effect." In a version of life imitating art, some jury consultants say they deliberately pick jurors who are familiar with the *CSI* series and the kind of forensics it publicizes. One district attorney is even worried that the police will have to do extra forensic work just "to placate CSI-educated juries" (quoted in Goehner, Lofaro, and Novak 2004).

Law and Order has broken all records for viewership and spawned the almost irresistibly compelling *Law and Order: Special Victims Unit,* known colloquially both on and off the show as "Special Vics." For those few who have not seen it, the show focuses on the detection and arrest of people suspected of sex crimes and on the dramatic dynamics of their prosecution. Interspersed throughout are quasi-factual tidbits about actual statutes and criminal justice procedures, giving the show a documentary gloss and leaving viewers—for better or for worse—convinced they have learned something. It helps too that the show advertises itself as based on true stories, which are "ripped from the headlines," to borrow the show's own violent verbiage.

Video-streaming technology has accelerated the trend, offering one titillating series after another. I admit to being enraptured by *Damages*, *Orange Is the New Black*, and *The Killing*, and my friends insist that *Breaking Bad*, *The Wire*, and New Orleans–based *Treme* are even better. Nearly all of these series feature violent crime and/or the detectives and police who sometimes bring people to justice and sometimes join in the melee.

Elayne Rapping (2003) has written of the conservative ideological messages conveyed by these shows—the criminalization of social problems, the overrepresentation of people of color as criminal offenders, and the exaggerated focus on violent crime. In an article entitled "Looking beyond Caged Heat: Media Images of Women in Prison," Dawn Cecil (2007) reveals the sensationalized and sexualized image of women prisoners in documentaries, television news, and talk shows.

A heated debate has also been taking place about depictions of crime, homophobia, racism, and violence against women in video games (Freeman 2014; Suellentrop 2013; Sarkeesian 2014). Media critic and feminist Anita Sarkeesian has produced a number of You-Tube videos revealing the pervasive use in video games of themes such as "damsels in distress," which repeatedly show women as helpless hostages and victims of crime in need of rescue. These YouTube series are widely watched and have prompted loud and angry outcries from gamers whose reactions—including threats of rape and other forms of violence against Sarkeesian—echo the themes of the misogynist violence depicted in the games. "Gamergate," as the controversy is now called, has become such a hot topic it was the subject of a long segment on television's widely watched *The Colbert Report* (October 30, 2014).

SO, WE HAVE SEEN that violence, crime, and law permeate the media, from news programs and newspapers to fictionalized television shows and video games. But when we talk about law being everywhere, law and society scholars often mean something else. Beyond the hyperactive cop shows, celebrity trials, reality TV car chases, "pop torts," and video games, law is present in our lives in more mundane ways as well. It permeates popular culture to be sure, but just as surely it permeates our everyday, ordinary lives beyond the spotlight of the media or the ritual of the courtroom.

As did Malinowski, many law and society scholars find law even where there are no traces of formal law. Several decades ago Sally Falk Moore (1973, 721) wrote about the "semi-autonomous social fields" that are outside the formal legal system but "have their own customs and rules and the means of coercing or inducing compliance." Examples of such social fields are everywhere—from corporations to professional associations to voluntary associations, and to the structured interactive spaces among and between such groups. Moore analyzed the upscale ready-made dress industry in New York City as a "semi-autonomous social field" in which union representatives, contractors, and designers exchange gifts and favors in a way that often circumvents both the formal legal system and union rules. Making the case that this is indeed a legal order, she said, "There are strong pressures to conform to this system of exchange if one wants to stay in this branch of the garment industry. These pressures are central to the question of . . . the relative place of state-enforceable law as opposed to the binding rules and customs generated in this social field" (728). Moore's detailed description of these uncodified legal orders and their penetration into everyday life remains one of the most compelling in the field.

Clearly, law (or something like it) shapes the way we live whether we notice it or not. E. Adamson Hoebel and Karl Llewellyn (1941) emphasized this point long ago in their study of the Cheyenne who once inhabited the Great Plains of North America. Unlike Moore's research, their focus was on formal law; but like Moore, they highlighted the ubiquity of legal orders and law's often invisible presence. Mixing interviews with historical documents, they pieced together a picture of a traditional system of law organized around two main functions. The first was to set the parameters for ordinary life so people could "go around in more or less clear ways" (20). In this function, law stayed largely behind the scenes, like a theater prompter who is invisible as long as everyone remembers their lines. But, said Hoebel and Llewellyn, "trouble cases" inevitably arose—for example, in the form of disputes or egregious violations—and then law made a flamboyant entrance to clean up the "social mess" (20).

As Hoebel and Llewellyn found with the Cheyenne, law in contemporary Western society sets the ground rules and mostly stays in the background, commanding attention only when trouble comes. We nonetheless sense its routine strictures, as, for example, when I am intimidated into leaving the annoying labels on my mattress, or concede to a credit check, or even more routinely when I stop for the red light on my quiet street at midnight with no other cars in sight. The impulse to abide by law's restrictions may vary across time, culture, social class, personality type, and punishment severity (a topic of what are called compliance studies), but even violators usually modify their behavior to minimize detection. It is this everyday nature of law—its ability to influence our most mundane activities and even to determine what those activities *are*—that makes it such a powerful resource for those who would shape the socioeconomic order to their advantage, as we saw in the previous chapter.

If law shapes how we live, it also shapes how we talk, and so how we think. At the most basic level, law creates conceptual categories and determines their contents and boundaries. For decades, there has been a heated debate in the United States about whether immigrants take jobs away from citizens. Beyond the specifics of that debate, consider how law shapes the thought process that underlies it. Without immigration law, there is no category of "immigrant" (as there wasn't when European explorers "immigrated" to the shores of what was to become the Americas). The point may seem trivial until we recognize how much a part of natural reality this legal category and others like it seem, and how critical to our very thought processes.

Susan Coutin's (1994) analysis of the 1980s sanctuary movement in the United States underscores this power of language and legal categories. She shows that while sanctuary workers resisted the government's definition of which illegal aliens were true "refugees," they continued to use these legal classifications that are so much a part of our linguistic and cognitive repertoire. Sanctuary activists redefined the *contents* of categories, and so at one level replaced government's legal authority with that of the community, but at the same time they reinforced the legitimacy of the categories themselves. Even this radical movement that was intent on shaking up legal meaning "both resisted and furthered repression" (299), illustrating once again the cognitive power of legal classifications.

So it is with many of the categories that are the building blocks of thought. Not just "criminal," "prison," "felony," or "illegal alien," but less combustible words like "contract," "capital," "private property," "mortgage," "welfare," "spouse," and "discrimination" are the creatures of law. Law not only defines their boundaries and content but also brings them into existence in the first place. They become routine parts of our vocabulary, but their origins in law—and so their essentially invented nature—remain obscure to us. Even words like "brother-in-law" that noisily declare their legal origins somehow manage to settle in to the natural order of things. By the same token, relationships that lack a name lack a certain cognitive solidity. There is no word in English for me to call the parents of my son's wife. To my son, they are his "in-laws." But there is nothing for me to call them, and so they reside somewhere out there on the hazy fringes of family.

Law and society thinkers who study the concept of race point out that race and racial categories are not fixed, natural realities but are instead sociolegally constructed. Critical race theory scholars show that law has historically been a central protagonist in defining racial categories and that the boundaries of these categories have shifted over time to accommodate political realities and conventional wisdoms. For example, the first citizenship law in the United States in 1790 declared that only "free White persons" could become U.S. citizens. So it was critical to define who was "white" and on what grounds. Over the decades (before the racist exclusion was finally repealed in 1952), the courts came to many conflicting decisions on the subject. As Ian Haney López (1996, 203–8) reports in his book *White by Law*, the courts have variously declared that "Chinese are not White," "persons half White and half Native American are not White," "Hawaiians are not White," "Burmese are not White," "Japanese are not White," "Mexicans are White," "Native Americans are not White," "persons half White, one-quarter Japanese, and one-quarter Chinese are not White," "Asian Indians are probably not White," "Syrians are White,"

"Armenians are White," "Syrians are not White," and "Filipinos are not White." The courts may have had trouble deciding what "white" actually meant, but they played a key role in perpetrating the ideas of whiteness and nonwhiteness and their assumed basis in natural reality.

Feminist scholars have shown that the content and boundaries of sexual identification are also at least partly legal constructions. Many of these scholars document the role of law historically in defining what it means to be women or men and what their respective characteristics, capabilities, and rights are. Some focus on the historical exclusion of women in the United States from public life and from certain professions, on the basis of women's alleged timidity and irrationality and their capacity for motherhood (Taub and Schneider 1998). Others, like Judith Butler (1990), argue that the dichotomization of sex into male and female is itself a sociolegal creation. Pointing to a continuum of anatomical traits and body types, Butler contends that law and culture impose the male-female duality on that continuum and in the process naturalize it.

Not long ago, a transgender prisoner brought a lawsuit against the California Department of Corrections and Rehabilitation (CDCR) for deliberate negligence, after being serially raped by her cellmate and others in a men's prison. At the start of the San Francisco trial, most of a day was consumed with the prosecution and defense arguing the legal question of whether the inmate should be referred to with the feminine pronoun she preferred or the masculine pronoun that attorneys for the CDCR insisted upon (presumably in part because the latter was jockeying for an advantage with the jury, who might find it harder to imagine a man as a rape victim). Beyond the fact that the very term "transgender" naturalizes the male-female divide that the gender-variant person transgresses, the intense courtroom debate underscored the mutually exclusive nature of the gender categories and the emotional stakes in assigning them.

The ability of law to create social realities that appear natural by inventing many of the concepts and categories we think with means that it insinuates itself invisibly into our everyday worlds and wields extraordinary power. John Conley and William M. O'Barr (1998), in Just Words, reveal the subtle workings of linguistic power in the courtroom, where participants who do not use linear logic and masculine forms of speech are effectively silenced and technical legal language defines reality. The "powerless language" of many women and some men "reflects and reinforces their subordinate position in society" (66, 65). In the courtroom, their tendency to use "hedge words" such as "kind of" or "sort of," finishing sentences with a lifting up of their voices as if asking a question rather than making a statement, and other stylistic specifics—learned through years of subordination and its attendant hesitancies—undermines women's authority with juries and other courtroom players and reproduces inequalities of power. The fact that this power remains mostly invisible precisely because its products are so taken for granted makes it even more formidable. Whether in the courtroom, on the streets, or in the private space of family, law and the thought processes and power relations it contributes to draw much of their power from their quiet ubiquity.

The Italian social thinker Antonio Gramsci (1971) called this power to shape reality without calling attention to itself "hegemony." Contemporary law and society scholars point out that law is hegemonic because not only does it shape how we live; it also gives the shape of our lives a taken-for-grantedness. The term is usually used for weighty subjects like the power of the ruling class to impose its value system and worldview. It is often brought to bear, for example, to explain how subordinate people come to accept their subordination or how a society that promises freedom and equality retains legitimacy despite its perpetuation of profound inequalities (Lazarus-Black and Hirsch 1994). To the extent that this subordination and these inequalities are made to appear part of the natural order of things through law and its associated cognitive processes and social structures, they go uncontested and derive further hegemonic power from their lack of contestation.

A similar process applies to the more trivial events of daily life. To give a couple of examples from the realm of traffic flows: I was recently in Ireland and found it almost impossible to drive as they do, on the "wrong" side of the road, and in one instance I ended up in a ditch. Upon my return, I exchanged many stories with other Americans and some Europeans, the common theme of which was twofold—the challenges of this driving experience and the conviction that the Irish drive on the wrong side. There is always a tongue-in-cheek quality to these conversations and accusations, but the extent to which law has ingrained in me which is the right side of the road was graphically conveyed by my landing in that ditch. My second example comes from closer to home. If I don't run the red light on my corner at midnight, it is not just because I am afraid the police will see me; it is also that deep in my frontal lobe somewhere "red light = stop" has taken up quiet, but no less forceful, residence.

Sociolegal scholar Tom Tyler (1990) asks "why people obey the law" and concludes that it is partly because we think of it as legitimate, fair, or just. The concept of hegemony takes this a step further. Not only do the categories and processes of law seem just; they seem natural. I consent to that credit check at Sears because it seems like a reasonable, legitimate thing for Sears to do; mostly though, it does not occur to me to question it, much less to ponder the sociolegal construction of the whole concept of credit. Only once have I thought long and hard about the meaning of "credit" in a capitalist society, and that was when my credit card company bizarrely informed me that my credit history was bad precisely because I paid all my bills on time and therefore owed no accumulated interest.

But if law is powerful and hegemonic, it also occasionally provokes people to contest that power and provides a venue for resistance. In fact, it is partly because law is the locus of so much power—both the formal, blatant kind and the more invisible, hegemonic kind—that people often turn to it as a tool of resistance. The transgender inmate, whose trial underscored the hegemonic quality of gender categories, effectively used the courtroom for a lesson on the ambiguity of those categories. Using law as a form of resistance, she not only sought material relief from the indifference of the CDCR but also briefly unsettled sexual categories and exposed their arbitrariness as the court argued for the better part of a day over whether she was a "she" or a "he." The judge finally intervened and announced that the plaintiff was to be considered female and should be referred to with the feminine pronoun. Ultimately, she lost the legal case against the CDCR, but a colleague who observed the trial and spoke to her afterward told me she was beaming even in the face of defeat, gratified not just that she had had her day in court but also that she had forced people to accept her femaleness, at least linguistically and for the duration of the trial.

James Scott (1985) wrote about small acts of everyday resistance as "weapons of the weak" among peasants in a Malaysian village. Others have extended the idea to daily acts of retaliation and sabotage, like a waiter spitting in a disrespectful customer's soup or a disgruntled worker surreptitiously dropping a wrench in the assembly line. People who are deprived of the power that comes with material resources or social status harness whatever is at hand to register their discontent, vindicate their lowly position, exact satisfaction for the wrongs done them, or simply rescue their dignity. As that transgender inmate found, the legal arena can sometimes be used for these purposes.

Sometimes law is not just the arena but also the tool. A good example of this can be found in the burgeoning prisons of twenty-first-century America. The unprecedented surge in incarceration in the United States has meant that prisoners are often crammed into quarters built for half as many, sleeping in tents set up in prison yards or triple-bunked in what were once prison gymnasiums. Rehabilitation programs have given way to warehousing, and increased mandatory sentences mean that many more prisoners are serving what amount to life sentences. As people serve out their long terms, the prison population is aging, and decrepit medical facilities are stretched even further beyond their meager capacity. Not long ago, the *Sacramento Bee* ran this description of medical facilities at San Quentin in California:

> To reach one of San Quentin's medical clinics, you must walk past a row of 20 maximum-security cells with inmates confined behind fine crosshatched wire, barely visible. The floor is strewn with trash, puddles of water and worse from the runoff of inmate showers from the tiers above. Soap and hair drip off the guardrails of the walkways, leaving a slippery mess to dance around as you approach the clinic, which is shoehorned into a converted cell. A mildewed shower curtain hangs in front of the clinic's entrance to keep the water from spraying directly into the medical area. . . . Inhumane is the nice term for the conditions. . . . The resulting patient health outcomes tell a gruesome story. (Sillen 2006, E1)

In the midst of the prison surge, the Republican Congress in 1996 passed the Prison Litigation Reform Act, designed to cut down on prisoner lawsuits. Among other things, it required prisoners with grievances to exhaust administrative remedies provided by the states' prison systems before accessing federal court to contest the conditions of their confinement. It was clear from the congressional debate that lawmakers saw internal administrative procedures as a way to reduce prisoner lawsuits, most of which they said were "frivolous."

And it worked. Federal lawsuits filed by prisoners plummeted from forty-two thousand in 1995 to twenty-six thousand in 2000, even as the prison population continued to rise. As I write this, the prisoner filing rate remains far below its pre-PLRA peak (Schlanger 2015, 157). The inmate grievance systems that are part of this decline in lawsuits are severely compromised as effective disputing mechanisms. State correctional systems control how the process works and often make it so complicated that few prisoners (or anyone else) can figure it out. Most states require the paperwork to be filled out just so, in strict accordance with all state guidelines, no matter how complicated; otherwise, the grievance will be screened out and the inmate deemed not to have exhausted internal remedies. In the 2005 case *Campbell v. Chaves*, one federal judge described prison grievance systems as "a series of stalling tactics, and dead-ends without resolution."

In California, inmates who want to file a complaint start the process by describing their grievance on a "602" form and depositing it in a grievance box. Inmates consider the system "a joke." One claims, "I've watched officers take 602s and using a lighter burn them in front of inmates and then deny having done so when asked about it by their supervisors." Another says he has seen staff throwing away prisoners' grievances before logging them in. And a woman reports that guards come into inmates' cells "and steal your stuff. . . . I turned in lots of 602s and they lost or ignored them, I never received any response. What are they going to do anyway? These men control us, it's their system, it's the way it is. We are a number to them, we're not even human." The prisoners are right to be cynical about it. The vast majority of these grievances are screened out or denied, and their appeals rejected (Calavita and Jenness 2013, 2015).

So, why are tens of thousands of these grievances filed every year in California alone? One inmate I asked looked at me as if the answer were obvious and said with a shrug, "It's all we got." I assume he meant that even if their chances of winning are slim, they take a shot at it anyway, like the lottery. But maybe filing a complaint is also about taking charge and telling one's story. In the context of captivity, where one's identity as an autonomous human being is under attack, filing a grievance may be an assertion of one's agency or ability to take action. A prisoner in solitary confinement recently wrote, "Every aspect of our lives is controlled, from when the light comes on in the morning to the little bit of property we're allowed in our cells. The system tries to make us into caged animals but we still retain the right to be persons who are humyn [sic]." In this context, prisoners might file grievances as a way to affirm their very humanity.

Some prisoners talk of filing grievances as a way to harass guards and officials, in a rare turning of the tables of who is in charge. Assuming that the forms are not simply thrown away, they produce an avalanche of paperwork for guards, wardens, and the entire prison system, as folder after folder of prisoner grievances pile up at the Sacramento Office of Inmate Appeals. I once overheard an inmate in a California prison yard telling another about something a guard had done, and that he was going to retaliate: "I'm gonna 602 his ass!" The fact that "602"—the administrative number of the grievance form—has become a verb in prison slang and means something you do to an official offers a powerful hint about its use as a weapon of the weak.

The point is, these grievance systems that Congress saw as a way to limit the power of prisoners to get to court may actually empower them at some level. Even though it is unlikely to succeed at changing conditions, filing a grievance may be a form of resistance—an assertion of agency, the catharsis of telling one's story, and the rare opportunity to exact revenge-by-paperwork on one's captors. So, law may contribute to hegemony as Gramsci explained, but it may also be used at the microlevel to fight back, or at least to fight for one's dignity.

Sometimes the victory eked out through resistance is more than symbolic or subjective and extends beyond the microlevel. Richard Abel (1995) writes of the ingenious and powerful use of law by opponents of apartheid in South Africa. As he tells us, law was a potent weapon not only for those who imposed apartheid on black South Africans but also for those who resisted it. And its power as a tool of resistance was related directly to its hegemonic power, in the sense that it was the cultural legitimacy of the rule of law in South Africa that enhanced its utility in challenging white elites.

Contributors to the edited volume *Contested States* (Lazarus-Black and Hirsch 1994) explore the uses of law by women in India to resist patriarchal relations (Moore 1994), the role of courts in the politics of slave resistance in the British Caribbean (Lazarus-Black 1994), and women in sixteenth-century Istanbul who stood defiantly at the "gates of justice" and negotiated protection under Islamic law (Seng 1994). In some cases, the impacts were confined to the individual protagonists, and in other cases their ramifications were far-reaching. In all of them, though, the previously disempowered obtained concrete changes through the deployment of laws that were otherwise used to subordinate them. Hirsch and Lazarus-Black (1994, 20) sum it up succinctly: "Law is at once hegemonic and oppositional." While law exerts enormous power by seeping into and through daily life, structuring our routines, our language, and our thought, at the same time it offers itself up as one of the sharpest instruments in our tool kits of resistance.

A *New York Times* article entitled "Tiny Voices Defy Fate of Girls in Yemen" tells the story of two young girls in Yemen who risked death to escape their violent, forced marriages (Worth 2008). The average age of marriage for girls in this conservative Arab country steeped in poverty is twelve or thirteen. Fathers sometimes force their daughters to marry as young as eight years old. The thinking apparently is that early marriage preempts a dishonoring kidnapping by a future husband. It is also understood locally that early marriage makes the wife more compliant. The local saying goes, "Give me a girl of eight, and I can give you a guarantee [that she will be a good wife]."

The article tells of two girls who rebelled against this custom. The *Times* reporter recounts the story of ten-year-old Nujood Ali:

> The issue first arose because of Nujood, a bright-eyed girl barely four feet tall. Her ordeal began in February, when her father took her from Sana, the Yemeni capital, to his home village for the wedding. She was given almost no warning. . . .
>
> The trouble started on the first night, when her 30-year old husband . . . took off her clothes as soon as the light was out. She ran crying from the room, but he caught her, brought her back and forced himself on her. Later, he beat her as well.
>
> "I hated life with him," she said, staring at the ground in front of her. The wedding came so quickly that no one bothered to tell her how women become pregnant, or what a wife's role is. . . .
>
> Nujood complained repeatedly to her husband's relatives and later to her own parents after the couple moved back to their house

in Sana. . . . On April 2, she said, she walked out of the house by herself and hailed a taxi.

It was the first time she had traveled anywhere alone, Nujood recalled, and she was frightened. On arriving at the courthouse, she was told the judge was busy, so she sat on a bench and waited. Suddenly he was standing over her, imposing in his dark robes. . . .

[The judge] invited her to spend the night at his family's house, she said, since court sessions were over for the day. . . .

When Nujood's case was called the next Sunday, the courtroom was crowded with reporters and photographers, alerted by her lawyer. . . . "Do you want a separation, or a permanent divorce?" the judge asked the girl, after hearing her testimony and that of her father and husband.

"I want a permanent divorce," she replied, without hesitation. (Worth 2008, A8)

The judge granted the divorce, and since then Nujood's lawyer has been contacted by other girls. As the reporter tells it: "One of them was Arwa, who was married last year at the age of eight. . . . Arwa described how surprised she was when her father arranged her marriage to a 35-year-old man eight months ago. Like Nujood, she did not know the facts of life, she said. The man raped and beat her." After several months, Arwa fled to a hospital and ended up in front of a sympathetic judge who dissolved the marriage. When the reporter asked her what had made her run away, "Arwa gazed up, an intense, defiant expression in her eyes. 'I thought about it,' she said in a very quiet but firm voice. 'I thought about it'" (Worth 2008, A8).

These two girls' actions triggered a movement against child marriage in Yemen, where many people are outraged at the violence and suffering the girls speak of. And their resistance will probably reverberate beyond that. Nujood told the *Times* reporter that she planned to be a civil rights lawyer or journalist. Like the Ottoman women who went to the "gates of justice" four centuries ago, Nujood and Arwa defied patriarchal customs and used the courts to do so. In the process, they freed themselves and launched a movement.

In *Law and Globalization from Below* (2005), editors Boaventura de Sousa Santos and César Rodríguez-Garavito and their contributing authors look at some of the other resistance movements that have been built like this from the bottom up. They include the struggles of landless peasants, marginalized immigrants, and workers in this period of relentless globalization. Reversing the conventional emphasis on the inexorable sweep of the neoliberal forces of globalization, the book reveals the many ways that those most negatively affected by globalization fight back, crafting legal strategies and forming advocacy networks. The results are some important local victories and the emergence of a counterhegemonic "global justice movement" (3).

One particularly powerful account in the book describes the local, national, and international opposition to development of the Narmada Valley in India (Rajagopal 2005). In this two-decade struggle, a coalition of local and global actors used law and international norms regarding human rights and sustainable development to oppose elites (including the World Bank) who supported the damming of the Narmada River and the flooding of tribal lands and farms. Contesting the displacement that the flooding would entail, its impact on local livelihoods, and its environmental effects, the coalition was both strategic and persistent. The outcomes were mixed, with the Indian Supreme Court first ordering the project suspended and later reversing itself, the World Bank withdrawing from the development project, and the World Commission on Dams being established as a venue for policy discussions about the impacts of dam development. Following the second decision by India's Supreme Court, in 1999, displacement continued. Rajagopal argues though that domestic and international norms concerning sustainable development have been advanced by this intense and visible struggle and that the resistance contributes in the long run to counterhegemonic globalism.

To be successful, such acts of organized resistance have to be tailored to historical and local contexts and they sometimes strategically avoid direct engagement with law. For example, Lynette Chua (2014) recounts the story of gay activists in authoritarian Singapore, where homosexual acts and even advocacy of gay rights are criminal offenses. Unable to turn to a rights discourse or any judicial reprieve, gay activists there use a potpourri of subversive tactics, including enhanced visibility through courting the media and exploiting cyberspace, and seeking cracks and fissures in official bans. Drawing from James Scott's concept of everyday resistance and expanding it to include organized collective action, Chua calls the strategy of these activists "pragmatic resistance." Her story of the increasing success of these strategic activists in this most unfavorable of legal and political environments underscores the counterhegemonic potential of such resistance.

Echoes of Foucault permeate this scholarship on resistance. Remember from chapter 2 that Foucault was interested in the social practices that constitute power relations at the local level. For him, the practice of power assumes at least two adversaries, each of whom is capable of action. Just as it is ultimately human beings whose actions and practices *produce* power, human beings are capable of resisting it. Prisoners in twenty-first-century California, twentieth-century opponents of apartheid in South Africa, eighteenth-century slaves in the British Caribbean, women in the Ottoman Empire, Yemeni child brides, opponents of dam development in the Narmada Valley, and activists for gay rights in Singapore all in their own way exploit law's power to contest their disempowerment.

In one final example of the power of people to carve counterhegemonic forces from otherwise oppressive contexts, legal anthropologist Laura Nader (1990) describes the "harmony ideology" among the indigenous Zapotec people in Oaxaca, Mexico. Nader tells us that missionaries and colonizers imposed ideas on the Zapotec about the dangers and dysfunctions of conflict and the superiority of harmony. This harmony ideology, with its strong value placed on compromise and cooperation, was eventually incorporated into the local society and legal order. The Zapotec then exploited this "rhetoric of peace" as a shield with which they protected their autonomy from encroachment by the Mexican state. It was in other words "both a product of nearly five hundred years of colonial encounter and a strategy for resisting the state's political and cultural hegemony" (2). In this example, the instrument of resistance was neither a courtroom nor law per se, but rather an ideology that permeated the sociolegal order—an ideology that was imposed from above and then retrofitted for counterhegemonic ends.

LAW AND SOCIETY scholars generally argue that beliefs and behavior are ultimately rooted in culture and social structure, which helps explain law's hegemony, but that people also have the capacity to resist, rebel, and at least temporarily subvert that hegemony. The law and society concept of legal consciousness ties this conceptual package together. Patricia Ewick and Susan Silbey (1998) and others who study legal consciousness are interested in people's beliefs about law and how they act on those beliefs. They pay special attention to the tension in legal consciousness between its role in reproducing legal hegemony and the agentive quality entailed in resistance. Mostly, though, studies of legal consciousness reveal the amazing capacity of law to roll with the punches, exhibiting a Zen-like flexibility that strengthens rather than diminishes its power.

People may recognize law as a tool that is wielded over them and may sometimes fashion resistance to that subordinating force, but our experiences with law and our interpretations of those experiences are full of inconsistencies and contradictions. These inconsistencies usually remain under the radar of our awareness, cause us no cognitive dissonance, and if anything contribute to, rather than detract from, law's hegemony. Law's basic legitimacy remains unquestioned, as our legal consciousness seems capable of expanding and morphing at a moment's notice. So, according to Ewick and Silbey (1998), the same person may think of law as impartial and objective in one instance, boast of manipulating it in the next, and then complain of its oppression, without posing any real threat either to our cognitive processes or to law's legitimacy.

I was reminded of this chameleon-like quality of legal consciousness recently when I was called to jury duty. At first, I complained that I couldn't spare the time. But once I got to the courthouse and was seated as a potential juror, I was awed by the majestic ritual. It was not just the judge's robes, the respectful silence, and the bailiff's formal demeanor, but the judge's meticulous explanation of due process and the obvious lengths to which the system goes to ensure adherence to that inspired principle. Now anxious to serve, I soon found myself strategizing over the best way to pass the voir dire process, during which those who are deemed potentially biased are excluded from the jury pool. Committed to not telling a lie, yet not wanting to reveal too much of my underdog sympathies, I thought carefully about how I might word my responses to the inquiries. As it turned out, the mental exercise was for naught, as the eerily clairvoyant prosecutor summed up my appearance, asked me nothing, and peremptorily excused me. Leaving the courtroom, I was troubled because I had figured out that this was a "three strikes" case, and that the defendant stood to go to prison for life for several small-time robberies committed to support a heroin habit. It struck me that I should have "resisted," at the very least making a statement protesting the three-strikes law in response to the judge's question about whether I could be impartial.

In the space of a few hours, I had alternately seen law as majestic, manipulable, and an oppressive system to be resisted. Probably because I was in law's formal living room—court—I became more than usually conscious of my fickle legal consciousness. But our sense of law, in all its majesty, manipulability, and oppressiveness, is not confined to courtrooms, prisons, or struggles of liberation; subtler examples can be drawn from daily life, as we dispute with a neighbor, apply for a driver's license, or seek reimbursement from our insurance company. All are part of legal consciousness, welded by social structure, infused with ideology, and—here is the larger point—ubiquitous.

The development of legal consciousness probably starts in early childhood, like just about everything else. Legal historian Harold J. Berman (2006, 1) once said, "A child says 'It's my toy.' That's property law. A child says, 'You promised me.' That's contract law. A child says, 'He hit me first.' That's criminal law. A child says, 'Daddy said I could.' That's constitutional law." Law is not only everywhere, but there is hardly a time in our lives before at least some dim consciousness of law.

As Berman (2006) and Ewick and Silbey (1998) reveal, lawlike rules are everywhere, setting the terms for human interaction and imposing penalties for violations. Michael DeLand (2013) found a compelling example of this as he participated in pickup basketball games in a park in Santa Monica, California. There are no officials refereeing these games, but no matter. As DeLand says, "Players create and sustain orderliness themselves" (657). They do so through an intricate, if informal, system of rules that dictate what a foul is, what constitutes a traveling violation, when a point counts, how and when a call can be contested—everything that keeps order (sort of) and allows the game to continue. At least as important, the rules confer significance on the game as not just "playing around." Borrowing from Erving Goffman (1974), DeLand observes that while these games are unofficial, they are taken seriously in part because they are "played in the 'key of law'" (657). There are even procedural rules about when a call can legitimately be made. DeLand notices, "Calls that are made 'too late' are often dismissed promptly and emphatically." He tells this story:

> After a series of fakes Rob laid the ball into the basket. As he ran back on defense Steve said that he thought Rob had committed a traveling violation. Jake, Rob's teammate, immediately yelled at Steve, "You gotta call it before the shot goes in though. You didn't say shit til' he already made it!" . . . There's no discussion! (668–69).

So when law and society scholars say that law is everywhere, they mean that it permeates popular culture but also that it is part and parcel of our daily lives and our very consciousness. Neighborhood-watch campaigns, the shouted rules of a pickup basketball game, and the Sears credit check share important aspects of official law and bear an uncanny resemblance to their more formally dressed sister. We sense this functional similarity when we talk about "taking the law into our own hands" or when we "lay down the law" to our kids, "read someone the riot act," proclaim that "his word is law around here," or stand at an intersection beside our friend's stalled car and direct traffic—even the shiest of us—with surprising aplomb and authority.

The *New York Times* ran a funny article about a small town in Nebraska where the confluence of law and everyday life is especially apparent (and clearly considered quaint by the urbane editors of the *Times*) (Barry 2007). It seems that in this prairie town of Chadron, Nebraska, citizens call the police department to report almost any type of activity that is a little out of the ordinary, and the dispatcher provides the local paper with a weekly report of these activities. The reports—from daily life to police, and back again to the weekly paper, where people keep abreast of community events—have the ring of a town diary chronicling the everyday: "Caller from the 900 block of Morehead Street reported that someone had taken three garden gnomes from her location sometime during the night. She described them as plastic, 'with chubby cheeks and red hats'"; "Caller from the 200 block of Morehead Street advised a man was in front of their shop yelling and yodeling. Subject was told to stop yodeling until Oktoberfest"; "Caller from the 400 block of Third Street advised that a subject has been calling her and her employees, singing Elvis songs to them"; "Caller from the 200 block of Morehead Street advised that a known subject was raising Cain again"; "Officer on the 1000 block of West Highway 20 found a known male subject in the creek between Taco John's and Bauerkemper's. . . . Officers gave subject ride home"; "Caller on the 900 block of Parry Drive advised a squirrel has climbed down her chimney and is now in the fireplace looking at her through the glass door, chirping at her"; and "Caller stated that there is a 9-year-old boy out mowing the yard and feels that it is endangering the child in doing so when the mother is perfectly capable of doing it herself."

Mocking tone aside, the article is a great illustration of the penetration of law and daily life. It reminds us that legal consciousness is not just about prisoners resisting their grotesque conditions or heroic women in the Ottoman Empire standing up to patriarchy. It is just as surely found in Chadron, Nebraska, where citizens call the police to let them know about a squirrel in the fireplace or Elvis on the telephone. Legal consciousness, like law itself, is everywhere.

This concept of the pervasiveness of law and legal consciousness can be misinterpreted in the context of the conventional wisdom that American society is too litigious. Let me set this straight. I do not mean that Americans are quick to sue. For one thing, the idea that law is everywhere is not for the most part about people using the formal levers of law; it is more fundamentally about the profound visible and invisible presence of law in every realm of life and thought. It is true that some of the examples I have given here—like the prisoners who file grievances and the girls in Yemen who go to court to contest their forced marriages—involve people turning to the formal law as a tool of resistance. The larger point, though, is that law permeates our lives in myriad ways even when we are not consciously engaged with "the law."

There is another problem with confusing the idea of the pervasiveness of law with the notion that contemporary American society is litigious. And that is that sociolegal scholars long ago put to rest the myth of American litigiousness. Felstiner, Abel, and Sarat (1980–81) point out that while people may be quick to complain, they are unlikely to mobilize law formally. They note the differences in "naming" a problem, "blaming" someone for it, and actually "claiming" compensation in court. While there may be quite a lot of naming and blaming, relatively few people go the extra step of filing a legal claim.

Haltom and McCann (2004) summarize extensive scholarly findings that support this. These findings show that, contrary to the conventional wisdom, the amount of product liability and malpractice litigation in the United States has not significantly increased over the past few decades. They then question what has given rise to the myth that contemporary Americans are quick to sue. Tracing the trajectory of celebrity torts—or torts that are so widely known about that they become household words—they document these torts' tour through the media, the often distorted nature of the story, and the interests these distortions serve. Haltom and McCann build a convincing case that prevailing ideas about American litigiousness are spread by a media eager to appeal to readers with dramatic and oversimplified tales of tort-happy complainants, and by economic elites who are interested in tort reform to immunize themselves from lawsuits.

So we end this chapter where we began. Law permeates our cultural vernacular, introduced to us over and over by a mass media less interested in accurate portrayal than in selling copy. Litigiousness is not the same thing as the pervasiveness of law, but the entrenched myth of American litigiousness provides a powerful example of the cultural, ideological, and economic moorings of legal consciousness.

In the next chapter, I pick up again on the ubiquity of law, its role in shaping our experiences and perceptions, and the powerful forces these reflect and advance, this time in the contentious arena of race. As we will see, law may be less overtly implicated in constructing race today than it was when the courts struggled to define who was white. But in small and large ways—many shaped by the kinds of invisible processes I have touched on in this chapter—law is far from color-blind.

CHAPTER FOUR

The Color of Law

A leading American psychologist reported in 1913 that 83 percent of Jews, 80 percent of Hungarians, 79 percent of Italians, and 87 percent of Russians were "feeble-minded" (Goddard 1917, 247). He arrived at this astounding finding by giving IQ tests to immigrants landing at Ellis Island. If the southern Italians who had worked as sharecroppers all their lives and had never left their hometowns before boarding the ship to America could not tell the test givers what was missing from a picture of a tennis court without a net (to cite one example), they were deemed "feeble-minded" or "morons." Similar tests were given to prisoners in the United States and to recruits in the U.S. Army, with similarly alarming results.

The theory that triggered this massive testing campaign, and that was reinforced by its results, was that feeblemindedness made people commit crime. Supposedly, the brain deficit was hereditary, which helped account for why crime rates were higher among African Americans and recent immigrants than among native-born Caucasians. The feeblemindedness theory was so popular in the first decades of the twentieth century that it was used to explain all manner of other social ills, from alcoholism to divorce, suicide, and poverty. Here at last was a "scientific" theory that explained why crime and poverty were endemic to African Americans, immigrants, and other people of color in the United States. Not coincidentally, given its neat fit with elites' own sense of superiority and its removal of societal responsibility for social problems, the research was funded and its results disseminated with the financial support of a wide swath of early twentieth-century captains of industry and finance (Rafter 1997).

Henry H. Goddard (1917, 266), the psychologist who directed the Ellis Island research, was a little worried that so many "defectives" were entering the country: "It should be noted that the immigration of

recent years is of a decidedly different character from the early immigration. . . . We are now getting the poorest of each race." But he found
a silver lining in the vast number of "morons" available to the newly
industrializing nation, reminding his compatriots, "They do a great
deal of work that no one else will do. . . . There is an immense amount
of drudgery to be done, an immense amount of work for which we do
not wish to pay enough to secure more intelligent workers. . . . May it
be that possibly the moron has his place?" (269).

Not everyone was convinced that this silver lining was enough to
justify the presence of this "poorer class of immigrant" (U.S. Congress, Senate Immigration Commission 1911, 38). The immigration
restrictions of the 1920s, which were targeted at the Southern and
Eastern Europeans then entering the country, were largely based on
this racist theory. In 1920, Lothrop Stoddard, author of *Revolt against
Civilization; The Menace of the Under-Man* (1922), and Harry Laughlin,
noted eugenicist from Cold Spring Harbor, came to testify at the
House Hearings on Immigration Restriction, and the House Committee appointed Laughlin its "expert eugenics agent." Johnson called
the new immigration "pernicious" and quoted a State Department
report in which Jews were said to be "abnormally twisted," "filthy
un-American and often dangerous in their habits" (U.S. Congress,
House Committee on Immigration and Naturalization 1920, 10). In
1923, Laughlin used army IQ tests and feeblemindedness data to argue that Southern and Eastern Europeans were of hopelessly inferior
racial stock (U.S. Congress, House Committee on Immigration and
Naturalization 1923, 1311). The following year, Congress passed the
Emergency Quota Act, which limited immigration from each European country to 2 percent of the number present in the 1890 U.S. census, cutting their numbers by more than half.

At the same time, alarmed policy makers launched eugenics practices to rid the United States of the feebleminded already in their
midst. Forced sterilizations and the warehousing of innocent people
in institutions for the feebleminded were carried out in the name of
limiting their reproduction. Sterilizations were first introduced in the
prisons of Indiana and eventually spread to thirty-three states. Justice Oliver Wendell Holmes Jr., a strong proponent of eugenics, put
the constitutional stamp of approval on forced sterilization in 1927,
when he helped decide a landmark U.S. Supreme Court case, *Buck v.*

Bell, involving a young woman named Carrie who had been involuntarily sterilized in Virginia and who purportedly had a feebleminded mother and daughter. "Three generations of imbeciles are enough," Justice Holmes famously declared. Subsequent scholarship revealed that neither Carrie, her mother, nor her daughter were mentally impaired or suffered from any mental illness, but these findings came too late for this family and for the many immigrants and others who were sterilized against their will. By 1941, over sixty thousand people, disproportionately African Americans and recent immigrants, had been subjected to the procedure (Gould 1985; Rafter 1997).

The feeblemindedness theory has long since been dismissed as based on shoddy science (although variations of it persist), whose primary virtues were its consistency with the racist assumptions of the day and its compatibility with the self-interests of the wealthy individuals and foundations that bankrolled it. There are few better examples of the interplay of race and law and the ways our preconceptions about race get naturalized as biological fact and inscribed in social policy. No matter that the theory was so glaringly defective as science, fraught as it was with racial biases and methodological problems; it formed the basis for eugenics policies, immigration restrictions, and criminal justice practices for decades, with scientists, policy makers, and practitioners turning a blind eye to its obvious defects. In turn, these laws and policies reinscribed and reinforced the racist assumptions they were founded on.

Angela Harris (2000) uses the term "race law" to refer to laws, like those based on the feeblemindedness theory, that maintain racial categories and shape interactions among racial groups. In the previous chapter, we saw how legal actors struggled historically to fix racial boundaries—for example, determining who was white for the purposes of naturalization—and how those boundaries shifted and continue to shift over time. If we look carefully at these struggles and unstable boundaries, a pattern emerges. Not only are the boundaries fluid and shifting, but the boundaries and their shifts are often driven by instrumental interests.

Richard Delgado and Jean Stefancic (2001, 6–8) call this phenomenon "interest convergence" or "material determinism," meaning that material interests produce the concept of race and determine the content of racial categories, including their shifts over time. We can see this material determinism clearly in the feeblemindedness movement and its funding by those more interested in promulgating excuses for inequality and its myriad dysfunctions than in scientific rigor. The theory may have been defective, but it was perfect as a way to explain the inequality from which these titans of industry and finance so abundantly benefited.

We do not have to look far for other examples. Most obvious are the economic interests that shaped slavery and elaborated its ideological justification in the form of racism against Africans. Paul Finkelman's (1997) edited volume *Slavery and the Law* provides a compelling picture of this stitching together of slaveholders' economic interests and their convenient ideological rationalizations for turning human beings into property, with law as the master tailor. Edward Baptist's (2014) *The Half Has Never Been Told* makes the case even more bluntly and with a broader lens: American slavery, and the legal regime that shored it up, were the central ingredients in the flowering of global capitalism (recall the theme from chapter 2 on the connections between law and economic form). More precisely, American cotton was "the world's greatest commodity" (xvii) in the nineteenth century. Picked ever more efficiently by slave labor overseen by legalized violence, it fueled England's textile industry and laid the material and cultural foundation for "the great economic and social transformations" (xvii) of the nineteenth century and beyond. In Baptist's telling, the story of American slavery did not end with the Civil War. Instead, the "compact [between Northern and Southern whites] of white supremacy" (xv), forged in slavery and the global economic interests it enriched, survived in the form of racist laws of segregation and economic exclusion well into the twentieth century.

This convergence of law, racism, and economic interests was apparent too in the extensive use of the criminal justice system to provide black convict labor to employers in the decades after slavery was officially abolished (Blackmon 2008), a subject we'll return to in chapter 6. This convict lease system was not confined to adults, as Geoff Ward (2012) makes clear in his award-winning book, *The Black Child Savers*. Ward traces the origins and development of "Jim Crow juvenile justice" in America, which effectively created an apartheid juvenile justice system from 1890 to 1950 and beyond. An integral part of this history dated back to the days of slavery, when "slaveholders were keenly aware of the profit value that black children represented" (35). While the Progressive Era brought reforms in the treatment of white juvenile offenders, black children were funneled into a horrifying network of special reformatories and work assignments. And as with the system of slavery from which it dated, this convict labor was justified through racist reference to the black juvenile's allegedly irredeemable nature and proclivity for manual labor. A federal engineer even claimed in 1912 that black offenders on chain gangs "benefitted [from the] outdoor manual labor" (quoted in Ward 2012, 100).

Shifting our focus to the western frontier, we see this same materially based racialization by the founding fathers. They were convinced of their "manifest destiny" to expand westward and were also conveniently convinced of the racial inferiority of the Native Americans they exterminated in the process. Reginald Horsman (1981, 300–301) summarizes this bond between racist ideology and self-interest in early America: "By the late 1830s pro-Indian and antislavery spokesmen were drawn almost exclusively from areas in which there were few Blacks and fewer Indians. . . . When basic interests were involved, intellectuals thought hard to discover why Blacks should be enslaved or Indians dispossessed." In other words, where there was an economic interest in exploiting slave labor or appropriating land, people could be counted on to develop theoretical justifications for doing so.

Economic interests were also complicit in the racialization of the Chinese in late nineteenth- and early twentieth-century America. Anti-Chinese racism had existed from the first arrivals of large numbers of Chinese during the California gold rush in the 1850s. Prior to the completion of the Central Pacific Railroad, for which cheap Chinese labor was a critical component, U.S. industrialists took an active role in tamping down the racism and limiting calls to restrict Chinese immigration. After the railroad's completion in the 1870s, the sudden silence of this powerful lobby paved the way for Chinese exclusion from immigration and citizenship.

The anti-Chinese racism that culminated in the first Chinese Exclusion Law in 1882 was fueled in part by the material self-interests of labor unions (Saxton 1971; Salyer 1995) and in part by political leaders who calculated that their own interests could be advanced by stirring the racist pot (Gyory 1998; Tichenor 2002). Fearing competition from large numbers of poverty-stricken Chinese immigrants and reeling from the economic downturns of the late 1870s, American workers lashed out against the racialized immigrants. California lawmakers and the U.S. Congress strategically fanned the flames—some say even lighting the match (Tichenor 2002).

The flames were ferocious. The congressional debate is worth quoting at some length, because it exposes the level of explicit racism rampant at the time and incorporated into law. Proclaiming the Chinese a "terrible scourge" on California and "a great and growing evil" (U.S. Congress, Senate 1877, viii, v), members of Congress pronounced the Chinese "an inferior race" and "a distinct race of people . . . wholly incapable of assimilation" (*Congressional Record* 1882, 1637, 1584). They were convinced of the biological basis of this inferiority even while deflecting challenges regarding the relatively light skin color of the Chinese. Thirty years before the Cold Spring Harbor eugenicists claimed to have located the "feeblemindedness" gene that would play a role in restricting European immigration, members of Congress trumpeted the "discoveries" of other pseudoscientists to justify restricting the Chinese: "The scientist who determined who belonged to the Caucasian race and who did not, did not determine it by the color of their skin but by the shape of their head and by their cranial development" (1710).

A few themes were repeated over and over in this race narrative. Among the most ironic, given the exploitation of Chinese workers by employers who paid them less than the prevailing wage, was the claim that Chinese workers had the biological capacity to subsist on below-subsistence wages and so were unfair competitors to American working men and women (*Congressional Record* 1882, 1636). One senator chimed in with his own version of survival of the least fit: "It may seem strange and improbable that the apparently insignificant, dwarfed, leathery little man of the Orient should, in the peaceful contest for survival, drive the Anglo-Saxon from the field" (1485). The Chinese were even said to require less food and air than normal: "His five thousand years' training to wretched frugality in competition with his five hundred million of fellow-Mongolians has taught him how to live upon the least possible amount of air and food" (1590).

Repeated references were made to African Americans, the experience of slavery, and lingering North-South hostilities thirty years after the Civil War. With a heavy dose of historical revisionism and self-congratulation, senators warned each other not to tackle another "race problem": "They [blacks] were a part of the people here; we could not send them abroad; and because we treated them with humanity, with righteousness, and with justice, shall we say that we are bound to extend to all the nations of the earth the same rights that we extended to them?" (*Congressional Record* 1882, 1713). Many said some version of "We have one race problem already unsettled in this country . . ." (1519), or "Because we have one evil, shall we fly to another?" (1645), or "Does anybody suppose for an instant that if the African were not in this country to-day we should be anxious to welcome him? Does any reflecting man believe that he is an advantage to this country?" (quoted in Gyory 1998, 228).

Some worried about the effect of the Chinese on African Americans: "The colored man is naturally superstitious, and how far he might be carried away from the Christian civilization after the Joss god of the Chinaman no one can tell. That he would be likely to fall into his vicious habits is greatly to be feared. Do not let these colored men be brought in contact with these Chinese people. . . . We are trying to build them up" (*Congressional Record* 1882, 1583–84). Pointing to the problem of the American Indian and calling them "savages," one leading senator warned President Chester Arthur (who had vetoed an earlier exclusion bill), "In other words, Mr. President, we would not permit the purity and sweetness of our national waters to be contaminated or polluted by the mingling of its pure streams with the impure from any source whatever" (3480).

The Chinese Exclusion Law was passed and signed by President Arthur in 1882. It suspended the entry of all Chinese laborers into the United States, barring immigrants on the basis of their nationality for the first time in American history. Chinese exclusion was not repealed until 1943, when it proved embarrassing in light of our alliance with the Chinese in World War II.

So, a group's racialization as nonwhite is often based on the material and economic interests of the labeling audience. At the risk of oversimplification, Africans were declared inferior in order to enslave them, American Indians were dehumanized to facilitate their removal, and the Chinese became a "yellow peril" after they had finished building the western railroads. But economics are related to racial constructions in a different way too: a group's location in the economic hierarchy of a society often determines group members' racialization in that society. More precisely, groups whose job it is to do the worst manual labor of a society are often ipso facto racialized as nonwhite—not just because of a vested interest in exploiting them, but also because cognitively race and economic status go hand in hand. And upward mobility often brings a change in racial status. One immigrant group after another in America was initially defined as nonwhite, experiencing "whitening" only after they became upwardly mobile. The Irish and the Germans in the 1850s, 1860s, and 1870s were thought of as nonwhite for several decades after their arrival in the United States. The Jews, Poles, and Italians who had been labeled feebleminded in the 1910s and 1920s came to be seen as white as they moved up the economic ladder, and by midcentury their racial whitening in the United States was virtually complete. In contrast, Italian immigrants performed cheap labor in Germany and Switzerland in the 1960s and 1970s and continued to be racialized there, long after they had moved into the white middle class in the United States. It seems that if a particular immigrant group is willing to—or condemned by destitution or illegal status to—perform low-wage work under precarious conditions, they are nonwhite in the public imagination regardless of skin color. This helps explain the continuing ambivalence about Mexican American racial identity despite Mexicans' official designation by the courts as white decades ago. Mexican immigrants are disproportionately concentrated in low-wage jobs in the United States and are so stereotyped as menial workers that the film title *A Day without a Mexican* evokes nervous laughter.

This link between a group's racial identification and its economic position apparently works even at the individual level. A study published by the prestigious National Academy of Sciences (Penner and Saperstein 2008) shows that in contemporary America people who are perceived to be white, and who self-identify as white, can fall out of that status if they become poor. Penner and Saperstein examined survey data from the U.S. Bureau of Labor Statistics that tracked twelve thousand Americans across time and found that even excluding Hispanics and those from a multiracial background from their sample, racial identification is not fixed, and whiteness is to some degree correlated with a person's economic status.

So far, we have seen that both law and economics influence the construction of race. Underscoring the constructed nature of racial categories, they multiply and contract over time, sometimes abruptly. Historically, groups that were considered nonwhite in America were assigned their very own racial classifications, with the numbers of categories and parameters veering wildly from one moment to the next. The Dillingham Immigration Commission Report in 1911 distinguished *forty-five* different races among immigrants to the United States. In 1990, the U.S. Census Bureau asked people to place themselves in one of six possible categories: white; black; American Indian, Eskimo, or Aleutian; Asian or Pacific Islander; and "some other race." Ten years later, American Indians were allotted their own category, and people were allowed to choose more than one racial identification; within each of the resulting sixty-three combinations there were "Hispanic" and "non-Hispanic" options, making for 126 possible racial classifications. Naomi Mezey (2003a, 1702) notes that the U.S. census historically played a big part in producing such ethnic identities. For example, she argues that the census produced the category "Asian American," consolidating the many different national origins and experiences that the identity encompasses. She concludes, "The racial categories of the census have made and unmade racial identity as the boundaries of those categories have shifted over time, making, for example, fair people black, and dark people white."

People are arguably more involved in their own racial identification today than in the past, with law and legal processes supplying their options and playing a supporting role. This interplay between official classifications and self-identity can be seen in the sorting that happens daily in the largest prison system in the world. The California Department of Corrections and Rehabilitation keeps its thirty-three state prisons rigidly segregated by race. Defying a U.S. Supreme Court order to desegregate, prison officials insist that keeping racial groups apart is imperative to safety given the prevalence of race-based gangs.

The sorting happens at the reception centers where incoming prisoners are given cell assignments. A close look at the process underscores the lack of clear race boundaries and their socially created nature. For one thing, race and gang affiliation get conflated, with "Hispanics" housed according to whether they identify with "Northerners" (a Mexican American gang in Northern California) or "Southerners" (a Mexican American gang in the southern part of the

state). Prisoners themselves often vociferously claim that the difference between the two is racial and based on "blood." Nationality is
also sometimes a stand-in for race. Ethnographer Philip Goodman
(2008, 759) observed this exchange at one reception center, between
an inmate and the corrections officer assigned the task of determining
prisoners' race for purposes of housing assignments:

OFFICER: Race?
INMATE: Portuguese.
OFFICER: Portuguese? [Pause] You mean White?
INMATE: Nah, I'm Portuguese, not White.
OFFICER: Sure, but who do you house with?
INMATE: Usually with the "Others."
OFFICER: We don't f—— with that here. It's just Black, White or
   Hispanic . . .

Two points. One, California prisons reinforce racial categories
through this sorting process and the segregated housing arrangements it produces. And two, as Goodman watched officers and inmates negotiate racial classifications, he saw once again the constructed nature of what is taken to be a natural, biological fact, and
law's complicity in that construction.

Law is also complicit in the subjective positioning of one group vis-
à-vis the other. Portes and Rumbaut (2001) give us personal accounts
of second-generation immigrants and the complex ways they put together an ethnic self-identity. One young Mexican American woman
in Southern California told them that her "Mexican ethnic identity was
'thickened'" when the anti-immigrant Proposition 187 passed by a
wide margin in California in 1994 (148).

In a different twist on this same theme, Soheir Morsy (1996, 176)
tells the story of a naturalized U.S. citizen of Egyptian origin who
contested the Immigration and Naturalization Service classification
of him as white. He explained his concern to Morsy, "Classification as
it is done by the United States government provides Whites with legal
ground to claim Egypt as a White civilization. . . . [W]e are fools if we
allow them to take this legacy from us." Like the Mexican American
woman in California interviewed by Portes and Rumbaut, this naturalized U.S. citizen's subjective identity as nonwhite is reinforced in
response to, and contestation of, law and legal processes.

These processes of racialization and identity construction are of course not confined to the United States. Suárez-Navaz (2006) describes the newly constructed identity of Andalusians as Europeans in the 1990s. She explains that poor Andalusian farmworkers in this southernmost region of Spain have worked side by side in the fields with North African migrants for decades but have come to identify as white citizens of the European Union and now disdain the North Africans. When Spain passed its first immigration laws in the 1980s and entered the European Union at about the same time, Andalusians began to see the immigrants as "others" with intolerable racial differences and criminal tendencies. In this case, laws hardened the subjective boundaries around Spaniards as white and immigrants as nonwhite others. On the other side of Spain in a large metropolitan area, a Moroccan told a researcher that when he calls about an apartment for rent, he is turned down because they can tell he is Moroccan: "They haven't even seen me yet . . . but they know I'm an immigrant by the color of my voice" (quoted in Agrela 2002, 111).

In Italy, sub-Saharan African immigrants are known as *vu comprà*, a derisive label mocking Nigerian street vendors who are said to approach people with this broken-Italian version of "Vuole comprare?" ("Do you want to buy?"). Reminiscent of the days of apartheid on other continents, a national politician from a right-wing party in Italy went on record in 2003 recommending separate train compartments for these so-called *vu comprà*, because, he said, second-class compartments had been reduced to "civil degradation due to the presence of so many immigrants" (quoted in Selva 2003, 27).

Jacqueline Andall's (2002) ethnography of African Italians in Milan, including some with Italian citizenship, is full of moving anecdotes documenting their experiences. One young woman, an Italian citizen of Senegalese descent, described what it was like to arrive at the airport in Italy after a vacation abroad: "I had just come back from London and the guy . . . was checking my identity card, he looked at me, looked at it, looked at me, looked at it, as if to say it just cannot be that this girl is from Italy." A young man who was seeking employment at a warehouse spoke of many Italians' inability to grasp the idea of black Italians: "I brought along my cv where everything is written down—where I was born, how old I am, what I have done. He [the employer] looked at me and said, 'But were you born here?'

And I said . . . it's written there. Then he said, 'But are you an Italian citizen?' and I said, again, yes, it's written there, I was born here. Then he said, 'So you speak Italian?' At that point [after an entire interview in Italian] I just looked at him and said no and left" (quoted in Andall 2002, 400). In these Southern European nations that have a long historical experience with emigration and whose people have themselves been racialized over the centuries, the categories have been shuffled and redrawn, but the process of racialization and its links to law remain intact.

THESE STUDIES of racial identity and the role of law in shoring it up underscore some of the key concepts of critical race theory. While critical race theorists have various emphases, most agree that race is "not objective, inherent, or fixed" but is instead a "social construction." And racism is "ordinary" in the sense that it is "the usual way society does business," and so it is entrenched and "difficult to cure or address" (Delgado and Stefancic 2001, 6–8). Studies on the multiple and contingent nature of racial identity also confirm another critical race theory idea. That is, we are all formed of multiple experiences and incorporate numerous identities and social realities.

Critical race theorists call this "intersectionality." In other words, each of us exists at the intersection of our race, gender, sexual orientation, class, and other such statuses. As Delgado and Stefancic (2001, 9) put it: "A white feminist may be Jewish, or working-class, or a single mother. An African American activist may be gay or lesbian. A Latino may be a Democrat, a Republican, or even a black—perhaps because that persons' family hails from the Caribbean. . . . Everyone has potentially conflicting, overlapping identities, loyalties, and allegiances." We could add that a second-generation immigrant in Italy may be black and Italian; an Andalusian farmworker may be both poor and a proud citizen of the European Union; and a woman born in Southern California may identify as a woman, an American, and after Proposition 187, a Mexican. This intersectionality complicates considerably sorting practices like those observed by Goodman (2008) in California prisons, where "it's just Black, White, or Hispanic."

Kimberlé Crenshaw (1998) describes the repercussions of intersectionality for women of color and the ways law compounds them. She notes first that race and gender tend to be mutually exclusive categories in people's minds. We think, for example, about "women" and "people of color"; the intersectional experience of women of color remains invisible in this formulation. Crenshaw in part blames white, middle-class feminists for this invisibility, since they have typically used their own middle-class white, female experiences as the standard of womanhood. In the process, women of color become not quite "women," and their experiences are marginalized.

But Crenshaw reserves her harshest criticism for the courts. Using three appeals court cases to make her point, she shows that the law has recognized the special location of women of color—their particular intersectionality—only when it further disempowers them. In *DeGraffenreid v. General Motors* (1983), five black women took General Motors to court to challenge the company's seniority system, which they argued discriminated against black women. Because GM had a promotion system that relied on seniority and because no black women had been hired prior to 1964, black women were effectively locked out of the competition for promotions. But the Ninth Circuit Appeals Court affirmed the lower court finding that since both white women and black men had been hired before 1964, there was neither a valid sex discrimination claim nor a valid race discrimination claim under the Civil Rights Act. Further, the court wrote that Title VII of the Civil Rights Act did not recognize compound status claims, and so there was no recourse for these women in the law.

In *Moore v. Hughes Helicopter* (1982), the same Ninth Circuit used a black female plaintiff's compound status as a reason to exclude her from representing women in a sex discrimination suit, arguing that her status as a *black* woman may have made her experience unlike that of other women. And in *Payne v. Travenol* (1982), the Fifth Circuit affirmed a lower court decision to exclude two black women from representing blacks in a race discrimination suit, on the grounds that their compound status as black *women* may have made their experience different from that of black men. The point Crenshaw makes with this trilogy of circuit court cases is that compound, or intersectional, status was highlighted when it disempowered women of color (as in *Moore* and *Payne*) and disallowed as legally irrelevant when it might have empowered them (as in *DeGraffenreid*).

All of these critical race scholars show that the meaning of race is socially constructed and that law is a key architect. A second-generation critical race theorist, Osagie Obasogie (2010, 2014), takes this a step further. Drawing from his interviews with blind and sighted adults, Obasogie reveals that the *visual* features we take to be central to definitions of race are themselves constituted from microlevel social practices and interactions, and that these are so effective that the blind "see" race in the same way as the sighted. In other words, it's not only that the meanings attached to various phenotypes are socially constructed, as previous critical race theorists had argued. Rather, borrowing from the work of art historians, Obasogie argues that we actually "see" that which we have been trained to consider relevant. As he puts it, "Experience structures visual observation" (2010, 590). And this happens from the "inside out" through routine microlevel interactions, not only from the top down through legal and social structural imperatives.

TO SUMMARIZE so far, there is extensive evidence that law played a role historically in constructing categories of race and their meanings; that in the modern period it is part of the process whereby people come to identify with one race or another; that the intersectionality of multiple, socially constructed statuses complicates that identification and can lead to further disempowerment through law; and that the visual cues of race are not self-evident but are learned through social practices and interactions.

A tragic illustration of such practices, and their consequences, can be found in police violence against men of color. Perhaps the most notorious example of the last decades was the brutal beating of Haitian immigrant Abner Louima, perpetrated by New York City policemen in 1997. Louima had been arrested on a disorderly conduct charge and transported to a Brooklyn police precinct, where he was beaten and brutalized with a broom handle, leaving him with critical internal injuries. An emergency room nurse doubted the police department's initial contention that Louima's multiple and severe injuries were the result of "abnormal homosexual activities" and reported the assault to the police department's Internal Affairs Bureau. Widespread media attention and street protests followed, and eventually the two officers who were directly implicated received prison terms.

In the second decade of the twenty-first century, there is no sign that police violence against minorities is abating. On August 9, 2014, a white police officer in Ferguson, Missouri, shot and killed Michael Brown, an unarmed nineteen-year old black man. The police officer, Darren Wilson, had ordered Brown to move out of the street onto the sidewalk. Some witnesses say that words were exchanged and the policeman, still in his patrol car, grabbed Brown by the shirt and opened fire. Others say they saw Brown lean into the patrol car, hit Wilson, and reach for Wilson's gun. At this point, Officer Wilson shot Brown. Brown ran, then turned back, and Wilson eventually fired five more times, killing him. The killing, and the subsequent failure to get an indictment of the police officer, sparked months of protest in this small suburb of St. Louis and across the nation, and reopened a national conversation about race in America. In the meantime, shootings by police—sometimes captured on cell phone videos—are reported with what seems like greater and greater frequency. Police killings of unarmed black men in America, a long-standing problem with roots in the overt and officially sanctioned racism of yesteryear, have clearly not disappeared in this "postracial" age.

Let's turn now to a less dramatic, but more routine, area of law—racial profiling—where "the color of law" is brilliantly on display. Racial profiling, like race itself, is a slippery concept, and it is important to get our terms straight. One kind of racial profiling begins with the perpetration of a specific crime. Let's say that a robbery has been committed, and the suspect is described as a Latino male, approximately five feet eight, between the ages of twenty and thirty. Law enforcement might stop and question those fitting that description, including a large portion of the Latino men in the area.

Another type of profiling does not begin with a specific crime but involves the broad-brush application of racial stereotypes. For example, young minority men are perceived to be potentially criminal not because they fit the profile of a particular perpetrator but because they fit the profile—the stereotype—of an offender in general. African American men are stopped by highway patrols so frequently they have coined the tongue-in-cheek term "DWB"—"driving while black." The 148-mile New Jersey Turnpike is considered by law enforcement to be a major route for drug smuggling in and out of New York City and a critical connection for New York–Florida drug traffic.

On this stretch of road, minorities make up only 30 percent of motorists, but they constitute 78 percent of those who police stop and search for drugs. While the police target minorities, there is evidence that they find illegal drugs more frequently on the white motorists they stop. This is consistent with an Amnesty International USA report on racial profiling in 2004 that cites surveys in which respondents were asked whether they had been the target of racial profiling. Forty-seven percent of non-Hispanic blacks responded they had been targets of profiling, 23 percent of Hispanics said they had, and only 3 percent of whites said they had experienced it.

The New York Civil Liberties Union reported data from the New York City Police Department (NYPD) on how often people are stopped and frisked. The data show, for one thing, that the NYPD has become much more aggressive in stopping people in recent years. In the first three months of 2008 (when the study was conducted) they stopped 145,098 people, meaning that by year's end they would stop 600,000, compared to a little over 97,000 in 2002. This despite the fact that only 13 percent of the stops led to an arrest of any kind. More relevant here, of the 145,098 people stopped in that three-month period, 87 percent were black or Latino. In central Harlem, where residents are predominately people of color, people are stopped much more frequently by the police than in the Upper West Side, which is predominately white, even though the two areas have roughly similar crime rates. In a three-month period in 2006, the police stopped over 2,300 people in the Harlem precinct but just over 400 in the Upper West Side precinct.

The *New York Times* joined forces with the New York Civil Liberties Union in this investigation, and their reporters interviewed people whom the police had stopped. One African American man in Harlem was questioned by the police just half an hour before being interviewed by the reporters. He said he was stopped by two patrolmen sitting in a van near his house. On this hot summer day, he carried a bag holding a can of soda and a cup with ice in it. The police ordered him over to the van so they could look inside the bag. Finding only the soda and cup with ice, they let him go, but one of them told him, "Oh, yeah, that's the type of stuff people have when they're doing something" (quoted in Williams and Grant 2008, A16).

It is not only blacks who get targeted. The Amnesty USA report documented the profiling of Arab men in the United States after 9/11.

In the immediate aftermath, immigration authorities and the police rounded up over 1,200 noncitizens from Arab and Muslim countries and detained them. Some were deported, but none was ever charged with terrorism or other crimes. The report tells the story of Moham-med Ali, a resident of Denton, Texas. Ali was stopped by the police while driving home from the video store and warned that one head-light was brighter than the other. He told an Amnesty hearing that the officer asked him, "'Well, I was wondering if you had any dead bodies or bombs in there, in your car, Mr. Ali?' . . . They walked around the car, looking in the windows, and asked me if they could do a search of the car. And my answer was no, I don't have any dead bodies or bombs in there, and you're not going to look. Then they asked me again, same question, and I proceeded to say no again. They asked a third time, and I said no again. . . . And then the officers went ahead and searched the car anyway." The police arrested Ali for having a small pocketknife in the side pocket of his passenger door, but the case was eventually dismissed in court.

Even whites can be targets under the right circumstances. In Texas, the police have developed a profile of the typical gun owner and stop and search cars accordingly. Cracking down on the illegal transport-ing of weapons, they single out white men who fit what the American Civil Liberties Union calls the "Bubba profile." The power of this ste-reotyping is underscored by the fact that I need say no more—you, the reader, know exactly what "Bubba" looks like. Bubba examples aside, the stereotypical association of young men of color with criminality lies at the heart of racial profiling in law enforcement.

The impact of such profiling and targeting is starkly revealed in Victor Rios's 2011 book *Punished: Policing the Lives of Black and Latino Boys*. Drawing from interviews and observations of forty boys of color in Oakland, California, Rios shows that the targeting of these boys as delinquent is widespread, has long-term consequences, and is not confined to law enforcement. Expanding on David Garland's (2001) "culture of control" concept, Rios argues that a "youth control com-plex" marks these boys at a very young age. The juvenile justice system is part of this complex, but so are schools, families, commercial es-tablishments, and community centers. The monitoring and targeting of these boys criminalizes them, both metaphorically and literally, as they rotate in and out of detention facilities.

Even those institutions that are presumably set up to help them often reinforce their delinquency. Rios writes, for example, that six of these boys on different occasions had been victims of violence at school and stayed home to recuperate. When they returned to school, they found they had been accused of truancy and expelled. The boys were convinced the schools pushed them out for fear they would engage in retaliation. Such expulsions are one more mark, one more sign of their delinquency, one more reason for ever-closer monitoring. These control measures further limit the life chances of these boys, affect their self-image as delinquent, and elicit subcultures of hypermasculinity and crime.

This kind of racial profiling and stigmatization does not depend on individual bias. Instead, it is institutionalized, and as such it exerts a power far beyond that of individual intention. As Charles Epp, Steven Maynard-Moody, and Donald Haider-Markel (2014) show in their book *Pulled Over*, the disproportionate police stops of minority drivers—such as those on the 148-mile stretch of New Jersey Turnpike just described—cannot be ascribed entirely to individual officer prejudice. They are the product of police department policies that since the 1970s have made investigatory stops based on vague suspicions a centerpiece of their crime control activities. Institutionalized policies such as these ensure that culturally dominant stereotypes get enshrined in everyday police practices. In the works of both Epp and colleagues and Rios, what we see are institutionalized practices that differentially affect people of color, whatever the individual intentions of the practitioners.

These institutionalized stereotypes and practices are particularly visible when contrasted with stereotypes of conformity. When I was a PhD student at the University of Delaware, I did a research project at a police station in a nearby city. It involved my interviewing arrestees after they were booked and before they had their bail interviews. The bail interviews took place in the same basement room where I was doing my research. It was a hot, dingy room with a musty smell that I still remember these many years later and a fan whirring (mostly ineffectively) in the corner. If physical locales tell us anything about the status of the administrative functions going on within, then these bail interviews of primarily inner-city minorities clearly ranked near the bottom. Over time I came to know the unfortunate clerk who spent his days in this basement room interviewing his even lower-status "clients."

One day there was a lull, and since neither of us had anything to do, we took the opportunity to relax and chat. Moving from my usual location across the room, I sat next to the clerk's desk—in the same metal, fold-up chair that defendants routinely used for their bail interviews. As we sat there talking, a police officer from upstairs came through the door on his way to the exit on the opposite side of the room, which led presumably to some other equally miserable administrative quarters. With hardly a glance and continuing on his hurried trajectory across the room, the officer muttered with visible annoyance, "What's she doing here?" Like a bolt of lightning, I was struck by how profoundly privileged I am in my white, middle-class female persona and how potent a disguise it is should I commit a criminal offense. Here I sat in precisely the same spot where day after day, hour after hour, defendants sat for their bail interviews, and yet I was not even conceivably one of them. I have to admit the thought ran through my head that I could probably get away with a lot if I wanted to. The corollary to my potent shield against criminal suspicion is the equally potent criminal profiling of others. While I could get away with a great deal, by the very same logic, others are suspect whether they do the deal or not.

These collective biases and the practices that enshrine them constitute racial profiling writ large and are a major factor in discrepancies in incarceration rates. As we saw in chapter 2, sociolegal scholars have written a lot about the rapid increase in the number of people incarcerated in the United States and a corresponding rise in the proportion of minorities in prison. Having held steady for decades at an overall rate of about 150 people imprisoned for every 100,000 U.S. residents in 1970, the rate had increased to more than 700 per 100,000 by the turn of the twenty-first century—a spectacular and historically unprecedented increase that did not coincide with comparable increases in the crime rate. And the rate at which racial and ethnic minorities are incarcerated has outpaced this overall increase. While 1.7 percent of white men between the ages of twenty-five and twenty-nine were incarcerated in 2000, 13.1 percent of non-Hispanic black men and 4.1 percent of Hispanic men in that age range were in prison.

A vast and growing literature offers an array of explanations for this dramatic turn of events. The culture of control described by Garland (2001) and discussed in chapter 2 is certainly one thread in the intricate weave of factors responsible for the current mass incarceration. Other related factors include the interests of political actors anxious to fuel and then capitalize on the fear of crime (most notably, Beckett 1997), the economic benefits of the prison binge to key players (Parenti 1999; Gilmore 2007), and the interplay of institutional, political, and historical factors, many of which play out at the local level and vary by states (Savelsberg 1994; Barker 2009; Lynch 2010; Page 2011; Campbell and Schoenfeld 2013; Campbell 2014; Schoenfeld 2009).

Percolating through these analyses is the issue of race, an issue that many scholars say is the central ingredient. Michelle Alexander (2010) calls this era of mass incarceration "the New Jim Crow," in which race discrimination is carried out under cover of felon discrimination. Loïc Wacquant (2010, 74) points out that this "mass incarceration" is more accurately the "hyperincarceration of (sub)proletarian African American men from the imploding ghetto." According to these analysts, the fact that mass incarceration of men of color came on the heels of the civil rights movement was no accident. Western (2006, 4) offers a multifactor explanation but ultimately links "the punitive sentiment unleashed in the 1970s" to both "rising crime and civil rights activism in the 1960s." Murakawa (2006) details how conservative politicians tapped the anger of Southern whites over judicial decisions such as Brown v. Board of Education, successfully conflated black civil rights activism and black criminality, threatened judges who were perceived to be soft on crime, and ultimately set off the incarceration surge. Weaver (2007, 230–31) is even more direct, arguing, "Several stinging defeats for opponents of civil rights galvanized a powerful elite countermovement. . . . What the literature usually treats as independent trajectories—liberalizing civil rights and more repressive social control in criminal justice—were part of the same political streams."

One consequence of these tangled threads of racial profiling, institutionalized racism, and mass incarceration is that fear of crime and race anxieties get subliminally tangled up. An article titled "Television and Fear of Crime" reported that television programming that features African American offenders increases not only whites' fear of crime but also that of African Americans (Eschholz, Chiricos, and Gertz 2003). This link between fear of crime and racial fears was dramatically revealed in the infamous Willie Horton incident. In the 1970s, Massachusetts had a furlough program that released prisoners for periods of time as part of their rehabilitation. An African American prisoner named Willie Horton, who was serving a life sentence for murder, committed an armed robbery and rape while on furlough. In 1988, the presidential campaign of George H. W. Bush ran a television ad against Democratic opponent and former governor of Massachusetts Michael Dukakis that featured a mug shot of Horton, with a voice-over saying ominously, "Every suburban mother's greatest fear." The ad—using thinly disguised code words for race and playing on fears of African American criminality—is widely regarded as having been central to Dukakis's defeat. The Willie Horton ad arguably surpassed in importance even the Democratic candidate's own missteps, such as being photographed in a military tank looking like Howdy Doody or replying without passion to a hypothetical question about what he would do if his wife were raped. He might have survived these, but not the specter of Willie Horton.

Racial stereotyping and the high imprisonment rate of African Americans has political consequences of another kind too. Almost all states bar those serving prison sentences from voting, and thirteen states permanently disenfranchise ex-offenders who have served their time. Overall, 3.9 million Americans are barred from voting because of these laws, with 1.4 million of these being former offenders. Because African Americans have a disproportionately high incarceration rate, felony disenfranchisement has the greatest impact on the African American vote. Jeff Manza and Christopher Uggen (2006) have written about how state laws that disenfranchise prisoners and former felons have effectively nullified the voting rights of millions of African Americans. In seven states, one out of every four African American men are barred from voting because of a current or former felony conviction. While nobody has produced a smoking gun of intent, it is interesting that the increase in the number of African Americans and other racial minorities behind bars—many of whom are permanently disenfranchised as a result—coincides in time precisely with their acquisition of real voting rights and other civil rights after the struggles of the 1950s and 1960s.

Manza and Uggen reveal that the disenfranchisement of former felons, who disproportionately vote for Democrats, has influenced the results of presidential and congressional elections. The most conspicuous example of this is in Florida, where four hundred thousand ex-offenders are barred from voting and 31 percent of black men in the state are disenfranchised. In the hotly contested Gore-Bush presidential election of 2000, the hundreds of thousands of mostly African Americans who were expunged from voter registries in Florida on the grounds that they were former felons represented far more votes than would have been required to swing the results of the election in Florida, and so the nation, to Al Gore.

At first, it is surprising to learn that Florida's former governor Charlie Crist has signed a law restoring voting rights to many former felons. But the devil is in the details, as they say. Under the new law, each individual must apply to have his or her rights restored, and there are two formidable barriers. First, 30 percent of those who might otherwise be eligible are denied on the grounds that they still owe some monetary restitution to victims—and in a classic catch-22 they cannot pay off the restitution because having one's rights restored is a prerequisite for many jobs. Second, at the same time this reenfranchisement bill was signed, the state *reduced* the budget of the Parole Commission, which restores voting rights, by 20 percent and cut nine positions from its staff. As a result, in the summer of 2008 there was a backlog of sixty thousand former felons waiting for their rights restoration, and four thousand more were added to the backlog each month. By the time of the presidential election in November 2008, the backlog had reached seventy-six thousand, most of them African Americans and the vast majority potential Democratic voters.

Former convicts pay for their crimes well past their period of incarceration in another way as well, and this too is compounded by race. In *Marked: Race, Crime, and Finding Work in an Era of Mass Incarceration* (2007), Devah Pager presents evidence that men (the study was limited to men) who have been in jail or prison are often closed out of jobs, housing, loans, and other such necessities and resources. Furthermore, these ongoing penalties are distributed differentially by race. In her study, Pager arranged for matched pairs of young men to look for work in Milwaukee. Similar in every way except their race and status as former felons, the men in these matched pairs got very different reactions from potential employers. Predictably, white men who had been in prison were less likely to find employment than white men who had not. More surprising, white men who had done time had comparable job search experiences to black men with no record. Both white men with a record and black men with no record were three times as likely to find work than were black men who had done prison time.

The connections between and among crime, race, and incarceration clearly have powerful material, political, and cultural effects. They also have powerful subjective effects, discernible in the disparate meanings we attach to the commission of crimes depending on who the perpetrator is. When whites and others who are not generally thought of as criminal types commit an offense, it is considered out of character and so may be subliminally downgraded to a mistake or aberration; instead, when those thought to be prone to criminality confirm their nature by actually committing an offense, their demonization is complete. When suburban white children take up arms and kill scores of their teachers and classmates, as in the Columbine massacre and other such tragic incidents, a national debate is opened up on how we collectively fail our children and/or on the details of psychiatric malfunction; but teens killing teens in our poor, minority urban neighborhoods are written off as gangsters and thugs.

Do the following thought experiment: Imagine that Bonnie and Clyde were black. Bonnie Parker and Clyde Barrow, along with others in the Barrow Gang, traveled around the midwestern United States during the Great Depression of the early 1930s, robbing banks, small stores, and gas stations and killing those who got in their way. Despite their gang status and violent crimes, they are celebrated in folklore, song, and film. The cryptic but revealing tag line of one Bonnie and Clyde movie, starring Hollywood darlings Warren Beatty and Faye Dunaway, was "They're young. They're in love. They rob banks." Hard as I try, I cannot imagine a comparable fairy-tale version of violent black gang members.

A contemporary real-life love story echoes the tale of Bonnie and Clyde as rebellious lovers whose romantic appeal is enhanced by their flaunting the law. Roger Dillon, twenty-three, worked for an armored car company when he and his sweetheart, Nicole Boyd, twenty-five, made off with $7.4 million in cash and checks from the company's safe. Known for dressing in goth-style clothing and playing the fantasy game Dungeons and Dragons, Dillon and Boyd quickly became famous around Ohio and West Virginia. In January 2008, they earned a full-page spread complete with pictures of the baby-faced couple in the *New York Times* (Hamill 2008). The newspaper called them "A Goth Bonnie and Clyde." Their fame spread through call-in radio stations and online chat rooms, where more than one person expressed the sentiment, "*They are heroes*. Nobody was hurt. It's one for the working man or woman." (The public sentiment appears to have shifted once they were caught, and one ballad is now entitled "Dumb as Dillon.")

What about that crew of western bad boys that include the likes of Jesse James and Billy the Kid? A Confederate rebel before the Civil War, and later a gang leader, robber, and assassin, Jesse James was a legend in his own time, and after his death he was constructed as a kind of Robin Hood. The subject of dozens of ballads, books, and films, Jesse James is even lionized in an episode of television's *Little House on the Prairie*. Another outlaw and killer, Billy the Kid, achieved notoriety only after the publication of his biography by the sheriff who killed him. But scores of songs now attest to his celebrity status, including one by Jon Bon Jovi, "Blaze of Glory." These outlaws (not "criminals") are honored in American folklore as rebels who lived life large, literally "outside the law" that constrains more conventional, timid folk. Even the anonymous former inmates of Alcatraz—long ago closed down, but still the most frequently visited tourist attraction in San Francisco—have achieved something like collective outlaw fame.

Not one of these notorious bad boys (and girls) was a person of color. A few revolutionary figures like Eldridge Cleaver and other Black Panthers, and even Mumia Abu-Jamal who was sentenced to death for allegedly killing a Philadelphia police officer in 1981, have their supporters. But these are mostly political figures, unlike such "daring desperadoes" as Bonnie and Clyde who are celebrated solely for being outlaws. It is not a stretch to say that political actors like the Black Panthers are criminalized in the public imagination, while criminals like Bonnie and Clyde, Jesse James, and Billy the Kid are turned into folk heroes, nonconformists who had the courage to live on the wild side.

MOST CRITICAL RACE THEORY scholarship examines the role of law in creating and enforcing these kinds of racial categories and conceptualizations and the resulting experiences of people of color.

But a growing body of literature within this genre explores what is called "white consciousness." This literature helps us understand, among other things, how conceptualizations of whiteness get constructed as so normative that even violent outlaws become pillars of Americana. In an early contribution to this literature, David Roediger (1999, 8) wrote in *The Wages of Whiteness: Race and the Making of the American Working Class* that "working class formation and the systematic development of a sense of whiteness went hand in hand for the U.S. white working class." For Roediger, white workers in America came to see themselves as a distinct class through their distancing from blacks and a disdain for the preindustrial work that blacks were associated with. As unskilled, dependent labor was identified with the slave labor of blacks, immigrants who performed such labor were the targets of racist contempt. This identification of immigrant labor with slave labor helps explain how and why large segments of the white working class in America were vehemently anti-immigrant in the early twentieth century. The larger point Roediger makes is that whites developed their own sense of identity largely in contrast to the racial other.

In *White Nation*, Ghassan Hage (2000) describes whites' self-identity in Australia as the master race. Hage followed the course of a conversation played out in graffiti on the campus of the University of Western Sydney. One writer had scrawled, apparently to some imagined immigrant audience, "Go back to your own country!" Soon, a respondent chastised, "This is their country, too! We are a multicultural society in case you have forgotten." A week later came the response, "Fuck multiculturalism!" Then, in turn, "Fuck you, you racist turd!" Hage argues that whatever their differences, these white graffiti authors share a view of themselves as the "masters of national space," "enactors of the Law," and "'governors' of the nation." In contrast, the common perception of "ethnics" (as immigrants in Australia are called), is that they are "people one can make decisions about: objects to be governed" (16–17).

Related to this idea of whites as "masters of national space" is the assumption that they are the standard in comparison to which blacks and/or immigrants are differentiated. Ruth Frankenberg (1996) conducted a series of interviews with white women in the United States to explore how they conceived of their whiteness. She found that even among these women who consider themselves enlightened on issues of race, "white" and "American" are almost synonymous (in a version of Italians' inability to envision black Italians). When they spoke generically of "people," they were almost invariably referring to white Americans. Illustrating that nonwhites were considered deviations from the normative standard, one woman referred to her Jamaican, Rastafarian daughter-in-law playfully but without apparent irony, "She *really* comes with diversity" (quoted in Frankenberg 1996, 69, emphasis in original).

THE CONCEPT of race has gone hand in hand with the concept of America as a national territory. The European discovery of the land and the displacement of indigenous peoples who were declared savage and childlike; the enslavement of Africans to work the land; the arrival of one cohort after another of destitute and racialized immigrants—throughout American history, race has been used to justify the suppression and exploitation of those declared inferior. Its power lies in its association with natural, biological fact: race has been, and is, conventionally thought of as ingrained in our bodies and phenotypically displayed.

But law and society scholars scrutinize this concept of race and find it suspicious. The self-interest and the self-declared racial superiority of those who have obliterated, displaced, and exploited others are a red flag. The fickle and shifting boundaries of racial categories give us further clues that something is up. Upon close investigation, it turns out that race is one of those taken-for-granted categories that is socially constructed, with much of its foundation resting on law.

If you have any lingering doubts about the socially constructed and fluid nature of race, ponder the following. Christopher Columbus (in real life, Cristoforo Colombo), the European "discoverer" of America and so its legendary father figure, was born and raised in Italy. Four hundred years after his mythical discovery, he would have been declared racially inferior—maybe even feebleminded—in the land he discovered. The restrictive immigration quota laws of the 1920s were devised to keep out the likes of Cristoforo Colombo.

Law and society scholars who study race focus on many different aspects of the phenomenon and use many different methodologies, only a few of which are sketched here. But we tend to converge on one paradigmatic point. As we saw in chapter 2, a core idea in law and society is that laws and legal systems are shaped to, and simultaneously shape, the contours of society. Following similar logic, the form and content of race and racism are contoured to extant social realities and instrumental interests, with law often being the matchmaker that ensures the union.

CHAPTER FIVE Many Laws, Many Orders

The gym I frequent is a franchise of a national chain. Recently, it established a new policy for gaining access. We used to have to show our membership cards and identification, but this routine was replaced last year with a high-tech machine. To open the turnstile now, I digitally enter my phone number and place my right index finger on a small infrared glass that scans it. The other day I noticed a stern warning on the counter next to the fingerprint scanner: "All members must show membership cards and photo IDs to gain entrance." Right behind it, but less obvious, was another advisory: "Members no longer need to show cards and IDs." Perplexed by the inconsistency and ever curious about such insignificant details of life, I asked the staff about the dual signage. It turns out that the policy of corporate headquarters is inflexible on this matter: all members must show membership cards and IDs, and local chains must post signs to that effect. But my particular gym—with its new electronic system of telephone number and fingerprint scanning (itself an illustration of the penetration of lawlike processes into our everyday lives)—has no need for the old-fashioned cards and has its own policy that reflects this local reality. Their solution is to post both signs.

Legal pluralism is like that—two or more sets of laws and legal practices operating (more or less) at the same time in the same place. The most familiar and straightforward example of legal pluralism for the American reader is the U.S. system of federal, state, and local laws. In every city, town, hamlet, and county across the United States, people go about their daily lives facilitated by, confronted with, and otherwise navigating a complex web of legal jurisdictions. These systems are often nested in and/or are complementary to each other (unlike my contradictory gym rules), with each jurisdiction having its own responsibilities. For example, the federal government establishes federal income tax rates, and every April we send our checks to the Internal Revenue Service. Most states have their own income tax laws too, and the local property tax system within each city or county completes this picture of tax-law pluralism. This plurality is incremental, with one tax system layered on top of the other and not in direct competition with it. The federal government also has a slew of regulatory agencies, and many states have parallel agencies of their own. For example, the federal Occupational Safety and Health Administration oversees the workplace conditions of American workers, and most states have their own workplace safety agencies as well. In these cases, federal and state responsibilities are worked out through reams of technical guidelines and customary practices.

In some policy realms, the federal government sets a floor for state policies or a default position. Minimum wage laws are a case in point. While the U.S. Congress sets, and the president signs into law, a federal minimum wage standard, each state can set a higher minimum wage for workers in that state. The federal minimum wage in 2015 was $7.25 an hour, but in California the mandatory minimum was $9 an hour. In addition, some cities have set their own minimums above the federal or state floors. For example, as of May 1, 2015, the minimum hourly wage in San Francisco was $12.25. Some states have minimum wages lower than the federal (it must be said, meager) standard, but in that case the federal minimum applies by default. Issues arise from time to time as to which jurisdiction trumps the other in a particular legal arena. Local policies relating to the treatment of immigrants provide a good example of such jurisdictional conflicts. A number of states and cities have passed laws and ordinances against renting housing to undocumented immigrants, barring children of undocumented immigrants from public schools, and otherwise making life difficult for those without legal status. They are often challenged and sometimes voided because immigration law in the United States is constitutionally the sole prerogative of the federal government.

Sometimes it's not just a matter of contests over jurisdiction. State and local laws and policies cannot run afoul of the U.S. Constitution, just as they have to be consistent with their own state constitutions. California voters passed Proposition 209 in 1996 to amend the California State Constitution. The ostensible purpose was to make it illegal for public institutions in the state to discriminate on the basis of race, sex, or ethnicity. Discrimination was already illegal under the federal Civil Rights Act of 1964, and the real goal of Prop 209 was to eliminate affirmative action for minorities and women in California (more on this in chapter 7). The measure was quickly appealed on the grounds that it conflicted with federal equal-protection standards, under which minority outreach and other proactive programs are endorsed as a way to open up business and educational opportunities to historically excluded groups. Prop 209 survived most of these legal challenges, but officials in California's institutions of higher education, which frequently get infusions of federal monies, still struggle with the delicate task of reconciling this state law with federal mandates for outreach to disadvantaged minorities and women. And, unlike my gym and its ID protocol, they usually do not have the luxury of simply ignoring the conflicting national policy.

Consider too the medical-marijuana proposition passed by California voters that same year. The measure permits the cultivation and use of marijuana for the treatment of pain and other side effects of major illnesses, when prescribed by a doctor. Because the growth, sale, and use of marijuana is illegal under federal law, federal indictments and prosecutions have proceeded against medical-marijuana cultivators, dispensaries, and users in California. And the U.S. Supreme Court has upheld the right of the federal Drug Enforcement Administration to enforce the federal laws against marijuana possession and distribution even when their targets are engaging in legal activity under California law. In this case, it is not that federal law has declared California law void; rather, there are two separate and conflicting laws.

Sometimes the Supreme Court completely invalidates the laws of local jurisdictions as violations of the U.S. Constitution. In 1976, the District of Columbia (Washington, DC) City Council passed the comprehensive Firearms Control Regulations Act of 1975. Enacted at a time when homicides in the city were at historic levels—there were 242 homicides that year, mostly by firearms—the measure was one of the strictest gun-control laws in the nation. It prohibited private citizens from owning handguns and automatic and semiautomatic weapons and required people to register their long guns (such as hunting rifles). It also mandated that all permissible firearms in the home be kept unloaded and locked, presumably ensuring the safety of children and others who might be tempted to toy with them but also making them effectively useless as a defense against intruders. The homicide rate in Washington declined in the years immediately following passage of the law but began to climb again in the 1980s, and today there is considerable controversy about the law's impact. Truth be told, it probably did not deter many who were intent on homicide, since guns were plentiful in nearby Baltimore, Maryland, and other neighboring cities.

Whatever impact Washington's law did or did not have, it was declared unconstitutional by the U.S. Supreme Court in *District of Columbia v. Heller* (2008). The Court's majority found that the ban on firearms violated the Second Amendment to the U.S. Constitution, which, they said, "protects an individual right to keep and bear arms." The Court further declared that the "unloading and locking" requirement of the law constituted a de facto prohibition on the possession of guns for self-defense and was therefore also unconstitutional.

The right of Washington, DC, to govern itself had been called into question before. The District of Columbia is unique in that it is not within any state. The U.S. Constitution carves out a special niche for the capital city, placing it under the jurisdiction not of a state government but of the U.S. Congress. In 1973, Congress passed the District of Columbia Home Rule Act, which finally provided for a local governance structure in the form of a mayor and city council. It was this city council that passed the firearm ban. The Supreme Court's nullification of this law was in part related to Washington's unusual status, and it is a good example of the sometimes complicated landscape of federalism.

The convolutions of the American federal system can also be seen in the realm of death penalty policy. Frank Zimring (2003) argues that much that is wrong with the practice of the death penalty in the United States is traceable to the idiosyncrasies and ironies of U.S.-style federalism. Historically, state criminal law and its practice, including laws relating to the death penalty, were the exclusive province of state governments. The U.S. Supreme Court case *Furman v. Georgia* in 1972 dramatically changed that. The majority in that case found that the vast variability in states' death penalty practices and the lack of consistent national standards constituted a violation of the Eighth Amendment's prohibition of cruel and unusual punishment. When the Court approved some states' newly minted death penalty laws in

1976, a set of federal standards was thereby implied, including a set of guidelines to be given juries on how to choose between life imprisonment and a death sentence.

According to Zimring (2003, 68), this gave birth to a "Frankenstein's monster." For one thing, state variability in the practice of the death penalty was not reduced, in part because so few of the states' practices are ever brought before the Supreme Court. Twelve states have no death penalty; seven have it but don't use it; and a handful of states (88 percent of them in the South) are responsible for the vast majority of actual executions. In fact, Zimring shows, the concentration of executions in the South is greater now than it was prior to *Furman* (77). Furthermore, the system of state trials and appeals but federal controls contributes to the delays for which the practice of the death penalty in the United States is famous, with most executions taking place more than ten years after the initial sentence.

It works like this: The typical capital trial is held in state court, followed by appeals in state appellate courts. Only after state appeals are exhausted can a writ of habeas corpus be filed in a federal district court. It takes at least a decade to get to this point, the case having had to percolate through the state system before accessing the federal courts, which as Zimring points out, is where the relevant constitutional questions are raised. Since the relevant issues are those related to *Furman* and U.S. constitutional law, the exhaustion-of-state-appeals requirement achieves little else than to give symbolic deference to state courts. Ironically, says Zimring, because the federal review is "last-in-line," that is where popular resentment for the delay is concentrated. As he puts it, "So the most vulnerable stage of the review process is also the most critical stage for any of the quality controls on state capital punishment outcomes" (79). It is a system that satisfies no one, piques the resentment of many, and is profoundly "dysfunctional" (67). Not least of the reasons is the multiple layering of, and frequent disconnects among, a plurality of jurisdictions.

COMPLEX SYSTEMS of administrative law permeate and crosscut each one of these layers. "Administrative law" generally refers to the legal order that establishes, interprets, and implements the rules and regulations of administrative agencies, with the prototype being federal agencies such as the Social Security Administration or Immigration and Customs Enforcement. The administrative law context provides an especially good example of legal pluralism for several reasons. First, it is a highly decentralized field of law, with many regional players having decision-making authority. Second, administrative law adjudicators exercise substantial discretion, although they tend not to be institutionally independent of the agencies whose actions they adjudicate. Third, and related to this, there is little independent oversight or appeal. The result is that there is often enormous disparity in legal outcomes across regions and adjudicators.

This disparity is evident in the processing of disability claims by the U.S. Social Security Administration (SSA). Jerry Mashaw's (1983) book *Bureaucratic Justice: Managing Social Security Disability Claims* reveals both a massive caseload of urgent appeals by the disabled applying for federal disability funds and the discretionary and disparate processes that yield decisions on those claims. According to Mashaw, this is "the largest system of administrative adjudication in the Western world" (18). Thousands of administrative law judges across the United States hear hundreds of thousands of appeals of the SSA's initial decisions. Aside from the structural bias inherent in the fact that the judges are themselves employees of the SSA, Mashaw and others point out that it yields vastly disparate decisions, according to the proclivity of the individual judge.

A study of asylum decision making depicts a similar administrative system, with even more "eye-popping disparities" (Taylor 2008, 475). People who wish to claim asylum in the United States must start with an application and interview with an asylum officer in the Department of Homeland Security. Those who are unsuccessful at that level (the majority) are referred to an immigration judge in the Executive Office for Immigration Review. Here, they are processed for removal from the United States and are given another opportunity to state their asylum claim. If the immigration judge remains unconvinced, the claimant can appeal to the Board of Immigration Appeals (BIA), also housed in the Executive Office for Immigration Review. If claimants fail there, they can petition the circuit court of appeals in their jurisdiction.

This complex four-tiered process is fraught with hurdles for the claimant, not least of which is navigating the dizzying bureaucracies and their idiosyncratic requirements. More important for our purposes, there is a huge amount of discretion and correspondingly large discrepancies in legal outcomes. The authors of a study titled "Refugee Roulette: Disparities in Asylum Adjudication" (Ramji-Nogales, Schoenholtz, and Schrag 2007) tracked hundreds of thousands of decisions across four levels of review for several years and found striking variation in outcome by region, the nationality of the claimant, and the individual adjudicator. Chinese asylum applicants in the Atlanta Immigration Court in Georgia were successful only 7 percent of the time, whereas 76 percent of Chinese asylum seekers in the Orlando Immigration Court in Florida were successful (Ramji-Nogales et al. 2007, 330). And rates were sharply different among judges in the same court. In the Miami court, one adjudicator was convinced by only 5 percent of claimants from Colombia, while his colleague down the hall granted asylum in 88 percent of the Colombian cases he heard. Similar disparities were documented across all four levels of review.

The study makes it clear that these administrative decisions are profoundly influenced by adjudicators' individual preferences and attitudes. But Taylor (2008, 479) points out that it also affirms the "strategic model of judging." That is, administrative judges are affected by the institutional, structural, and political pressures they face. For example, Ramji-Nogales and colleagues (2007, 355–56) note that in 2002 then attorney general John Ashcroft issued orders to streamline BIA decision making by reducing the number of cases heard by panels of judges and increasing the number presided over by a single judge. In part because the grant rate of single judges tends to be lower than that of panels, favorable BIA asylum decisions declined in every region subsequent to Ashcroft's order. By 2005, single judges decided most cases, and brief, negative decisions were the norm. The attorney general's order apparently had two effects. First, it altered the structural context of immigration appeals by limiting the use of the panel system, which generally produces more favorable results. Second, it sent an implicit political message favoring fast, negative asylum decisions.

In addition to this kind of direct intervention, administrative law scholars have long observed the potential institutional biases associated with courts hearing appeals of decisions from within their own agency. This lack of independence creates a conflict of interest that Taylor (2008, 481) says "has bedeviled administrative law from its inception." While reforms stressing institutional independence have been implemented in some administrative law arenas, independent administrative courts remain in the minority, and their adjudicators are still by no means fully insulated from political pressures.

Disparate decisions can be found in all court systems in the United States, as federal, state, and local jurisdictions and their various levels of appeal are shaped by their institutional contexts and the leanings of their judges (more on the forces affecting courts in chapter 7). But the plurality of judicial decisions is arguably even more pronounced in the administrative law realm, where the rules of the game are often amorphous, oversight can be lax, and political-institutional independence severely circumscribed.

These various legal regimes provide good examples of pluralism at work, including the struggles, discrepancies, and adaptations it often invokes. But there is more to it than that. Crisscrossing these governmental legal systems in the United States are legions of private security firms, surveillance systems, and neighborhood associations that add their own layer of lawlike fiats and processes. In some cases, such as the privately contracted prisons and detention facilities that some states rely on, public and private jurisdictions are functionally intertwined. In other cases, such as private store security personnel, their jurisdictions remain separate from, but are arguably the functional equivalent of, public law enforcement. The average shopper may not care whether the police or a private guard stands at the Target exit to check her receipts. But in both the private prison and Target, an intricate set of rules and practices govern which type of social control agent is authorized to do what.

Gaps in the rules of public-private jurisdiction occasionally surface, and accountability sometimes falls through the cracks of these multiple legal orders. One case like this involves the private security firm Blackwater Worldwide. Blackwater was contracted by the U.S. State Department early in the Iraq War to guard diplomats and high-level officials. Like the tens of thousands of other private security forces in Iraq, the rules Blackwater operated under were vague, to say the least. Not subject to military regulations and explicitly exempt from Iraqi law—until a revision of Iraq's laws took effect in January 2009—they sometimes appeared to skirt all accountability. Blackwater personnel were sometimes not even liable under U.S. laws that applied to other civilians contracted by the military. This partial legal limbo became evident following a 2005 incident in which Blackwater personnel in a helicopter dropped a dangerous riot-control gas (whose use by actual military personnel is severely restricted) at close range on a Baghdad checkpoint, choking Iraqi civilians and U.S. soldiers alike. It is still unclear what their intention was. Some observers on the ground speculate they might have wanted to clear the traffic at the crowded checkpoint so their convoy could get through. What is clear is that the vague rules of engagement for these security forces left gaps in their accountability.

Two years after the gas incident, Blackwater personnel opened fire on seventeen unarmed Iraqi civilians, triggering passionate protests by the Iraqi government and frustrating those who repeatedly attempted to hold the security firm and its personnel accountable. Five Blackwater guards were finally indicted by an American prosecutor in late 2008, but only after demands from the Iraqi government and expressions of international outrage (Robinson 2008). In October 2014, a jury in federal district court in Washington, DC, found four of the five guards guilty of murder, manslaughter, and illegal weapons possession (Apuzzo 2014), and six months later they were handed long prison terms (Apuzzo 2015). But the story does not end there. As I write this, the verdict is scheduled to be appealed. The main issue: whether or not the U.S. Justice Department can even bring this case against Blackwater, over which the department's jurisdiction is unclear since the company was under private contract to the State Department at the time.

Less sensational than Blackwater, homeowners' associations are an example of private regulatory forces that affect many Americans' daily lives. In 1965, there were just five hundred homeowner associations in the United States, but by 2007 their numbers had grown to over 230,000. In some areas, the vast majority of new homes are under the jurisdiction of these associations. In California, when neighborhoods were hard-pressed for public funds after Proposition 13 curtailed property taxes in 1978, homeowners' associations began to operate like substitute tax collectors to ensure infrastructural maintenance. Usually governed by boards of directors, the associations are quasi-corporate in nature, but they function like mini-governments, setting fees for landscaping and maintenance, and issuing directives on what homeowners may or may not do with their properties. Besides the usual limitations on house color and height, some associations in Orange County, California, restrict the amount of time a garage door may stay open, prohibit hanging laundry outside to dry (what are they thinking in this time of energy shortages and global warming?), and forbid washing or tinkering with a car on one's property. In one notorious case *Fountain Valley Chateau Blanc Homeowners' Association v. Department of Veteran Affairs* (1998), a homeowners' association required an elderly man with Hodgkin's disease to submit to a home inspection that resulted in a reprimand for his sloppy housekeeping and an order that he "clear his bed of all papers and books, discard 'outdated clothing' and remove the papers, cardboard boxes and books from the floor area around his bed and dresser." The court censured the homeowners' association, comparing it to "some parent nagging an errant teenager."

Not surprisingly, many lawsuits have been lodged by people who chafe at such intrusions. A voluminous record of legal findings specifies the respective rights of residents and homeowners' associations, within the context of state and federal law. It is a body of law that is still evolving, and as recently as 2003, one judge referred to an overzealous homeowners' association as a "banana republic" that used techniques of enforcement similar to the "Spanish Inquisition" (AHRC News Services 2003). What better illustration of legal-normative pluralism at work, particularly since many of the most restrictive homeowners' associations operate in places like Orange County, California, where so many people subscribe to libertarian principles of small government, minimum regulation, and maximum individual freedom. While some of these homeowners' association edicts are voided in court, others continue to govern the minutiae of daily living for their residents.

HOMEOWNERS' ASSOCIATIONS operate at the most local level, and so can be thought of as the inside layer of the regulatory-legal onion. Working our way outward from this most local level, we find a plethora of municipal regulations. In *Everyday Law on the Street*, Mariana Valverde (2012) describes the complex web of regulations and permit policies in Toronto. She and her team of researchers did ridealongs and engaged with and observed enforcement officials, city councillors, neighborhood associations, and local activists as they maneuvered to enact and enforce regulations relating to such things as street-food vendors, affordable housing, the taxi permit system, begging, and noise.

Among her many findings, Valverde reports that these regulations are so numerous and the value commitments underlying them so varied that they frequently conflict with each other and on occasion backfire. For example, the spoken commitment to racial/ethnic diversity and the policies that trumpet it operate in tension with a number of unspoken moral judgments and prejudices, with the latter coming out on top. As one illustration, Valverde tells of people who come in front of the Toronto Licensing Tribunal for the purpose of renewing a rescinded taxi or truck license. She shows that the tribunal rewards those who conform to the Anglo-Christian ethic of remorse for the behavior that resulted in the rescinded license, while displays of suffering and emotion by African immigrants who seek license renewals are seen as forms of manipulation. Whatever commitment to diversity the members of the tribunal might espouse, their unspoken and presumably unreflected-upon prejudice in favor of Anglo-Christian morals and customs time and again sabotages that commitment. Important for our discussion of legal pluralism, Valverde demonstrates that a veritable cacophony of municipal regulations, and their underlying moral commitments, produce an irrational and chaotic system of governance that is only barely functional and that, at the end of the day, is grossly unfair.

Supranational jurisdictions reside at the outermost ring of this regulatory-legal onion. For example, the European Union, with representatives from its twenty-eight member states, enacts a broad set of policies and guidelines that local laws are supposed to be consistent with. Often considered only advisory and sometimes not accompanied by enforcement mechanisms, these regulations nonetheless can be controversial, particularly when they contradict local customs and practices. In a region of the world that is justifiably proud of its culinary achievements, among the most contentious EU regulations are those that pertain to food and drink. For example, raw-milk cheeses and other artisanal foods are the target of EU regulations, and producers in some countries are pushing back. A threat to cloth-bound cheddar cheese from the United Kingdom made headlines a few years ago. An EU order in 2004 banned methyl bromide, which is crucial to destroying cheese mites during the maturation of the unique cloth-bound cheddar, because of its effect on the ozone layer. A temporary exception was carved out for UK cheddar makers but has now expired and is still controversial. The controversy is not only about wanting to preserve this one delicious cheese; it is about national sovereignty and the preservation of local traditions that are threatened by laws imposed from afar.

Globalization has meant that there are more and more such su-pranational legal institutions impinging in various ways on local practices. Free trade agreements like the North American Free Trade Agreement are put in place and enforced by international regulatory bodies. At the global level, the World Trade Organization (WTO) sets the parameters for trade negotiations and hears disputes among its 151 members worldwide. In this era of the unprecedented international movement of goods, a frequent complaint by member states is that other states are "dumping" goods on their markets at below-market rates, creating unfair competition for local companies. Argentina has alleged that ceramic floor tiles from Italy were being dumped in Argentina; the European Union charged India with dumping "cotton-type bed linens"; Guatemala has complained about cement from Mexico; and Mexico filed a complaint against the United States for dumping high-fructose corn syrup. The United States is among the most prolific filers of antidumping allegations, contesting hot-rolled steel products from Japan, stainless-steel plate from Korea, and lamb from New Zealand. While these disputes have many lawlike features, the WTO has only "quasi-binding" enforcement mechanisms, and its decisions often remain largely symbolic (Conti 2008, 147).

By one recent count, there are about 125 international institutions that issue directives with various degrees of binding power on sovereign states. International law is especially active when it comes to setting human rights standards. A prime example is the United Nations' Convention on the Elimination of All Forms of Discrimination against Women, which by 2014 had been signed by more than 188 countries. As Elizabeth Boyle (2002) has shown, female genital cutting is among the practices that are implicitly prohibited under this convention. The procedure involves the excision, or cutting away, of all or part of the female external genitalia and is mostly performed on young girls, often under unsanitary conditions and without anesthesia. Steeped in religious and cultural significance, the practice is widespread in Central Africa, where the majority of women have undergone the procedure, but it can be found in various forms in roughly twenty-five different nations.

In recognition of the violence done to women by genital cutting, the World Health Organization, UNICEF, and other international bodies and nongovernmental organizations (NGOs), issued a joint resolution against the practice in 1996. Resolutions like this and the human rights principles they are based on rarely have the force of what is sometimes called "hard law." But they can have direct and indirect impacts, at times through coercion and at other times by seeping into local discourse. Boyle (2002) documents the different roles of players at various levels and locations in the genital cutting controversy, from international institutions with "soft" legal authority to NGOs, sovereign nation-states, and local officials. She shows the myriad noninvasive ways that international governmental institutions such as the United Nations have attempted reform without directly usurping national sovereignty and cultural prerogatives, while nongovernmental actors such as Amnesty International have been more direct, as they are less constrained by nation-state protocols. Boyle's book is a classic in the study of international legal and normative pluralism and the ways the various levels within these normative orders relate to each other.

Sally Engel Merry's (2006) *Human Rights and Gender Violence* explores some of this same ground but casts a wider net, examining the many aspects of gender violence and the supranational norms that counter it. Emphasizing the multifaceted nature of international human rights discourse and its sometimes unanticipated effects, Merry exposes the potential of human rights demands to buttress the power of (in some cases, nondemocratic) states, even while they protect women from violence. There are few better examples of the legal pluralism literature, and specifically of the ways supranational legal norms need to be (and, ultimately, one way or another, are) nested in and contoured to the local context.

Boaventura de Sousa Santos (1995, 263) talks about "globalized localisms" to describe the exportation of all sorts of artifacts, including law, from the local contexts where they are produced to become global phenomena. He points to the export of human rights concepts devised in the West as an example, as well as the global use of English as a universal language, the globalization of American patent and copyright laws, and the spread of Coca-Cola and fast-food chains like McDonald's. But he also speaks of "localized globalisms," which refer to local phenomena that have been refashioned by global processes imposed from above. He includes in this category things like the impact of free trade agreements on developing countries; austerity programs and natural resource depletion to pay down debts to global powers; and transformations of local legal systems to jibe with global imperatives. For Santos, there is a pattern to these globalized localisms and localized globalisms, such that affluent countries specialize in exporting the former, while poor developing countries are subject to the latter. The result of these processes and their asymmetrical distribution across wealthy and poor countries is a series of "class, national, gender, ethnic, religious, [and] generational conflicts" (263). These two phenomena—globalized localisms and localized globalisms—may be analytically distinct and may even operate asymmetrically in practice, but in both cases the global and the local intertwine and reconfigure each other.

Law and society scholarship also examines fragmentation between and among the multiple international regimes that have emerged. For example, the various global agreements on trade enforced by the WTO may be at odds with aspects of international agreements relating to climate change, such as the Kyoto Protocol. Van Asselt, Sindico, and Mehling (2008, 437–38) point out that industries in the European Union, which has signed the Kyoto Protocol, are held to emission standards that industries in countries that have not signed the protocol are free to ignore, creating potential competitiveness and trade inequities. One proposed solution is to put a "border tax adjustment" on non-Kyoto nations that would increase the cost of their goods and level the playing field. But this solution, say Van Asselt and colleagues, would probably conflict with WTO laws governing free trade. Such conflicts are important not just because they create policy impasses but more broadly because conflicting rules may produce incoherence and jeopardize the credibility of international legal regimes. Van Asselt and colleagues are ultimately optimistic that this international legal pluralism can be dealt with through discussions of potential incompatibilities when accords are first entered into and through political negotiations should conflicts emerge after the fact.

THESE ARE ALL vital topics for law and society scholars. Probably because we are especially drawn to issues involving asymmetries of power (and, as we saw in the last chapter, the racialization of those on the wrong side of that asymmetry), lately it seems that a preponderance of scholarship looking at legal pluralism explores colonial and postcolonial contexts. Pathbreaking studies have examined the transporting of European legal systems to colonized territories beginning in the sixteenth century and the plural and multilayered normative systems that resulted. Many of these studies focus on the material and ideological interests served by this transplantation and its accompanying legal pluralism.

In *Of Revelation and Revolution*, John and Jean Comaroff (1997) discuss the imposition of the European concepts of private property, debt, contracts, and wages in colonial South Africa. Economic development of the land required capitalist laws of contract for the colonial elite, and new laws were also installed to produce a class of wage laborers for the extraction of wealth. Laws that took land from subsistence farmers on one hand and set the parameters for wage labor on the other, provided both the coercive force and the rules of engagement needed for the transformation to colonial-style capitalism. At the same time, the new legal regime reformulated notions of individuality, work, and self-discipline, so that over time these prerequisites for a wage-labor system would come to be internalized and naturalized, thereby "replac[ing] one hegemony with another" (Comaroff and Comaroff 1991, 311). This was not just the colonization of a territory but "a persuasive attempt to colonize consciousness" (313).

As the Comaroffs and other legal anthropologists have shown, European law in the colonial context had other ideological dimensions as well, for example, providing an important legitimating tool to the white colonizers (Mertz 1988). Racialization of the colonized and/or exterminated has always been a key element of the legitimating story line. The "white man's burden," "manifest destiny," and lengthy elaborations on these early sound bites provided authority for the colonizing agenda and are found throughout legal documents of the colonial era and beyond.

I used the word "transplantation" to describe the importation of European legal systems into their colonized territories. I probably should have borrowed the botanical term "grafting" instead. Legal systems and laws were not imported in toto but were grafted onto the local reality over time and in the process went through varying degrees of molecular change. Consistent with the law and society idea that types of societies and types of law are mutually constituted, scholars of legal pluralism describe the ways European legal traditions were adapted to local realities in colonial Africa, the Americas, and Asia. This sometimes meant that indigenous legal systems and European systems produced a hybrid in the colonized territory. As ordinary people from European and indigenous backgrounds confronted each other in the colonial context, legal orders were produced that were effectively "a combination of the two" (Comaroff and Comaroff 1991, 313).

Sometimes dual systems emerged, with Europeanized institutions used by colonial and local elites, and indigenous practices—which were almost always racialized as primitive—used by everyone else. South Africa provides an especially conspicuous example of multiple systems of justice operating in the same geographic space. Before European settlers and colonists arrived in South Africa, a patchwork of tribal laws and legal processes existed. Dutch settlers beginning in the seventeenth century brought with them their version of civil law, which was largely replaced by a common law system when British colonists achieved dominance in the nineteenth century. By the mid-twentieth century, the Afrikaner National Party, with its strong Dutch roots, had ascended to power and reverted to some aspects of the civil law system, among other things doing away with the jury system the British had installed (Gibson and Gouws 1997; Friedrichs 2001, 245–47). Throughout these almost four centuries of colonial rule, alternative systems of popular justice also operated. These tended to handle the grievances of most members of the black townships who largely shunned the formal, European system (Nina 1993). Hund and Kotu-Rammopo (1983) describe in detail the justice meted out in one black township where gangs and tribal courts rendered judgments guided by indigenous law. Nancy Scheper-Hughes (1995) reveals the violent proceedings in a squatter camp, where one form of execution involved the burning of a tire around the accused's neck, causing a slow and painful death. While popular forms of justice often involved mediation and extensive negotiation among parties, they clearly should not be romanticized.

These were more than just parallel legal regimes. Colonial and indigenous legal practices were dialectically linked, with each having repercussions for the other. The Comaroffs show that the transformation of consciousness that European colonizers brought to South Africa formed the basis for a distinctive black identity that later fueled antiapartheid politics. And the Western legal codes and practices furnished a counterpoint and sense of coherence to disparate tribal traditions, thus providing an indigenous consciousness of "law and custom" where none had previously existed (Comaroff and Comaroff 1991, 212–13).

The transformative links are sometimes more concrete, as when indigenous people harness aspects of imposed legal systems to their advantage. In chapter 3, I mentioned the concept of resistance and law as a weapon of the weak. The importation of Western law into colonial territories on one hand provided the colonizers with a powerful lever for the extraction of wealth and for maximizing control. But it was also periodically appropriated by the colonized to fight back. Women in Hawaii used colonial law to contest the violence that was part of traditional patriarchal relations; colonial law was also central to the politics of slave resistance in the British West Indies in the eighteenth century; and women in sixteenth-century Istanbul went to the courthouse, an affront to customary gender practices, to challenge their subordination by local and colonial male authorities.

Shelley Gavigan's (2012) *Hunger, Horses, and Government Men* provides an excellent example of this exercise of resistance by indigenous people within legal pluralism. In this study of the introduction of criminal law on the Canadian plains and its imposition on First Nations people following the Indian Act of 1876, Gavigan reveals that indigenous people were not only criminalized by the new laws as other scholars have noted; instead, indigenous leaders used the new courts to extract benefits. Gavigan does not downplay the deleterious effects of this imposition of Western law. In one example, she writes of finding in the archives the case of one indigenous man who was put on trial for stealing a horse, at a time when horse theft had only recently been made a crime and in this young man's culture was an approved way of gaining status. But her research into what she calls the "low law" of the Canadian plains—that is, the legal cases that made their way into regional courts as opposed to the "high law" of the upper courts—reveals the dexterity of indigenous leaders in using the new legal system to advance First Nation interests whenever they could.

Contemporary examples exist too. In the Pacific nations of New Zealand and Vanuatu, indigenous people regularly adapt Western principles of copyright and trademark to shore up local sovereignty and indigenous identity (Geismar 2013). As Geismar (2013) shows in her book *Treasured Possessions*, even as these two nations are substantially different in size, economic structure, and the percentage of the population that is indigenous, in both places "global forms of cultural and intellectual property" are "redefined and altered by everyday people and policymakers" (1). The result of this "indigenous intervention" is to heighten indigenous entitlement to cultural artifacts and styles, provide more space for their voices in museums and auctions, and prioritize self-determination and cultural sustainability.

If European—and later, American—legal systems have influenced those of indigenous peoples in colonized territories and beyond, the influence has sometimes been reciprocal. For example, law and society scholars who study the emergence of alternative dispute resolution in the United States have shown that its roots can be traced to the more informal systems of justice practiced in places like rural Mexico and China. In the face of burgeoning court costs and lawyers' fees, mediation is an increasingly popular alternative to litigation. The Justice Center of Atlanta, Georgia, advertises its mediation services on its website: "Mediation brings the two sides of a dispute together to listen, speak, and understand each other. . . . [W]e empower people to find the common ground that may have existed all along, but was hidden by anger, or fear, or misunderstanding." It took a while, but when the conditions were ripe (in this case, escalating legal costs), the conciliatory dispute resolution processes practiced in some postcolonial contexts have migrated and become central elements of the U.S. legal system, lauded not just for their low cost but for their emotional benefits.

In her book *Law and Societies in Global Contexts*, Eve Darian-Smith (2013) integrates the two dimensions of legal pluralism I've discussed so far and analyzes them through the concept of hegemony (remember this concept from chapter 3). The first of these dimensions has to do with the myriad levels of law, both formal and de facto, in one location. What counts as law here is not confined to official products of the state but includes popular artifacts as well. The second dimension relates to the multitude of global legal regimes, none of which is entirely disconnected from the others or is even a discreet place-based entity. Instead, "domestic law is . . . constitutively linked to issues of global economic, political, and cultural power" (378). Darian-Smith makes two main points about these dimensions of legal pluralism. One is that while law is always and everywhere multifarious, some of this law and legal knowledge is "silenced, ignored, or deemed irrelevant," while other versions—notably elite Euro-American versions—achieve hegemony. But this is not an altogether pessimistic reading of legal pluralism, because Darian-Smith's second overarching point is that recognition of this pluralism opens up spaces for local resistance, as well as for counterhegemonic sociolegal studies.

As you can see, the concept of legal pluralism covers a lot of ground, goes a lot of places, and some might say is a little undisciplined in its travels. Partly for this reason, some scholars reject the concept of legal pluralism altogether, arguing that it is imprecise, the term conflating concepts such as global, transnational, and international when referring to any legal regime that crosses national borders (Halliday and Shaffer 2015). Halliday and Shaffer also object to what they argue is an unhelpful emphasis on conflict among scholars of legal pluralism who generally "adopt a normative commitment against the establishment of a hierarchy of legal institutions and norms" and who, they argue, oppose international legal orders as a destructive force that kills off local alternatives (27). While this objection may be an overgeneralization, and ignores much of the work cited here on the potentially liberating effects of legal pluralism, Halliday and Shaffer's critique underscores the complexity of the concept and its many uses.

Others, like Boaventura de Sousa Santos (1995), while not rejecting the concept of legal pluralism, have instead attempted to systematize the field. Santos's six "clusters" of types of law in capitalist societies within a global context help bring some order to this slippery concept of legal pluralism. These clusters are domestic law (the norms and practices of the household), production law (regulating wages, working conditions, and workplace conduct), exchange law (regulating the marketplace—my gym and its ID requirements fit here), community law (local norms and values), state law (such as criminal law—this is the realm we usually think of as "law"), and systemic law (the global rules and norms that regulate relations among and between capitalist powers and subordinate, or "peripheral," nations). These are by no means independent, autonomous entities, neatly circumscribed from each other. They often bleed into each other; they sometimes intersect and overlap; and they may be in conflict or neatly nested.

When there are conflicts between these different levels of law, social movement actors who are pushing for radical reform can play one level off against the other. Heinz Klug's (2000) analysis of the democratization of South Africa after the official system of apartheid fell reveals the advantages activists can secure by pragmatically borrowing from diverse sources. According to Klug's analysis, two aspects of the adopted legal system were especially important to South Africa's postapartheid rebuilding. One was a constitution that included a strong bill of rights. The other was the granting of broad legislative review powers to the judiciary. This faith in the judiciary as ultimate arbiter was particularly surprising, says Klug, because it placed a limit on majoritarian rule in a country that had long suffered from its absence and might have been expected to celebrate majoritarianism.

This incorporation of external legal concepts and institutions bears some resemblance to earlier legal transfers into colonial territories. The difference, Klug says, is that rather than having foreign legal notions imposed from afar by colonial powers in this case local actors proactively borrowed from the many available legal doctrines and forms and strategically interpreted them for their own internal purposes. The result was a utilitarian "hybridization" that, according to Klug (2000, 180), gave enormous power to the judiciary and has led to "the civilization of potentially unnegotiable political conflicts."

Klug's analysis of South African reconstitution illustrates perfectly many of the empirical findings I've related so far regarding legal pluralism. It demonstrates the transplantation and diffusion of certain political-legal arrangements, such as democratic constitutionalism; the establishment and global ascendancy of the human rights movement; and the importance of local context and legal tradition in the playing out of these developments within specific localities. The broader point Klug's book makes is that there are many orders and dimensions of law, and this legal pluralism may have profound consequences for social change in a wide variety of contexts, including the colonial, postcolonial, and newly democratic.

Abolition of the death penalty around the world and its relationship to human rights discourse is a case in point. When the UN General Assembly issued the Universal Declaration of Human Rights in 1948, with the "right to life" as a central principle, most countries still retained the death penalty. By the time the declaration had been signed by enough member countries in 1976 to become de facto international law, the number of abolitionist nations had risen dramatically. And today the vast majority of the world's countries no longer impose the death penalty.

David Johnson and Franklin Zimring (2009) look at this pattern and reveal the substantial impact of international human rights discourse on the abolition of the death penalty. But the integration of international legal principles into the domestic realm is by no means a simple affair. As we have seen in other contexts, local culture and tradition often push back against the wholesale adoption of Western legal principles. In other cases, Western and indigenous legal regimes are dialectically linked, transforming both. Johnson and Zimring add a further ingredient to this mix, showing that in Asia, it is the nature of the political regime that determines which countries do away with the death penalty. More authoritarian countries—such as China, North Korea, Singapore, and Vietnam—still impose the death penalty, while less authoritarian Nepal, Bhutan, Cambodia, and the Philippines have abolished it.

In some ways, Johnson and Zimring's analysis offers hope to those interested in abolishing the death penalty worldwide. For they show that it is not entrenched local cultures or even assertive nationalism that accounts for the continued use of this most extreme of punishments, but that it is related to the arguably more malleable element of state power. And given the rapid ascendancy of human rights discourse and the kind of popular democratization that Klug (2000) traced in South Africa and that we have seen in embryonic form around the globe (as I write this, pro-democracy demonstrations are erupting in Hong Kong, and in Burkina Faso democratic protests have forced a regime change), worldwide abolition of the death penalty is not beyond the realm of possibility. Of course, given the mixed results of the popular uprisings in the Arab Spring beginning in 2010, it would be foolish to be overly optimistic about the fate of these democracy movements and associated death penalty policies. But a glimmer of hope exists even in China, where the vast majority of the world's official executions take place. A San Francisco–based organization working for human rights in China reports that executions in China have fallen by 90 percent in three decades, from 24,000 in 1983 to 2,400 in 2013 (Tatlow 2014).

Studies like these that investigate the dynamics, effects, and crosscurrents of global human rights discourse, international law, and "transnational legal orders" (Halliday and Shaffer 2015) seem to dominate the scholarship on legal pluralism these days. But, as we conclude this chapter, let's return to the more general concept. The study of legal pluralism underscores the multiplicity of normative orders and the diversity of legal systems at all levels, from the top down and the bottom up, often operating side by side. Some are formalized (federal minimum wage laws, transnational trade agreements), some are unwritten and unspoken (the American practice of tipping waitstaff), and some are hybrids (the "soft" legal authority of NGOs). Tamanaha (2001, 193) even argues that statements like "Law is . . ." make no sense, since "law" includes a lot of qualitatively different phenomena going by the same name.

It is still open to debate in law and society circles whether it is productive or counterproductive to bestow the term "law" on rules, norms, and practices that vary widely in their degree of institutionalization and in their modus operandi. There is even some debate whether lawlike systems that are not codified and do not involve state actors qualify. But the very fact that the formalized law of the colonial powers and the indigenous justice systems of colonized peoples— some of which were decentralized, informal, and uncodified— crossbred seems to suggest (if my rudimentary biology is correct) that they are of the same species.

At first glance, the concept of legal pluralism that is so much a part of law and society scholarship today appears to muddy the waters of the "type of society–type of law" paradigm we saw in chapter 2. If societies have numerous, sometimes conflicting, legal and normative orders, then it is less clear that a given type of society inexorably yields a particular legal form. Recall from chapter 2 that this is the argument Tamanaha made against the mirror paradigm of law and society. But a closer look might vindicate that paradigm. Studies of legal pluralism might even corroborate it. For one thing, legal pluralists have shown us that while a formal system of law may be imported into territories by a colonial power, these societies often also retain their customary ways of handling disputes. For another, this body of scholarship reveals that systems of law crafted from afar cannot simply be imposed in toto on different social contexts. Instead, imported legal institutions and codes get significantly reshaped to fit the local reality. This tailoring—sometimes deliberate and at other times emergent—together with the retention of traditional mores and practices, tends to confirm the law and society idea that law and the society it is embedded in are not just intimate but also alchemical partners.

To sum up, studies of legal pluralism have taught us that multiple legal and normative systems often operate simultaneously. Sometimes it is simply a matter of a division of labor among jurisdictions, as with the U.S. federal, state, and local distribution of legal authority. Sometimes legal systems overlap but do not compete or conflict, as with the occasionally seamless integration of private security guards and local police. Sometimes gaps are exposed across multiple jurisdictions so that legal actors like Blackwater personnel escape accountability altogether. Sometimes there is cross-fertilization, as with many colonial and postcolonial systems. And sometimes competing systems find themselves on a collision course, as is the case with international human rights conventions against female genital cutting and local cultural and religious traditions in some societies.

When legal orders conflict, one of them may be nullified, if not officially then at least in practice. The dual posting of signs at my gym is an example of two jurisdictions with policies directly at odds with each other and the de facto nullification of one of them. Although the corporate policy of checking IDs remains on the books, in practice it is ignored—by all but the inquisitive law and society patron who momentarily miffed the staff by drawing attention to the discrepancy. Disconnects like this between law as it is written and law as it's practiced are the topic of the next chapter.

CHAPTER SIX The Talk versus the Walk of Law

The Cliffs of Moher rise dramatically from the Atlantic Ocean on the western coast of Ireland. At their highest, the Cliffs measure 214 meters (702 feet) and climb so steeply and abruptly from the rocky beach below that the scene is both spectacular and a little scary. The air is chilly, and powerful winds often blow in from the ocean, adding to the atmosphere of rugged beauty. This is the most visited tourist attraction in Ireland, and on any given day you will see brave souls from around the world admiring the sight from along the extensive cliffside walkway. The low railings protecting the walkway end halfway up and a large sign reads "DO NOT PROCEED BEYOND THIS POINT." But the pathway beyond the sign is well worn. Families, couples, and solo backpackers continue on, mostly oblivious. On the day I was there, one American family seemed playfully aware of their transgression, having their picture taken while peering out from behind the sign. Park officials are available for information, and security guards patrol the huge parking lots. But nowhere is there any indication of walkway enforcement, and it is clear that the public is not in *practice* barred from the foot-worn path.

Gaps between the law-on-the-books (the sign indicating no access) and the law-in-action (the de facto policy of granting access) are a central concern in law and society research, and the pervasiveness of these gaps is one of the field's founding ideas. Sometimes the issue is routine nonenforcement. For a historical example, remember the vagrancy law passed in the aftermath of the bubonic plague in medieval England. As Chambliss (1964) showed, the vagrancy law—devised to expand the workforce and contain the upward spiral of wages resulting from labor shortages—lay dormant for a century after the conditions that produced it had subsided. Instead of repealing the statute, it was easier just to ignore it.

For a contemporary example, consider the sharing of copyrighted files on the Internet. A 1997 law in the United States makes peer-to-peer (P2P) swapping of any copyrighted Internet files, not just music, a federal felony punishable with fines of up to $250,000 and a three-year prison term. There is a reason you may not have heard of this law that was signed by President Clinton almost two decades ago: There have been almost no P2P prosecutions. This year alone, tens of millions of online users like yourself (and me, once I can figure it out) will exchange billions of files, and it's a safe bet we won't be caught. Capturing the carefree enthusiasm of file sharers, one responded to an online news story about the law (quoted in Borland 2004), "Long live P2P!" Like the signs on the Cliffs of Moher, this law is transgressed routinely and without consequence. There is a law on the books against what we are doing, but, happily for music and film buffs and the iPod industry, it has not made its way off the books into real life.

Usually the gap between law-on-the-books and law-in-action is more subtle and textured than that. In 2008, the U.S. Government Accountability Office (GAO) issued a report criticizing the Wage and Hour Division of the U.S. Department of Labor for lackadaisical enforcement of laws relating to overtime pay and wage complaints. The report notes that in the decade from 1997 to 2007 enforcement investigations declined by a whopping 37 percent. The GAO also uncovered evidence that the division mishandled workers' complaints. In one case, a truck driver had complained that he worked fifteen hours of overtime every week and was not compensated with overtime pay. It took the Labor Department over a year and a half to put an investigator on the case; the investigator waited six months to begin work and then declared that the two-year statute of limitations was up. In another case, when a swimming-pool maintenance worker complained he had not received his paycheck, the department investigator dropped the case after the employer derided him and announced he had no intention of paying the back wages. A woman filed a charge that she had not been paid for over a year by the nursing home she worked for; the department closed the case after the company claimed the woman's room and board were sufficient payment and that anyway they didn't have the money to pay the wages they owed her. These were not isolated cases. The GAO found thousands of cases like these and concluded that the Wage and Hour Division was not engaging in effective enforcement. Unlike the pathway access at the Cliffs of Moher where the law-on-the-books is completely voided in action, this nonenforcement of labor laws is partial and sporadic. But it is meaningful and patterned nonetheless, and figuring out the pattern and its logic is what interests law and society scholars.

Sometimes the pattern reveals selective nonenforcement. The original law against vagrancy, for example, was never meant to apply to everyone but was targeted at the lower classes to coerce them into the agricultural workforce. While the law ostensibly was neutral in terms of its class referents, there was little doubt who was to be caught and why. This reminds me of a famous quote from the Scythian philosopher Anacharsis. More than 2,500 years ago, Anacharsis quipped, "Laws are like spiderwebs that will catch flies, but not wasps or hornets."

The use of vagrancy laws to channel people into the workforce made its way to the new American continent, where race targeting was added to the mix. After the Civil War in the United States, vagrancy arrests were used in the South to keep freed slaves in a state of agricultural servitude. In *Slavery by Another Name*, Douglas Blackmon (2008) exposes this system of neo-slavery that lasted into the 1940s. Here's how it worked: Tens of thousands of African Americans were arrested on trumped-up charges of vagrancy and other amorphous crimes. They were then sold into bondage to the highest bidders, who put them to work in coal mines, railroads, brickyards, plantations, lumberyards—anywhere captive labor could be of use. According to Blackmon, even the U.S. Steel Corporation participated in this labor scheme. As in the prior slave system, the captives were often bought and sold multiple times by their "employers." Over the course of almost a century, this convict-labor trafficking constituted a windfall for the private sector and for Southern state treasuries. Blackmon (2008, 1–2) begins his exposé by telling the true story of Green Cottenham, an African American man in Alabama who was sold into forced labor:

> On March 30, 1908, Green Cottenham was arrested by the sheriff of Shelby County, Alabama, and charged with "vagrancy." Cottenham had committed no true crime. Vagrancy, the offense of a person not being able to prove at a given moment that he or she is employed, was a new and flimsy concoction dredged up from legal obscurity at the end of the nineteenth century by the state legislators of Alabama and other southern states. It was capriciously enforced by

local sheriffs and constables, adjudicated by mayors and notaries public, recorded haphazardly or not at all in court records, and . . . was reserved almost exclusively for black men. . . .

After three days behind bars, twenty-two-year-old Cottenham was found guilty in a swift appearance before the county judge and immediately sentenced to a thirty-day term of hard labor. Unable to pay the array of fees assessed on every prisoner—fees to the sheriff, the deputy, the court clerk, the witnesses—Cottenham's sentence was extended to nearly a year of hard labor.

The next day, Cottenham, the youngest of nine children born to former slaves in an adjoining county, was sold. Under a standing arrangement between the county and a vast subsidiary of the industrial titan of the North—U.S. Steel Corporation—the sheriff turned the young man over to the company for the duration of his sentence. In return, the subsidiary, Tennessee Coal, Iron & Railroad Company, gave the county $12 a month to pay off Cottenham's fines and fees. What the company's managers did with Cottenham, and thousands of other black men they purchased from sheriffs across Alabama, was entirely up to them.

This powerful and disturbing book makes it clear that the convict-labor system amounted to a return to slavery in all but name. Fabricated charges and targeted enforcement of vague offenses like "vagrancy" were key to this neo-slavery. The system was put together most obviously to provide a cheap labor force to a wide variety of employers and industries. But it was also part of a broader effort by some Southern whites to return African Americans to a state of intimidation and dependence. In this sense, it was the criminal justice equivalent of lynchings and Ku Klux Klan raids. Except that, unlike those victimizations, these mass arrests of African Americans had the added advantage to those interested in subjugating them of reinforcing racist ideas about blacks' predisposition to criminality. As we saw in chapter 4, racism, ideology, and material interests came as a package, carefully wrapped by the hand of Law.

Loitering laws—which make it illegal in certain public venues to stand in one spot doing nothing—are a lot like vagrancy laws in that they prohibit behavior that many of us engage in and therefore encourage discretionary (and discriminatory) action on the part of law enforcement. I recently saw a "No Loitering" sign in a public park in Southern California; I asked myself what constitutes loitering in a park, where the point precisely is not to move on, but to linger. As far as I could tell, everyone here was loitering.

The ability to enforce the law against some people and not others is the very logic behind the enactment of some laws. Certainly, the vagrancy laws were useful to those who wished to reinstate slavery after the Civil War (although as Blackmon tells it, law enforcement used any statute they felt like and then concocted the evidence). More recently, in the civil rights era of the 1950s and 1960s in the United States, anti-loitering laws were used to break up sit-ins and protests. In one famous case, Martin Luther King Jr. was arrested and jailed on loitering charges in Montgomery, Alabama, where he was picketing a business that refused service to African Americans. If you look for "Martin Luther King arrest" on Google Images, you will find several poignant photos of this arrest and others like it. And when the Montgomery bus boycott in 1955—sparked by Rosa Parks's refusal to give up her seat at the front of a bus—dragged on for a year, the black community organized carpools; they were arrested for loitering at designated carpool pickup points in a thinly veiled effort by law enforcement to break the strike.

A white male student of mine told me he did an impromptu experiment when he was in high school. In the experiment, he and some friends tried to get charged with loitering and were utterly unsuccessful. He described the experience to me:

> I'm from a town of about eighty thousand, strongly divided along racial lines, and that day my friends and I were just out and about when one of us made a comment on the "No Loitering" signs, and so eventually, being who we were, we started talking about how none of us really knew exactly what loitering was. So as we went around that day, we tried actively to "loiter," and no matter where we went no one seemed to care that we were standing around. I mean, I've seen small groups of young black men approached by store/mall security for just standing around like us, not even being rowdy, and we eventually came to the conclusion that whatever loitering was, we couldn't do it.

Unlike this student, some young men are considered to be loitering as soon as they show up in public. In the 1990s, Chicago issued an injunction against alleged gang members, prohibiting them from appearing together. This law, which was technically a law against loitering (defined in this statute as "remaining in any one place with no apparent purpose"), was struck down as unconstitutionally vague by the U.S. Supreme Court in *City of Chicago v. Morales* (1999). "Gang injunctions" have since been passed across the United States, with a concentration in Southern California. To pass constitutional muster, they target accused gang members by name and designate the specific areas where they are prohibited from gathering. In Los Angeles, these injunctions are in effect against presumed members of all major gangs. A Tulare County Superior Court judge ordered an injunction against a Latino gang that will affect at least five hundred people. The injunction, which is based not on criminal activity but on association, prohibits such everyday activities as riding in cars, walking down streets, and sitting in front yards. A similar injunction in the San Fernando Valley covers almost ten square miles. However laudable the crime-fighting intentions of these measures, it is important to notice that they target kinds of people, not the actual criminal activity. (Recall that the surge of "mass misdemeanors" in New York City discussed in chapter 2, was also aimed at populations thought to be in need of "management.")

This kind-of-people targeting is also clear in the case of drug laws, as Doris Marie Provine (2007), Bruce Western (2006), and others have shown. There has been a particularly notorious discrepancy in U.S. drug laws: beginning in 1986, people convicted of possessing five grams of crack cocaine with intent to distribute got a mandatory five-year prison sentence, while it took five hundred grams of powder cocaine to receive a comparable sentence. The Fair Sentencing Act of 2010 reduced the sentencing disparity in federal law from the previous ratio of 100 to 1, to a still substantial 18 to 1. The disparity has profoundly discriminatory effects since blacks and Latinos are more likely to possess crack cocaine, and whites are more likely to use and deal the powder variant. This racial difference is apparent in federal court statistics on drug-dealing prosecutions, which show that 82 percent of defendants prosecuted for dealing crack are African Americans, while they account for only 27 percent of those prosecuted for dealing powder cocaine. Conceding the drug policy's discriminatory impact, the U.S. Supreme Court ruled in *Kimbrough v. United States* (2007) that judges are permitted to use their discretion on a case-by-case basis to set lower than the mandatory sentence for crack offenders. Despite this chipping away at the disparity, federal law still enshrines this disparate treatment of drug offenders.

As alarming as this statutory discrepancy is from the point of view of fair and equal treatment, just as disconcerting but far less commented on is the unequal enforcement of what appear to be racially neutral drug laws (Provine 2007). A team of social scientists in Seattle found that blacks and Latinos were disproportionately arrested for drug possession in that city relative to their actual drug use (Beckett, Nyrop, Pfingst, and Bowen 2005). They also found that the police were blind to drug transactions involving whites. The precinct captain of a white Seattle neighborhood went on record saying that whites in his area never do outdoor drug transactions, yet Beckett and her team of social scientists observed many drug transactions there by whites in a relatively brief time.

Across the United States in New York City, 54 percent of the people arrested for marijuana possession from 1997 to 2006 were black and only 14 percent were white. This despite the fact that 36 percent of New York's population is white (and only 27 percent is black), and a larger percentage of whites report using marijuana (Levine and Small 2008). New York's mayor Bill de Blasio has installed a policy whereby people caught in public with twenty-five grams or less of marijuana will not be handcuffed and booked but will simply be issued a ticket for unlawful possession. In announcing the change, the police commissioner went out of his way to note that people with outstanding warrants, subjects of open investigations, or those with no identification will still be arrested. Given the disproportionate number of people of color in these categories, it is unclear whether this new policy will ameliorate or amplify discrepancies in drug arrests. Noted academic and activist Cornel West and others have called the reform a "sugar pill," designed only to placate those outraged by the history of racially tinged marijuana enforcement in New York (quoted in Grynbaum 2014, A24).

What we learn from these various statistics and patterns is that laws that are neutral on their face are applied disparately. It may even be the main virtue of certain laws—vagrancy and loitering being conspicuous examples—that they are pliable and in practice can be bent toward certain populations. Some laws are so vague and the offending behaviors so relatively trivial (what is loitering?) that their principal merit is that they lend themselves to this bending and so achieve what is otherwise impermissible under the constitutions of most Western democracies—the criminalization of certain kinds of people.

In a different twist on this theme, but underscoring its basic point, some states have turned to an unusual strategy to facilitate drug prosecutions (Barnard 2008). Twenty-nine states in the United States have passed laws imposing taxes on illegal drugs, partly in the hopes of enhancing tax revenues but mostly because it is easier to prosecute tax evasion than drug dealing. The rare drug dealer who actually chooses to pay taxes on his wares in some states gets special stickers to post on his (illegal) merchandise that admonish, "Say no to marijuana" (the irony of this seems comical until you realize the parallels with the surgeon general's statement on every pack of cigarettes sold in the United States that "Smoking causes lung cancer . . ."). Predictably, few people—other than stamp collectors who covet the bizarre tax stamp—pay the tax. One young drug dealer in North Carolina was apparently meticulous about paying his taxes, using the questionable logic that if he is caught, he won't have to forfeit his inventory, since he will have paid taxes on it. The broader point is that states passed this legislation *not* under the assumption that drug dealers would actually pay their taxes; instead, legislators passed the laws precisely because they assumed—and hoped—they would be violated, since it is the dealers' tax *evasion* that is useful to prosecutors looking for a way to secure convictions.

Other laws target kinds of people to eliminate from public view "undesirables" and the social problems they embody, such as the bundle of policies that "banish" (Beckett and Herbert 2010) certain people from designated areas of Seattle, discussed in chapter 2. Other examples can be found in the myriad policies designed to rid an area of homeless people. Laws against "illegal lodging" and "anti-camping" measures are designed to deter the homeless from sleeping in doorways of businesses and camping out in parks. Municipal restrictions also limit the ability to feed homeless people outside. Fort Lauderdale, Florida, has been at the forefront of the effort. Spearheaded by local businesses and the U.S. Chamber of Commerce, a new law there requires toilets to be available and written authorization from property owners before food distribution can take place (Alvarez and Robles 2014). But middle-class picnickers and night-sky enthusiasts can rest assured they won't be charged under any of these ordinances, however technically similar their behavior might be to that of the less fortunate who sleep in public parks. A homeless man in one city in Florida where a law made it illegal to lie down in public was reportedly so annoyed at the blatantly selective enforcement that he called the police to report a family having a picnic (Alvarez and Robles 2014). In the case of a similar ordinance in Santa Ana, California, the city council has taken pains to distinguish between using blankets to *cover* oneself as the homeless are likely to do (which is forbidden) and using blankets to *sit on* as middle-class picnickers occasionally do (which is allowed).

THE DISPARATE TREATMENT implicit in vagrancy, loitering, and anti-camping laws reflects the economic interests and biases of class societies, joined in the United States and other racialized societies by racial stereotypes. Sometimes such law-on-the-books and law-in-action gaps are the result not so much of class or race biases—or even ulterior motives like those implicit in the drug dealers' tax— but of structural dilemmas faced by policy makers and enforcement agents. For much of the past century, the U.S. Immigration and Naturalization Service (INS) (now Immigration and Customs Enforcement, or ICE) was derided as dysfunctional and lambasted for its inability to control the borders. A Pulitzer Prize–winning journalist (Crewdson 1983, 114) once called the INS "the worst-managed, least effective federal agency in Washington." More than twenty-five years later, a *New York Times* (2009a) editorial said federal immigration enforcement was "out of control," adding that ICE and the Border Patrol are "botching their jobs" (A26). Another editorial, criticizing ICE under President Obama, declares that nothing has changed: "That shambling machinery lurches on" (*New York Times* 2009b, A20). And a study of the agency by the nonpartisan think tank Migration Policy Institute paints a "portrait of dysfunction" (paraphrased by a *New York Times* reporter; Thompson 2009, A19). Decade after decade and reform after reform, the immigration agency remains one of the most widely criticized federal agencies in the United States.

Close inspection tells us the agency is not simply chronically inept or mismanaged. Instead, it has the misfortune of sitting at the fault line of a structural contradiction between the economic demand for cheap immigrant labor and political demands for border control. Immigration officials are stuck between the rock of economics and the hard place of politics—"damned if they do and damned if they don't," as a former president of the union representing employees of the immigration agency once put it (quoted in U.S. Congress, Senate Committee on the Judiciary 1980, 559). While they are charged with rounding up and deporting illegal immigrants, historically they have faced enormous obstacles in the form of backlash from employers who stand to lose their workers in these roundups.

In the mid-twentieth century, it was the Border Patrol's explicit policy not to interrupt farm production. The immigration commissioner assured the House Committee on Agriculture in 1947 that he recognized it was the "duty" of the agency "to protect valuable and necessary crops" by not deporting undocumented farmworkers (quoted in U.S. Congress, House Committee on Agriculture 1947, 36). Confronted with an institutional mandate to control the border that conflicted with the economic realities of immigrant labor, the Immigration Service followed the course of least resistance, retreating into token gestures that did nothing to threaten the interests of immigrant employers.

The bracero program established a system of imported Mexican farmworkers (called "braceros") for U.S. agriculture that lasted from 1942 to 1964, with the INS the chief overseer of the program. Here potentially was an ideal solution to the agency's structural dilemma. INS officials soon learned that if they provided growers with easy access to braceros, they could reduce the number of illegal immigrants, thereby allowing for the technical enforcement of immigration laws without incurring the wrath of farm employers. But it was against the law to simply transform illegal Mexican farmworkers into braceros on the spot; instead, braceros had to be contracted and brought in from Mexico.

To expedite employers' access to braceros and as a solution to the problem of undocumented farmworkers already in the United States, the INS devised an ingenious plan. They escorted illegal immigrants across the Mexican border and brought them back five minutes later as braceros. The ritual of having illegal aliens step across the border and come back as legal braceros was referred to ironically by immigration officials as "a walk around the statute"(quoted in *New York Times* 1951, 34; see also Calavita 1992, 41). The playful term suggests they knew full well they were circumventing the inconveniences of the law-on-the-books. Confronting the practical advantages of contracting illegal immigrants directly as braceros versus the legal requirement that braceros be imported from Mexico, officials' creative response attests to the truth of the adage that necessity is the mother of invention.

A lot has changed in the past half century in the field of immigration, but much remains the same. Immigration, both legal and illegal, has increased dramatically. Almost 12 million undocumented immigrants are estimated to live in the United States; they are more likely to be settled in the United States than shuttling back and forth across the border as they did in the past; and they are more evenly distributed across the United States than they once were. Also changed is the post-9/11 political climate, with its enhanced national security fears and popular sentiment against porous borders. These changes, rather than transforming the structural contradiction faced by the immigration agency, intensify it. With undocumented immigrants now less concentrated in agriculture and central to a wide variety of manufacturing and service sectors, their economic utility is even more pervasive; at the same time, fears about uncontrolled borders resonate broadly and deeply in the post-9/11 climate.

Reflecting this new environment, the budget of Immigration and Customs Enforcement grew from $4.2 million in 1975 to more than $5 billion in 2014, and its staff size almost quintupled. The number of Border Patrol agents increased from about 4,500 in the mid-1990s to over 21,000 by 2014. Despite these vast increases in budget and staff, certain types of enforcement have plummeted—notably, employer sanctions.

Sanctions against employers who knowingly hire undocumented immigrants were written into law in the 1986 Immigration Reform and Control Act, ostensibly as a way to reduce job opportunities to illegal immigrants and so reduce the flow. But enforcement started out spotty at best and dropped steadily from there. In 1988, the year after the law went into effect, the INS inspected the records of 9,500 of the nation's 7 million employers; in 2003, only about 2,000 employers were inspected. The number of employers who were fined fell from 1,200 in 1988 to one-tenth that in 2003. As the ICE budget soared and enforcement of employer sanctions dwindled, the pattern came to map perfectly onto the economic and political contradiction that has always restrained enforcement, evoked popular outrage, and condemned the agency to derision. The gap between the law-on-the-books and the law-in-action follows the contours of this contradiction and the institutional dilemma it poses for the immigration agency. I should note here that employer sanctions audits have increased considerably during the Obama administration, but fines remain low and are almost always reduced further by the lone administrative law judge assigned to employer sanctions cases.

Employer sanctions were doomed from the start. To secure the support of the U.S. Chamber of Commerce, growers' associations, and other employer groups, Congress inserted the word "knowingly" into the prohibition against hiring unauthorized workers. The law also stated that checking workers' documents was an "affirmative defense" against prosecution, even if the documents turned out to be false. In other words, the act of requesting documents from workers and keeping them on file was immunization against prosecution because it would allow employers to argue they didn't "know" of their workers' illegal status. The New York Times reported an immigration raid at a rag-exporting plant in Houston, Texas, where ICE arrested 160 immigrant workers who appeared to be unauthorized to work (Evans 2008). A lawyer for the company prepared the ground for its defense under the employer sanctions provision: "If we have an illegal employee, we don't know it" (quoted in Evans 2008, A15). The statute was flawed from the beginning in order to accommodate employers' concerns, and the lack of enforcement struck the last nail in the coffin.

This is what law and society scholars call a "symbolic law." Murray Edelman (1964) used this term to refer to policies that have little impact on objective conditions but serve the purpose of placating the public. They are, in other words, empty political gestures. In the case of employer sanctions, lawmakers confronted the economic reality of cheap immigrant labor and pressure from the employers and industries profiting from it, versus the political pressure exerted by public demands that Congress regain control of the border. The least painful solution was to announce loudly that action was being taken but to pass a law that was hobbled by loopholes. It is revealing that by the time the employer sanctions provision was passed in 1986, Congress had accommodated employer concerns so thoroughly that the U.S. Chamber of Commerce and growers' associations withdrew all opposition to it.

Before leaving this concept of symbolic law, here is one more example from the immigration arena. California voters passed Proposition 187 in a landslide in 1994. The proposition, as stated on the ballot, would have barred all undocumented children from attending public schools in California, required teachers and administrators to report "suspect" children, barred undocumented immigrants from receiving nonemergency health care, and required health-care personnel to report "suspect" patients. The law was never implemented because the courts immediately declared it an unconstitutional violation of the federal monopoly on immigration lawmaking and because its ban on public schooling for undocumented children was a violation of the equal protection clause of the Fourteenth Amendment (a 1982 Supreme Court case—*Plyler v. Doe*—had already established the latter).

Despite its conspicuous unconstitutionality and the predictable court injunction against its implementation, proponents urged people to vote for it. More accurately, people were urged to vote for it *because* it would not be implemented. The week before the election, I heard a major spokesman for the measure being interviewed on the radio. He complained about opponents who warned of increasing crime and gang activity if hundreds of thousands of children could not go to school. The spokesman told his radio audience it was "ridiculous" to paint such scary scenarios, since everyone knew the constitutionality of the proposition would be challenged immediately. In other words, he told his listeners, you can vote for the measure with peace of mind since it will not be enforced. And Californians did vote for it, en masse. The vast majority (78 percent) told exit pollsters they voted for it "to send a message" that they were fed up with illegal immigration; only 34 percent said they voted for it to keep people from using state services, and a mere 2 percent said they wanted to bar undocumented children from public schools (*Los Angeles Times* 1994, A22; see Calavita 1996). Proposition 187 was pure symbolic action. As with employer sanctions, serious opposition was muted by the implicit—and sometimes explicit—understanding that a political message could be sent without exacting any real change. In fact, it was the anticipation that it would have no concrete effect that allowed it to win so handily.

Sadly, even though Proposition 187 was never enforced, its symbolic, anti-immigrant message unleashed hostility and discrimination and caused widespread fear among immigrants. The *Christian Science Monitor* wrote that a fifth-grade teacher in California asked her mostly Latino students to report their parents' immigration status. A school security guard told two Latinas who were born in the United States, "We don't have to let Mexicans in here anymore" (quoted in Munoz 1994, 19). A worker at McDonald's insisted on seeing immigration documents before serving a customer. A pharmacist refused to fill a prescription for someone he suspected was undocumented. A customer at a restaurant asked to see the green card of the cook, saying, "It's a citizen's duty to kick out illegals" (quoted in Munoz 1994, 19). Pregnant women said they were afraid to seek prenatal care for fear of deportation. In one tragic case, an eight-year-old child died because his parents were afraid to take him to the hospital (Martinez 1994; Romney and Marquis 1994). While the law-on-the-books may have been voided by the courts and met none of its stated goals, it nonetheless had profound social and material consequences for immigrants and for many U.S. citizens.

LAW AND SOCIETY scholar Janet Gilboy (1992) has written about pressures of another kind in the immigration arena. In the early 1990s, Gilboy spent thousands of hours observing and talking with immigration inspectors at O'Hare airport in Chicago as they sorted arriving foreign nationals according to whether they were admissible or inadmissible. With tens of thousands of foreigners coming through the airport every year, these low-level officials have to make quick decisions: Do arriving passengers appear potentially dangerous? Are they likely to remain in the United States indefinitely or violate the terms of their visas? Are they who they say they are?

Gilboy was interested in the cues and profiling techniques that officials engage to facilitate this mind-numbing people processing, but she was more fascinated by how officials respond to important special interests. She found that every so often arriving passengers are supported by powerful outsiders who pressure the agency to admit them despite faulty or suspect paperwork. According to her research, even when there is no external pressure ahead of time, inspectors learn to recognize which cases might lead to potential trouble for their already-beleaguered agency down the road.

Young women coming to work as nannies or au pairs for the summer on a tourist visa, which does not authorize a person to work, are typical. An inspector explained to Gilboy that employers of nannies are wealthy and have powerful connections. He described one incident in which an inspector was about to bar from entry someone who claimed she was a tourist because he discovered incriminating documents indicating she intended to work as a nanny. She signed a statement admitting as much and was ready to depart when supervisors changed their minds and let her enter. "There's too much pressure from outside," the inspector told Gilboy. "If they make a wrong decision, then they [employers] call congressmen, and they call [the district director], and then back to us" (quoted in Gilboy 1992, 287).

Gilboy observed that these anticipated congressional interventions often led to a less-than-rigorous application of the law, especially in cases where there will be little public anger if the laxity is exposed. She summarized the officials' perception that there is probably little public support for "tough handling of an 18-year-old Scandinavian girl coming for the summer to babysit, or for stringent application of fiancée visa rules to a woman arriving with joyful expectations of marrying a U.S. citizen, or for a forceful stance for taking permanent residence cards from elderly people living out their last years outside of the country" (285).

No doubt some of this scenario changed with 9/11 and heightened security concerns. But these frontline officials day in and day out still make discretionary decisions that are designed to minimize trouble for their organization by warding off anticipated interventions, avoiding negative consequences, and not alienating potentially powerful constituents. In the process, some of the crossed t's and dotted i's of the law-on-the-books slide quietly off the page.

This practice of protecting institutional self-interests, and in doing so shaping real law, is of course not confined to immigration officials. Moving away from the immigration arena, sociologist Bob Emerson (1991) shows us how other bureaucracies minimize trouble for themselves by paying attention to the priorities and needs of other agencies in their orbit. In a study of agencies and officials who handle referrals, like courts and high school counselors, Emerson found that they develop a lot of "interorganizational knowledge" that allows them to read into the meaning of a referral and the priorities of those who made it. Decisions about how to treat the referral are made partly on the basis of these interorganizational understandings. In the end, says Emerson, a range of "practical factors . . . lead to decision outcomes that on a formal, ostensible level 'do not have to be'" (209). For example, "in complaints brought by the Child Welfare Department to a juvenile court charging a youth with runaway, court staff often learned that the charge was simply a device to get the 'runaway' held temporarily in detention until a new placement could be found" (Emerson 1969, 60–61). Contingencies and idiosyncrasies like this, not technical legal criteria, are often the deciding factors in how a case is dealt with.

As we saw in chapter 5, administrative law judges play key roles in setting the parameters of such decisions and in hearing cases on appeal. And we saw there that in the arenas of both immigration and asylum law and disability claims, adjudicators produce discrepant outcomes. The point here is twofold. First, frontline officers in the immigration service and in social services, like the Child Welfare Department described by Emerson, exercise substantial discretion, but their actions are partially circumscribed by the courts, which mediate between law-on-the-books and law-in-action on the ground. Second, administrative law courts are themselves sources of variable law-in-action. Much like the "street-level bureaucrats" (Lipsky 1980) whose decisions they hear on appeal, courts produce outcomes that are variable, contingent, and buffeted by extralegal forces. The asylum study is a perfect example of the conceptual link between legal pluralism and the books-action gap. For, as we saw in that study, the plurality and variability of administrative law outcomes expose the contingent process through which law-in-action is made.

ONE FINAL ARENA where we can clearly see institutional actors and enforcement agents effectively making law is in police work. Sometimes, this decentralized lawmaking is relatively benign, as when police departments use their discretion to interpret ambiguous statutes. To take one example, in California there are a series of laws on so-called hate crimes that impose more severe sentences on those whose animus against certain specified groups (notably, those identified by race, gender, sexual orientation, or nationality) contribute to their motivation to commit a crime. From 1999 to 2001, sociologists Ryken Grattet and Valerie Jenness (2005) did interviews with officials from 397 police and sheriff departments across California to see how these laws were being implemented.

Showing us once again that the law-in-action is not just an animated version of the law-on-the-books, they found enormous variation in how these organizations interpret California's hate crime statutes, starting with the very definition of hate crime (on which the laws are remarkably vague). According to Grattet and Jenness (2005), police and sheriff departments sometimes follow the lead of other agencies in defining hate crime, sometimes look to state guidelines for advice, sometimes seek approval from national professional associations, and sometimes turn to the local community. One police chief told Grattet and Jenness that she regularly seeks help from "organized groups that speak for the types of folks we police" when figuring out "how best to proceed" (927) on hate crime law and other new laws.

Regardless of which organizational network or community they are most attuned to, these departments are constructing legal meaning. This departmentally specific legal meaning is then codified in each jurisdiction's "hate crime general orders." These localized orders serve as the department's de facto hate crime law. Because they represent local interpretations of what the law-on-the-books means, and serve as rough blueprints for on-the-ground enforcement, these general orders might be thought of as "law-in-between," to borrow a phrase Jenness and Grattet (2005) use in another context. All law enforcement agencies in the state enforce the same California hate crime statutes, but in practice thousands of local hate crime general orders interpret them, thus transforming the abstract and ambiguous protocol into a patchwork of different policies. It is an open question how these policies are actually implemented on the street in specific encounters, which is arguably where de facto law happens, and which is driven in part by these departmental policies and in part by the discretionary decisions of individual officers.

In other cases, de facto police lawmaking is much less benign. Many police studies show us that law enforcement agents sometimes "take the law into their own hands" not just by virtue of their discretionary decision making but through corruption and misconduct. One of the most notorious instances of police misconduct in the United States involved the Rampart Division of the Los Angeles Police Department in the late 1990s. The Community Resources against Street Hoodlums (CRASH) was the anti-gang unit of this division, which in retrospect appears to have itself engaged in gangster behavior. Investigations, aided by the testimony of an implicated officer, Rafael Pérez, revealed that officers in the CRASH unit had systematically engaged in unprovoked violence and corruption, including homicides, beatings, the framing of suspects, perjury, drug dealing, and bank robbery. The scandal cost Los Angeles $125 million to settle over 140 civil lawsuits, and more than 100 criminal convictions were overturned when it was discovered they had been based on officer perjury or planted evidence.

This is not an isolated case of law enforcement breaking the law and in the process opening up a chasm between the formal law and law as it is practiced. Studies in Britain and the United States consistently find extensive misconduct by the police, sometimes spiked with their racial hostilities. It is usually not haphazard or without its own logic but instead is linked to agency subcultures, municipal politics, institutional dysfunction, and in some cases explicit policies of political harassment (Cain 1993; Seron, Pereira, and Kovath 2004). Various studies of the police in Mexico, Argentina, and Brazil expose the connections between their violent practices and national policies of brutality against oppositional and subordinate groups (Chevigny 1999; Botelo and Rivera 2000; Hinton 2005). Police violence seems to have actually increased in these Latin American nations following their formal democratization—suggesting that democracy has ushered in not just constitutional principles of justice and equality, but their ever more routine suppression as well.

Sometimes police misconduct is motivated by self-interest pure and simple, in an environment that encourages an "everyone for oneself" mentality. A study of the police in Russia (Gerber and Mendelson 2008) found that widespread corruption and violence—called "predatory policing" by the study's authors—is the aggregate result of individual officers pursuing their own economic interests. With the collapse of the Soviet Union, institutional chaos, deficient training, department underfunding, and poverty-level wages, police officers use their seemingly unrestrained discretion Wild West style to extract personal benefits.

SO FAR we have seen the gap between the talk and the walk of law in selective enforcement, in the discretionary application of certain laws, in the structural-institutional dilemmas of enforcement agencies, and in police discretion and misconduct. Moving to another level of theoretical abstraction, critical legal studies (CLS) exposes this gap by investigating the lapses of broad legal principles of the sort that undergird democratic societies. CLS developed within the law and society field in the 1970s, with one of its main goals being to reveal the disconnects between foundational legal principles of capitalist democracies and their realization. David Kairys's (1998) exposé of the myths of free speech in the United States, mentioned in chapter 1, is a good example of this approach. In that article, Kairys reveals the rhetoric versus the reality of the free speech principle and at the same time shows us the ideological work done by this principle despite its failure to live up to its promise.

Another Kairys (1982) piece explores deviations from stare decisis (literally, "let the decision stay"), the common law principle that requires judges to be guided by precedent decisions. Stare decisis is one of the fundamental building blocks of the Anglo-American legal system. Kairys's examination of how well this key precept lives up in practice to its promise on the books has powerful ramifications for the workings of the legal system as a whole. Examining three U.S. Supreme Court decisions on the issue of free speech rights in shopping malls, Kairys argues that the Court was guided by precedent only when it served the decision it preferred for ideological and political reasons.

The first of these three cases, *Amalgamated Food Employees Union v. Logan Valley Plaza* (1968), was triggered when members of the union were escorted out of a shopping mall by security personnel after picketing a store they had a labor dispute with. The liberal-leaning Warren Court upheld the free speech right of the picketers, arguing both that shopping malls are for all intents and purposes public spaces even though technically private property and that to deny the picketers access to the mall would effectively deny them the right to picket their employer.

By the time it heard a similar case in 1972, the Warren Court had become the Burger Court and included four relatively conservative justices who had been appointed by President Nixon. In *Lloyd v. Tanner* (1972), Vietnam War protesters had been ordered to leave a shopping mall after handing out antiwar leaflets. The Burger Court held against the free speech rights of the protesters, prioritizing instead the mall owners' property rights. To avoid the appearance of overturning the precedent set in *Amalgamated*, the Court "distinguished the precedent," arguing that the two cases were different since in *Lloyd* the antiwar protesters—unlike *Amalgamated* picketers whose employer was located in the mall—had no particular need to leaflet at that location.

The clincher came with *Hudgens v. National Labor Relations Board* in 1976. Once again, as in the 1968 *Amalgamated* case, the issue was the right of labor unions to picket their employers at a mall. This time, the Burger Court determined that the mall's private property rights trumped the speech rights of the labor union. And to avoid the appearance of deviating from the precedent set in *Amalgamated*, the Court argued that *Lloyd* had reversed that precedent in 1972 (even though the same justices had taken pains at the time to explain they were not doing that). Deviating from apparent precedent while insisting they had no choice but to follow what they said was the new precedent set by *Lloyd*, Justice Stewart, writing for the majority, disingenuously insisted, "Our institutional duty is to follow until changed the law as it is now, not as some members of the Court might wish it to be" (quoted in Kairys 1982, 12).

Kairys uses this trilogy of cases to show that what constitutes a precedent is in the eye of the beholders, and the beholders come from distinct perspectives that shape their point of view; that legal decision making is thus based not just on legal reasoning but also on political and ideological points of view; and that the rhetoric of law may be used to mask deviations from its own principles. From this perspective, the announced legal principles are majestic, but the practice is decidedly plebeian, firmly rooted in such earthly forces as ideology, politics, and economic convenience. And the majesty of the principles in turn *obscures* the pedestrianism of the practice and the power inequalities it secures.

TO SUM UP, law and society scholars who study the books-action gap focus on legal meaning making in police stations, in border enforcement, in the courts, on the street, in shopping malls, and everywhere else that law is literally en-acted on a daily basis. The studies reveal the multiple ways that laws-on-the-books and constitutional principles come to be interpreted and enforced, as well as their fundamentally indeterminate nature. At some level, the thrill is about catching law at violating itself—its promises eluded, its mandates subverted, its ostensible intent slipped. Snooping around a friend's house has its psychic rewards, as Peter Berger implied; and snooping around the dark corners of law's room and finding evidence of its failure to fulfill its promises can be heady stuff.

But it is more than that. In the process, we also discover law leaping from the confines of that room and boisterously affecting the lives of ordinary people: an arriving passenger is detained (or not) at the airport in Chicago, a homeless man is picked up in Seattle for loitering, a college student smoking marijuana is let off with a warning, an immigrant farmworker is escorted "around the statute" by the U.S. Border Patrol, a foster child is charged as a runaway in Florida, a New York drug dealer is prosecuted for tax evasion, a Russian is subjected to extortion by the police, and union activists are evicted from what now passes for public space but is private property. No amount of studying the law-on-the-books can predict or explain these events, and yet these are the legal phenomena that permeate and shape our lives.

It is not surprising that we want to understand this kind of law. At the end of the day—after laws are passed and lofty legal principles pronounced—this is the law that matters. But we also want to understand the *gap*, because it can provide us with clues about not just the workings of law but also the workings of society itself. As we have seen in the examples I give here, different kinds of gaps open up between formal law and real law, with different mechanisms at work. Some are the result of racial, political, or class biases; some are written into the law for instrumental purposes; some follow the contours of an institutional dilemma or structural contradiction; some are the products of organizational actors pursuing their institutional interests; some are the creatures of local police jurisdictions pragmatically hewing to community preferences; and some are the result of police corruption, aided and abetted by a collusive environment. There are a few constants though. Most important, the law-on-the-books is almost always ambiguous, and this commodious quality of law is exploited to construct legal meanings consistent with ideological, institutional, economic, or practical agendas.

The nature of law's journey off the books and into action, the parameters of these agendas, and the mechanisms of legal meaning making vary by social location and its attendant social processes. If we shadow law as it leaves the page, we follow it into some obvious locales like regulatory agencies, but we track it into some more unlikely hangouts too. If we observe closely and listen carefully to what transpires in these venues, we learn not only about the ways of law but also about institutional logics, racialization, tensions in the political economy, and the real dynamics of power.

Adding another element of intrigue, it is often difficult to tell at the outset how things will turn out, or why. Remember the pathways at the Cliffs of Moher. A large sign broadcasts the official rule: Sightseers must stay on the pathway and are forbidden from proceeding up the slope, where the views are most spectacular. But the forbidden path is well worn by tourists enticed by the views above and reassured by the hordes of other people casually forging ahead. What interests this law and society scholar-tourist is the complete disconnect between the sign and its application—literally in this case, between law's talk and its walk.

Two obvious questions come to mind: Why is there a total lack of walkway enforcement? And, given that there is apparently no incentive to enforce this rule, why have a sign (or rule) at all? The explanation I have settled on is that funds are inadequate for constructing a continuous railed trail, posting the sign is a protection against liability, and nonenforcement is an accommodation to the lucrative tourist trade. In this speculative scenario, the National Tourism Development Authority of Ireland confronts dueling institutional pressures related to funding deficits on one hand and the need to attract and accommodate tourists on the other. Posting a warning sign but then ignoring it might be a solution to this dilemma. Of course, we don't really know what the truth about this particular gap is. Maybe the cliffs beyond the sign are private property, and the tourism authority makes only a token gesture to keep people off with the feeble signage. Or maybe the low-level officials whose job it is to enforce the boundary have learned through trial and error not to harass affluent tourists and incur inconvenient downstream consequences. The range of scenarios we can conjure up confirms the wide variety of potential reasons for the gaps between law's talk and its walk, the diversity of possible mechanisms at work, and the richness of the rewards we stand to reap from sorting it out.

Before moving on, let's recap some of the themes we've touched on in these last chapters. You have probably noticed that some intersect each other and others overlap—remember, for example, our discussions of the "color of law" in chapter 4 and the race bias in law enforcement in this chapter. Weaving together a number of these key themes are a pair of riveting urban ethnographies: *On the Run*, by Alice Goffman (2014), and *Gang Leader for a Day*, by Sudhir Venkatesh (2008). These ethnographies examine in a close-up and personal way the interactions among poverty, race, law, and social order, and in the process illustrate several of the key points I've been making. Eschewing theory and abstraction, both Goffman and Venkatesh replace sociological analysis of those interactions with on-the-ground accounts of their daily effects. Both authors enmeshed themselves deeply in their subjects' lives over the course of many years without much regard for their own physical safety or legal liability. These are what you might call "extreme ethnographies."

Alice Goffman spent six years closely connected to, and sometimes living with, a group of young African American men in a poor neighborhood in Philadelphia that she calls "6th Street." She was especially close to Mike and Chuck—so much so that when Chuck was killed in a shooting outside a Chinese takeout place, she joined Mike and others to ride around looking for the killer with revenge on their minds. The book reads like a gripping action movie, except that it's real. Its revelations are many. For our purposes, what is relevant is, first, the vast surveillance and monitoring network that permeates this poor, black neighborhood and that is intimately linked to the culture of control and its selective emphasis on young minority men, as discussed in chapter 2 and again in chapter 4. Second, this network essentially criminalizes the vast majority of this population through the extensive use of arrest warrants for relatively minor offenses, as we saw in Ferguson, Missouri, and as discussed by Issa Kohler-Hausmann

(2014) in her concept of mass misdemeanors. Third, the police, as Goffman tells it, are not only proactive. She observed them beating, kicking, and choking suspects, as well as using threats of eviction or loss of child custody to elicit damning information from girlfriends and family members, in episodes illustrative of the gap between the majestic talk versus the banal walk of law.

These themes and others emerge in Venkatesh's (2008) *Gang Leader for a Day*. Working with some of the most renowned structural sociologists of poverty and race as a beginning graduate student, Venkatesh was unimpressed with their methods: "I liked the questions these researchers were asking, but compared with the vibrant life that I saw on the streets of Chicago, the discussion in these seminars seemed cold and distant, abstract and lifeless. I found it particularly curious that most of these researchers didn't seem interested in meeting the people they wrote about" (3). When he dutifully went into the field as a research assistant and began to ask his professor's survey questions— which, he says, were some version of, "How does it feel to be black and poor?"—Venkatesh was told by one young black man he encountered, "You shouldn't go around asking them silly-ass questions" (21).

Venkatesh abandoned the survey method and ended up spending the better part of six years hanging out in the Robert Taylor Homes in Chicago, at the time one of the most crime-ridden and violent housing projects in America. Built in 1962 and comprising twenty-eight high-rise buildings, Robert Taylor was home to some twenty-seven thousand people, the vast majority of whom were African American and poor. When Venkatesh ventured uninvited into one of the building's urine-soaked hallways for the first time and was held hostage overnight, it was controlled by the Black Kings, a drug-dealing gang led locally by the charismatic "J.T."

Remarkably, Venkatesh returned and gained the respect and apparent friendship of J.T., receiving unprecedented access to the workings of the gang and the larger community it controlled. A woman named Ms. Bailey was among the local leaders he met. Ms. Bailey was a formidable woman who acted as the unofficial "building president" and who did whatever had to be done for the physical and economic safety of the many women who offered local men sexual services in exchange for drugs and/or survival.

Venkatesh debunks a number of myths about gangs and their relationship to the communities where they operate. For one thing, he reveals that the Black Kings operated much as any business enterprise does, with meticulous bookkeeping, a keen eye for the bottom line, and a need for stability and predictability. Beyond that, he shows us a far more nuanced relationship between the gang and local residents than is usually portrayed by sociologists. While some residents are clearly tired of the violence and the iron hand with which the gang ran things, accepting the gang's control was a matter of survival. Not only did the gang drive the underground economy from which so many residents made their living; it ensured a minimum level of security. Time and again, Venkatesh reveals the lack of an official health and safety infrastructure at Robert Taylor, relating harrowing stories of, for example, the unwillingness of ambulance drivers to come to the neighborhood and the conspicuous absence of the police.

In this vacuum, the gang became the primary source of employment and crucial social services. As Venkatesh explains, the gang "worked as the de facto administration of Robert Taylor: J.T. may have been a lawbreaker, but he was very much a lawmaker as well" (59), setting policies about and collecting taxes on everything from prostitution to car repairs. The lack of formal employment and social and health services, and especially the absence of police, meant that local residents depended on the efficient, if sometimes violent, control measures exacted by the gang.

But the absence of police was not absolute. While J.T. and other leaders of drug gangs were not particularly concerned about being arrested—according to J.T., it was in the police's "best interest to let familiar faces run the drug businesses" (136)—lower-level street dealers were frequently arrested. And we soon find out that the police too were hustling. In one scene, Ms. Bailey, a pastor, and two policemen are shown mediating between leaders of the Black Kings and the Disciples, a rival gang. The Disciples had done a drive-by shooting that killed two children—an event that augured a possible all-out war and had scared off potential drug customers. The solution that more or less satisfied all sides was a practical one, with the Black Kings allowed to sell in the Disciples' territory for a week without interference, to make up for lost income. The pastor would later receive a "donation" from the Kings, and the police achieved a relative peace.

Other scenes involving the police are less sanguine. Four police officers drag a man from an apartment and demand to know where his prostitution proceeds are hidden, beat him until he tells them, and then leave with the money. In another of many such instances, five undercover police raid a party attended by J.T. and his gang, and leave with bags of cash and jewels. J.T. told Venkatesh, "As soon as they find out we're having a party, they raid it. . . . We make all this fucking money, and they want some" (231).

Venkatesh provides a glimpse inside a drug gang, and its interactions with local residents and law enforcement, that only long-term and deep embeddedness could achieve. Along the way, his account vividly illustrates the police corruption and selective nonenforcement that we have talked about in this chapter, as the police in Robert Taylor Homes selectively neglect, arrest, beat, and shake down drug dealers and local residents. It also reveals the everyday and everywhere quality of law, with or without a police presence, as the informal but all-too-real legal order imposed by the Black Kings and Ms. Bailey maintain control. And there could be no more compelling depiction of legal pluralism at work than the scene in which a pastor, two policemen, two gang leaders, and Ms. Bailey mediate the explosive dispute over a fatal drive-by shooting. Each of these participants represented their own particular legal and normative order, and the tense scene reveals the challenges of reconciling these multifarious layers of law and the sometimes unorthodox solutions deployed in the process. Finally, while Venkatesh consciously avoids any explicit structural analysis— finding it "abstract and lifeless"—the book nonetheless underscores the structurally embedded racial and economic inequalities of law, and their impact on the real-life characters of Venkatesh's stories. As we discussed in chapter 2 ("Types of Society, Types of Law"), the law these actors get mirrors their racial and social location. But we can go further. The type of law on display here—pluralistic, fragmented, and radically patterned by inequality—mirrors contemporary American society. In the next chapter, we turn to law and society scholarship that examines the potential for and limitations of efforts to alleviate that inequality.

CHAPTER SEVEN Law and Social Justice:
Plus ça change . . .

In the small town where I grew up on the Eastern Shore of Maryland, race relations in the 1950s were not much different from what they'd been after the Civil War almost a century earlier. The public schools were so segregated and the "colored" schools so geographically and socially isolated that white children like me were only dimly aware they existed. On Saturday afternoons, the town's one movie theater brought together the rambunctious children of white farmers, watermen, wealthy transplants from Washington and New York, landed gentry, and local professionals, for a weekly dose of cowboys and Indians; black children who could afford the twenty-five-cent ticket entered through the side door and sat in the cramped balcony. There were two black residential neighborhoods, one in town behind the jail and courthouse complex, where neat clapboard houses were interspersed with corner stores that served the sequestered population; the other was in a small rural settlement just outside town where servants for the area's sprawling estates lived, mostly in one- or two-room shanties with outhouses and no running water. In those few public places shared by blacks and whites—like the town's one-room bus depot—restrooms and drinking fountains were designated for "Whites only" and "Coloreds." This was not even the Deep South, but the iconic symbols of apartheid were everywhere.

Then, in 1954 and 1955, the U.S. Supreme Court declared in *Brown v. Board of Education* that school segregation violated the Fourteenth Amendment to the Constitution and that school districts had to desegregate "with all deliberate speed." The decision seemed poised to undo not just the segregation of schools but the whole racist system that had been in place for centuries in my hometown and across the country. Law professor and critical race theorist Derrick Bell (2004, 3) recalls that the decision was "the equivalent of the Holy Grail of racial justice." Newspaper editorials praised it as a salve on the wound of racism that would prove to be "profoundly healthy and healing" (*Washington Post and Times Herald* 1954). The *Chicago Defender* (1954) declared, "This means the beginning of the end of the dual society in American life and the . . . segregation which supported it." To underscore the continuing symbolic power of *Brown*, Bell (2004) tells a story of his participation at a Yale University graduation ceremony in 2002. Former civil rights attorney and federal district court judge Robert L. Carter was being celebrated with an honorary degree. His impressive achievements were read aloud to polite applause, but when his participation in *Brown* was announced, Bell reports that the audience spontaneously "leaped to its feet" (1) in a boisterous standing ovation.

But the *Brown* decision became "a magnificent mirage" (Bell 2004, 4). "All deliberate speed" turned out to mean deliberately slow. A decade after the decision, 98 percent of black children in most Southern states were still enrolled in segregated schools. Delaying tactics and phony integration schemes were finally prohibited by the Civil Rights Act of 1964. That same year, U.S. Supreme Court Justice Hugo Black declared in a landmark 1964 decision, *Griffin v. County School Board of Prince Edward County*, that when it came to school desegregation, deliberate speed was no longer sufficient. There had been "entirely too much deliberation and not enough speed," he said.

As the twenty-first century gets under way, public schools in most places in the United States are as segregated as they were before *Brown*, due in large part to the economic disparities of neighborhoods and white flight to private schools, both of which are exacerbated by limited spending for public education. A report by the Civil Rights Project at UCLA highlights the role of economics in the current segregation (Orfield and Lee 2007). According to this report, public schools are more segregated in the Northeast, where the gap between rich and poor is greater and more racialized, than in the South, where large proportions of both blacks and whites live in poverty. In 2005, 78 percent of black children in the Northeast went to schools that were predominately minority, a rate that has increased over the decades and that outstrips every other region.

Some aspects of the apartheid that shaped social and economic life through the 1950s have been undone by law. Even my childhood hometown now has an integrated public swimming pool. Other things have given way to the forces of modernity and the market-place—at least the now-ubiquitous multiplex movie theaters only have one entrance. And affirmative action policies have spelled incremental improvements in the representation of minorities in some workplaces and governmental offices.

But affirmative action's record is mixed. One reason for this mixed record is that affirmative action has been accompanied by a shift away from concerns for social and racial justice to a concern for diversity. In her book The Enigma of Diversity, Ellen Berrey (2015) closely examines discourses of diversity that surround a Chicago housing redevelopment project; that underpin affirmative action policies at the University of Michigan; and that permeate the human resources division of a Forbes 500 company. She reveals that an emphasis on diversity in these three venues signals an effort at inclusiveness, but that it is an inclusiveness valued primarily for the "excellence" that cultural difference may bring to a university, or the "strength" and competitive edge it may bestow on a corporation. Nothing in the diversity rhetoric or the individual inclusion policies it advances tamps down broad social and racial inequalities. In fact, the substitution of discourses of diversity for substantive discussions of social justice, Berrey argues, shore up existing power arrangements. As a result, economic disparities remain entrenched, jobless rates for minority youth rarely dip below double digits, exploding incarceration rates disproportionately affect African Americans and Latinos, and residential segregation is as pronounced as ever.

If neither affirmative action nor the marketplace have made a significant difference, what about the law? Why haven't law and the courts fulfilled the promise proffered by Brown? For Derrick Bell and many others, the failures of Brown epitomize the limits of law, and the courts in particular, to advance real social change. In The Hollow Hope: Can Courts Bring about Social Change? Gerald Rosenberg (1991) looks at the record on civil rights, abortion rights, women's rights, the environment, reapportionment, and rights associated with the criminal justice system. Since courts lack direct enforcement powers, he argues, their impact is dependent on the will of others. The courts, unlike the legislative and executive branches, are generally not beholden to voters and so are nominally independent of public opinion; but their inability to implement the changes they mandate means that their effectiveness is tied to the enforcement actions (or inaction) of others.

Focusing on *Brown v. Board of Education* in 1954 and the 1973 abortion rights case *Roe v. Wade*, Rosenberg (1991, 106) argues that in the United States "courts can matter, but only sometimes, and only under limited conditions." The U.S. Supreme Court, he goes on, cannot get too far ahead of political opinion or it triggers a wave of hostility that can set back the cause of change instead of advancing it. He points out that the *Brown* decision elicited mixed reaction, with most major newspapers praising it, but others calling it catastrophic. A front-page editorial in Mississippi's *Jackson Daily News* (1954) forecast bloodshed, stopping just short of inciting it: "Human blood may stain Southern soil in many places because of this decision but the dark red stains of that blood will be on the marble steps of the United States Supreme Court building. . . . White and Negro children in the same schools will lead to miscegenation. Miscegenation leads to mixed marriages and mixed marriages lead to mongrelization of the human race." The *Brown* decision, ahead of the curve of public opinion in the South, went unenforced by local officials there and acted as a lightning rod for resistance to the civil rights agenda. According to Rosenberg, it was not until Congress passed the Civil Rights Act in 1964, the Voting Rights Act in 1965, and the Elementary and Secondary Education Act in 1965 that some reforms were finally realized.

The context for, and outcome of, *Roe v. Wade* (1973), which declared that state laws barring a woman's right to abortion were unconstitutional, were strikingly different. Rosenberg argues that by the time the U.S. Supreme Court decided *Roe*, the American public already favored abortion rights. When market mechanisms took effect after the decision, there was an immediate increase in the availability of abortions in most states, with the exceptions being in states and counties where medical personnel were unwilling to perform them. In other words, changes did come in the wake of *Roe*, but they were not entirely due to the decision itself; they depended on a confluence of other factors, including public opinion and its many reverberations. Rosenberg's argument, then, is that the Supreme Court is nominally independent of public opinion and voter endorsement, but its landmark decisions ironically are effective only to the extent that the changes they mandate are already under way.

There is both bad news and good news here. As we have seen, judicial decisions are limited in their ability to accomplish progressive social change. They may even produce a backlash. But the good news is that courts with *retrograde* ideological preferences may not be able to impose their worldviews either and may in fact backfire. Much as *Brown* energized the racist resistance to civil rights, court decisions that hark to outdated, reactionary ideologies may occasionally be so repugnant that they end up advancing *progressive* worldviews.

Consider this bizarre sequence of events set off by an Italian Supreme Court decision. On February 10, 1999, Italy's highest court of appeals overturned the conviction of a driving instructor who allegedly raped his eighteen-year-old student. The court reasoned that the woman was wearing blue jeans at the time, which they said required assistance in their removal, and so the sexual intercourse must have been consensual. The decision set off a wave of protest across the political spectrum in Italy and around the world. Alessandra Mussolini, deputy of the right-wing National Alliance Party and granddaughter of former dictator Benito Mussolini, was outraged by the decision and organized a rally of female legislators and TV anchorwomen—all symbolically clad in blue jeans. Women in a large northern factory showed up for work en masse in jeans, and the women's Italian slalom-ski team wore jeans on the slopes at the Vail Winter Olympics. The following month, Italian parliamentarians, housewives, union officials, and advocates of women's rights joined forces with men and women in the United States and throughout Europe to declare "International Jeans for Justice Day." One legal scholar observed, "This decision has done what few legal decisions do: It has succeeded in making everyone agree. In opposition." The conservative Rome newspaper *Il Messaggero* ran a front-page story ridiculing the decision and lamenting that it "takes us back to the days when the victims of rape were put on trial instead of their offenders" (see Calavita 2001).

There is probably an element of hypocrisy in this universal outrage. I would wager that some people who publicly protested privately embraced the court's sexist opinion. But clearly the dominant, culturally acceptable narrative of rape is more progressive, more influenced by feminist sensibilities, and these judges had transgressed it. Unlike Supreme Court decisions in the United States, because of differences in the Italian system of law this was not a precedent-setting case and had no broad legal consequences. But it triggered a backlash that held up the judges' antiquated perspective to ridicule, and so arguably *advanced* women's rights. While law may generally be hegemonic, its orchestrating power is contingent on staying in tune.

Law and society scholarship in the United States came of age in the 1960s and 1970s, inspired in part by the era's vibrant social movements and the optimistic view that social change was possible, even inevitable. So, maybe it was predictable that many law and society scholars would explore the role of law in ushering in progressive change. But their findings were often disheartening. As Abraham Blumberg (1967, 16) wrote in the first volume of the Law and Society Association's flagship journal, *Law & Society Review*, "A particular decision may rest upon a legally impeccable rationale [but] be rendered nugatory or self-defeating by contingencies imposed by aspects of social reality of which the lawmakers are themselves unaware." In plainer words, a decision might be legally sound, but its impact can be nullified by social forces. As we have seen, one of those forces is an adverse political and ideological climate.

Other factors that limit law's potential for change are the institutional structure and procedural requirements of courts. In "Why the 'Haves' Come Out Ahead," Marc Galanter (1974) set out to understand how a legal system like that of the United States, while neutral on its face, systematically renders decisions that favor "the haves." He starts by noting that courts in the United States are "passive" institutions, meaning they do not initiate cases but wait for cases to be brought to them. He adds that the rules governing the courts and legal practice—for example, the intricate requirements of due process—are complex and cumbersome to navigate. Partly as a result, courts are overburdened and wracked with delays, and lawsuits are costly and time-consuming. These institutional and procedural aspects of litigation all advantage those with resources and the luxury of biding time.

Galanter reasons that there are two prototypical parties to litigation—those who have had and will continue to have multiple cases heard in court ("repeat players," or RPs) and those who have only one or very few ("one-shotters," or OSs). RPs tend to be large units with considerable resources, such as corporations or government entities, while OSs are usually individuals and their resources are by comparison more limited. By virtue of their repeat experiences, RPs have "advance intelligence" of how this complex system works and how to play it to their advantage. Also by virtue of their repeat status and abundant resources, RPs are more likely to have in-house attorneys who enhance their intelligence advantage. And because they expect to be back in court repeatedly, they are as interested in shaping the rules for the next time as they are in immediate victory. While rules of procedure are for the most part preordained, how they are interpreted is worked out in adjudication (it's the books-action gap again). RPs with expert knowledge know which rules are perfunctory and which to spend the time and resources tweaking. Over time, RPs are able to shape the interpretation of significant rules to their advantage and hire experts to marshal them through the process. Their stables of in-house lawyers also carefully screen which cases to proceed with, which ones are not worth the effort or may be lost, and how to set binding precedents that will be useful in the long run.

In contrast, one-shotters often have claims that are either too big or too little. Let's consider first the "too big" scenario. OSs may have so much vested in the big, once-in-a-lifetime lawsuit—like a workplace compensation claim—that they just want the best possible remedy as soon as possible. They do not have the luxury of, or much interest in, strategizing for the future, and neither do their lawyers. A public defender told me that occasionally he makes a legal move for a client that he knows may later serve as a constraining precedent, and that it "is going to make bad law," but he cannot forgo it. Doing so would sacrifice his client's immediate interests, which is unethical.

What about potential OS claims that are "too little"? Galanter says that many small grievances of OSs are not pursued because their potential payoffs are not worth the time and cost, especially given the slim chance of victory and the OS's limited resources. I am reminded of a minor incident that happened to me in Berkeley, California. Berkeley is by most measures a friendly, liberal town. The one exception is the town parking police, who have a reputation for being decidedly unfriendly. One day I returned to my car (after getting physical therapy for a painful back, so I was not in the best of humors) and found a ticket on my windshield. The ticket said I was being fined for a "missing front license plate." Concerned that someone must have removed my plate, I went to the front of the car and there it was—right where it was supposed to be and in plain sight. A trip to Berkeley's Parking Department to contest the ticket only elicited the insult that I had probably gone home to reattach my plate in the thirty minutes that had elapsed. Defeated and angry, I left the police station with ticket in hand, for the moment convinced I would never pay this unfair fine. But with no remedy in sight and under threat that the fine would double within thirty days, I paid on the twenty-ninth day. Granted, this was a mundane and trivial injustice, but at the time it raised my hackles. As Galanter says, many of us OSs have claims that are strong on principle but ultimately are not worth going to court for.

The dichotomy of the repeat player and the one-shotter is really a continuum; Galanter explains that real-life litigators often fall somewhere between these two prototypes. And most lawsuits do not involve one-shotters going up against repeat players. Probably the most common cases involve two one-shotters (e.g., parental custody cases, divorces, or neighbors suing each other), or two repeat players (e.g., two corporations in litigation, or a government agency versus a corporate entity). But cases pitting OSs against RPs are the most likely to have implications for redistributive change *and* the most likely to be won or lost on the basis of unequal resources, expertise, and the ability to play for the long haul.

Remember that lawyer friend of mine I mentioned on the first page who regularly asks me what "law and society" is? He told me of a case he was involved in, *Cassidy v. Chertoff* (2006), that is a great example of OSs challenging RPs. After the September 11 attacks, Congress passed the Maritime Transportation Security Act, requiring maritime vessels of a certain size and function to establish security procedures. In compliance with the act, in July 2004, the Lake Champlain Transportation Company ferry that links Grand Isle, Vermont, and Plattsburgh, New York, began random searches of people, cargo, cars, and personal items. Passengers on foot and cyclists were subject to searches of their bags, and those in cars were required to open their trunks and submit to a visual search of the car's interior.

Michael Cassidy and Robert Cabin, two commuters who took this ferry to work several times a week (Cassidy in his car and Cabin by bicycle), thought the searches were annoying and probably a violation of the Fourth Amendment. Backed by a small team of American Civil Liberties Union (ACLU) lawyers, they took their case to the U.S. district court in Vermont. The defendants were none other than Michael Chertoff, then secretary of the U.S. Department of Homeland Security; Thomas Collins, admiral commandant of the U.S. Coast Guard; Glenn Wiltshire, captain of the U.S. Coast Guard Federal Maritime Security Coordinator; and the Lake Champlain Transportation Company. The case was dismissed by the court and appealed to the U.S. Court of Appeals for the Second Circuit.

Suspicionless searches like those on the ferry are permitted under the Fourth Amendment only if they are deemed "reasonable," with reasonableness being gauged by balancing the intrusiveness of the search with some legitimate state interest. Since 9/11 and increases in security and law enforcement concerns, courts have allowed warrantless searches at highway checkpoints and Border Patrol stops, in New York subways, and in airport security zones. Over time, government agencies have established a vast array of precedents favoring security, or perceived security, over Fourth Amendment protections. The powerful coterie of government defendants in *Cassidy v. Chertoff* cited the long line of precedent cases they had a hand in establishing, and to which they turned for vindication.

The Court of Appeals, in an opinion written by Sonia Sotomayor, now a Supreme Court justice, upheld defendants' request for dismissal. Despite the plaintiffs' claims that the ferry searches were intrusive without being effective, that they were little more than "security theater," and that much more risky cargo ships with giant containers are regularly docked without inspection, the court found the searches to be a "reasonable means of complying with the Maritime Transportation Security Act." With two lone commuters against the U.S. Department of Homeland Security, the U.S. Coast Guard, and the transportation company, this was a classic case of one-shotters against powerful and resource-heavy repeat players who capitalized on their resources and the stock of precedents they had painstakingly secured in previous cases. We all know that the Fourth Amendment is meant to protect us from unreasonable searches, but what "unreasonable" means is determined in the course of adjudication when repeat players show up repeatedly and make legal meaning.

Galanter's work suggests that the deck is stacked against those who would use adjudication for potentially progressive or redistributive purposes. Rosenberg and others show us that those rare decisions like *Brown v. Board of Education* that might usher in real change can be nullified after the fact by an unfavorable political climate and other social or market forces. Law and society scholars have also shown that potentially progressive legislation can be neutralized when courts abdicate the interpretation of that legislation to large private organizations.

Lauren Edelman (2005) has written about how organizations deal with civil rights laws like those regulating workplace discrimination. Her theory can help us understand why such laws, and the courts that take part in implementing them, may be limited in their ability to radically change ongoing social arrangements. It goes something like this: Let's say that in 1964, when the Civil Rights Act made it illegal, among other things, to engage in sex discrimination in hiring and promotions, Corporation X employed only five women out of a payroll of five hundred. As this law and other similar workplace regulations increasingly formed the environment in which Corporation X operated, it set up its own legal department staffed with compliance professionals. As we saw in the previous chapter, laws are almost always ambiguous and open to interpretation. The job of these compliance specialists was to interpret the new laws and figure out how Corporation X could signal compliance and avoid prosecution. Their legal department and civil rights division crafted specific indicators of compliance with the new antidiscrimination law, among them establishing timelines for hiring more women. Over time, norms emerged within our hypothetical Corporation X, and collectively within the corporate world, as to what compliance meant and how to signal it. According to Edelman, a national survey shows that between 1964 and 1989 employers across the United States adopted a small handful of specific forms of compliance. Compliance then came to mean doing those particular things and following those particular procedures. In short order, having policies and procedures in place became symbolic indicia of compliance.

Because it was above all Corporation X, and its many thousands of counterparts around the United States, that first had to make sense of the new laws, and because they hired experts in legal meaning making for that purpose (echoes of Galanter here), their "organizational field" dominated cultural understandings of what compliance meant. In contrast to a "top-down" model in which the government imposes laws on institutions, the norms about compliance that developed within corporations were deferred to by the courts. As Edelman (2005, 342) says, "The law becomes what the interpreters make it." And the interpreters in this case are the organizations being regulated. It is an interesting twist on the law-on-the-books and law-in-action gap, with the entities that are subject to formal law acting as the practitioners who determine what the real law is. Edelman calls this the "endogeneity" of law. That is, laws are essentially made *inside* the organization, since their meaning is made there, rather than being imposed from outside. To the extent that organizations play a major role in shaping the meaning of laws, it seems unlikely they will produce radical progressive change.

Studies of the rise of judicial power around the world give us a good comparative barometer for this notion that law is limited as an agent of change. Those studies show that democratization in many countries has increased the power of constitutional courts, which is somewhat ironic since these courts are often a constraining force on the democratic institutions of majoritarian rule. In *Towards Juristocracy*, Ran Hirschl (2004) examines the reasons for the rather sudden adoption of judicial review (the ability of courts to void laws enacted by elected bodies on the grounds of their unconstitutionality) in the 1980s and 1990s in Canada, Israel, South Africa, and New Zealand. He concludes that it was a strategy of "hegemonic preservation" on the part of elites who feared a threat to their continued dominance at a time of democratization and rising "progressive concepts of distributive justice" (13). This rise of judicial power was in fact accompanied by declines in economic equality and ideological egalitarianism, a trend Hirschl says is apparent globally. It is difficult to make the case conclusively that the emergence of judicial review in these countries was the cause of this retrenchment, but at the very least these constitutional courts oversaw the trend away from "distributive justice."

Hirschl's analysis of the South African case is intriguing. When the Republic of South Africa adopted its permanent constitution and bill of rights in 1996, they included the judicial power of constitutional review. As Hirschl tells it, these review powers were designed to assuage the worries of the foreign investors who still largely controlled the economy that the majority-black population might marshal popular support for anticapitalist reforms. According to Hirschl, the strategy worked. While apartheid has been formally dismantled, economic disparities remain firmly in place (in a pattern that is reminiscent of the post–*Brown v. Board of Education* United States). In this telling, courts limit the ability of legislatures to enact radical reforms and are themselves subject to conservatizing forces, such as political pressure from elites and the built-in biases that Galanter and Edelman discuss.

Some U.S. constitutional scholars even argue that given these antidemocratic aspects of courts, their authority to nullify legislation enacted by elected bodies should be replaced by more overtly political constitution meaning making. Tushnet (1999, 154) claims: "Doing away with judicial review would have one clear effect: It would return all constitutional decision-making to the people acting politically. It would make populist constitutional law the only constitutional law there is."

Most provocative of all in this narrative of the limited capacity of courts to produce significant progressive change is a critique of the founding concept of liberal democracies—rights. Critical legal studies scholars lay out a broad critique of rights, despite what Duncan Kennedy (2002, 170) calls the "unpleasantness" of having to do so, given people's faith in rights and their association with the democratic process. The central criticism is that adjudication outcomes are contingent on politics, not just legal reasoning, and that adjudication in the name of rights often does more harm than good to progressive causes.

Stuart Scheingold (1974) coined the term "the myth of rights" to refer to the misplaced faith in rights discourse to advance social equality and empower the subordinated. He warned, "The myth of rights is . . . premised on a direct linking of litigation, rights, and remedies with social change" (5), but rights are a blunt weapon with a tendency to boomerang. They are blunt in part because much of the oppression of the disadvantaged today comes not from a failure to achieve formal rights but from systemic forms of subordination, like economic disparities. And litigation driven by rights discourse is almost completely ineffective at undoing systemic economic barriers.

Other systemic factors limit the potential of rights litigation as well. Take the example of efforts to prevent prisoner rape, or at least to hold officials accountable when it happens. In one of the first prisoner rape lawsuits to reach the U.S. Supreme Court, *Farmer v. Brennan*

(1994), a transgender prisoner, Dee Farmer, sued the warden at a U.S. federal prison for men in Indiana. Farmer had been brutally beaten and raped by her cellmate, and had contracted HIV. She argued that prison officials knew the risk of sexual assault when they placed her in the general population and that they turned a blind eye to her subsequent victimization. The court found for Farmer, noting that prison officials are liable for violation of the cruel and unusual punishment clause of the Eighth Amendment when they exhibit "deliberate indifference" to obvious risks of serious harm to inmates.

The nonprofit group Just Detention International has called the Farmer case "a pivotal civil rights victory" and Farmer an "unsung civil rights hero" (unpublished Listserv communication, 2014). The Farmer decision was quickly cited in subsequent prisoner lawsuits, a few of which have prevailed. But the narrow standard of "deliberate indifference" requires plaintiffs to demonstrate officials' state of mind and whether they knew or should have known of the significant risks of serious harm. Systemic prison overcrowding compounds the challenge, as both the risk of physical harm (including sexual assault) and the difficulty of proving that officials knew of specific individual risks have increased.

It is notoriously difficult to estimate with any precision the incidence of prisoner rape (Jenness, Maxson, Sumner, and Matsuda 2010), but the Bureau of Justice Statistics (BJS) revealed in 2013 that approximately 4 percent of the federal and state prison populations had reported a sexual assault in 2011–12 (Beck and Berzofsky 2013). And the rate among LGBT prisoners is roughly ten times the rate for straight prisoners (Jenness et al. 2010). The incidence has increased every year since the BJS began reporting in 2005. So, while the *Farmer v. Brennan* decision clearly set legal precedent, its material impact on prisoner safety is far less certain.

Rights are also blunt instruments for change, the argument goes, because rights talk is politically neutral, and progressive arguments about rights can invite the opposition to talk about counterrights. Carol Smart (1989) shows this in the area of reproductive rights for women. Describing the battle for legal abortions in England and Wales in the 1960s, she says the principle of "a woman's right to choose" quickly evoked comparable rights slogans from antiabortion groups who defended "rights for the unborn." Bringing this point home to me the other day, I saw a bumper sticker in conservative Southern California declaring, "Unborn women have rights too."

Remember the U.S. Supreme Court case *District of Columbia v. Heller* (2008), involving the gun-control law of Washington, DC, discussed in chapter 5. The firearms ban was challenged as a violation of the Second Amendment to the Constitution. The effort to overturn the law was initiated and funded by Robert Levy, a libertarian legal scholar at the conservative Cato Institute and a former money manager. Levy had been planning for years to bring a case like this. Carefully following the strategy used by Thurgood Marshall in *Brown v. Board of Education*, Levy said he wanted this to be a "grass-roots public interest case" that would protect the individual rights of "law-abiding residents of the District of Columbia [to] possess functional firearms to defend themselves where they live and sleep" (quoted in Liptak 2007). Levy tactically chose a case that would have broad appeal and resembled other civil rights cases, and the plaintiffs were also chosen carefully. Levy said, "We wanted gender diversity. We wanted racial diversity. We wanted age diversity. We wanted income diversity." In order not to arouse suspicion that this was just a self-interested case filed by the gun lobby, Levy and his team tried (not always successfully) to keep their distance from the National Rifle Association.

It worked. In a 5–4 decision, the Court ruled that the DC ban on handguns violated an individual's right to keep guns for personal use. The majority's written opinion focused on how to interpret the Second Amendment's rather contorted language, on how strong the government interest in the ban was, and above all, on the importance of individual rights. Antonin Scalia, author of the majority opinion, even included a lengthy reference to the importance of the Second Amendment to freed blacks after the Civil War. To validate his interpretation of the confusing language of the amendment, he turned to the Civil Rights Act of 1871 and the Fourteenth Amendment, which extended constitutional rights to African Americans. His choice of illustrations was not coincidental. Like Levy, Scalia chose his words carefully to associate Second Amendment rights with iconic civil rights struggles.

There may be no better example of the myriad uses that "rights" can be put to and their politically contingent outcomes. The conservative justices Scalia, Thomas, Alito, and Roberts as well as the more liberal Kennedy voted to extend to private citizens the right to own guns, while most of the liberals on the court voted against it. However you evaluate the decision from a constitutional perspective, this was a case in which conservatives marshaled civil rights arguments to suit their ideological purpose—a purpose almost unilaterally opposed by liberals, including those on the Supreme Court.

The New York Times (2008) criticized the Heller decision in an editorial where it also warned that one more conservative on the Supreme Court would endanger civil liberties, particularly in cases involving Guantánamo Bay detainees, eavesdropping, and warrantless searches. The next week, a letter to the editor from Adam Lang published on July 7 pointed out the newspaper's inconsistencies on rights issues: "While your editorial says a more conservative Supreme Court would remove more civil liberties, you chastise the court for upholding civil liberties in outlawing gun bans. Many people view gun ownership as a right protected by the Second Amendment. . . . One person's travesty of justice is another's civil liberty." Critical legal studies scholars could not have said it better. Rights talk is ambidextrous, pitching to the left or the right of the political spectrum.

After the Heller decision, the National Rifle Association sued the city of San Francisco for its 2005 ban on handguns in public housing. Strategically picking a gay man in San Francisco as the plaintiff and a ban in public housing as its focus, the National Rifle Association capitalized on the Heller precedent and the civil rights model that brought it success. The chief executive of the National Rifle Association told a New York Times reporter, "The Supreme Court has now said unequivocally that this is an individual right of the American people. . . . It can't be walled off by the political class. It would be the equivalent of saying you can have a right to free speech, but you can't have a right to free speech in public housing" (quoted in McKinley 2008, A9). The San Francisco Housing Authority smelled defeat and soon settled the lawsuit, agreeing to apply the ban only to illegal gun ownership, such as firearm possession by a convicted felon.

The California Civil Rights Initiative of 1996 is another example of using rights talk to advance a conservative agenda—in this case, to reverse liberal victories by appropriating their language. As I mentioned in chapter 5, the measure was placed on the California ballot as Proposition 209. Funded and directed by conservative African American businessman Ward Connerly and supported by Republican governor Pete Wilson, it was designed to eliminate affirmative action in government employment and public education. Nowhere did the text of the measure mention this goal. Instead, it borrowed heavily from the language of the civil rights movement, highlighting the issue of "discrimination." The key provision of Proposition 209 stated, "The state shall not discriminate against, or grant preferential treatment to, any individual or group on the basis of race, sex, color, ethnicity, or national origin in the operation of public employment, public education, or public contracting." The "Argument in Favor of Proposition 209" that was placed in the official electoral handbook began by associating the measure with the civil rights movement: "A generation ago, we did it right. We passed civil rights laws to prohibit discrimination. But special interests hijacked the civil rights movement. Instead of equality, governments imposed quotas, preferences, and set-asides. Proposition 209 is called the California Civil Rights Initiative because it restates the historic Civil Rights Act."

The initiative passed handily, and the fallout was immediate. African American enrollment rates at the state's public universities plummeted, with the drop most pronounced on the most prestigious campuses. In 2006, only 100 black students were among the 4,422 students in UCLA's freshman class. The following year, the number had doubled—to 200. At UC Berkeley, 108 black students were included in the 2005 freshman class. Never mind, said Connerly, at least there was no discrimination. Others also were unfazed by the results, and one state after another copied the California law. After winning initiatives in California, Michigan, and Washington, in 2008 Connerly took his campaign to Arizona, Colorado, Missouri, Nebraska, and Oklahoma, in what he called "Super Tuesday for Equal Rights."

So, rights talk can be used just as easily by conservative crusaders like Ward Connerly and lobbyists in the National Rifle Association as by progressives. The ACLU is the institutional embodiment of this inclusivity of rights and its pitfalls for progressive reformers. Defending both the right of the Ku Klux Klan to march in a Jewish neighborhood and the right of blacks to be served at a lunch counter, the ACLU is controversial on all sides of the political spectrum (Zackin 2008). This is precisely because the concept of rights that it defends is ideologically neutral and therefore politically fickle.

There is another problem with rights, and that is that they depend on interpretation; since they are never absolute. In her article on free speech rights and hate speech, Sarah Sorial (2013) shows that the interpretation of what constitutes illegal hate speech turns on whether people with expertise consider the speech in question a "reasoned argument" or an emotional "incitement." If it is the former, the speech is presumed to be part of an academic debate and therefore permissible; the latter is treated as illegal hate speech and penalized. The problem here is twofold. First, it discriminates against those who do not have the education or skills to seem authoritative and whose emotional arguments may appear to be inciting "rants" (60). Second, Sorial argues, those with racist or otherwise hateful and injurious views may be able to use the appropriate language and deploy "manufactured" authority to disguise their speech as representing a legitimate academic perspective. Sorial uses the example of Holocaust deniers in Australia and in Canada who "mak[e] their views seem as though they have serious academic merit" (72), by publishing books and presenting themselves as historians. She concludes her article—which is not a critique of rights generally, but rather a cautionary tale—"It is relatively easy to see a racist rant for what it is, but it is not so easy to identify racism that looks like scholarship or serious (civil) political debate" (73). In other words, the right of free speech is fluid, such that not only are the least powerful likely to be denied that right but also its exercise by the more powerful may inflict harm on others by authoritatively reinforcing racist convictions.

What's more, critics of rights point out that even in the hands of progressives, rights discourse can backfire. Having to make a rights argument in court requires people to simplify, narrow, and tame their agenda. At the very least, they have to employ legal logic and language and focus on a single, specific case. Broad, principled positions give way to narrowly constructed arguments that fit the case at hand. For example, a group advocating affordable housing as a human right will have to trim its stance to fit the tight parameters of acceptable legal discourse. The group might win a case by doing so (assuming everything goes its way and the various impediments we talked about earlier are not fatal), but the political commitment to affordable housing for all might be obscured in the process. Over time, the litigation strategy might even co-opt the larger principle driving the movement. This "losing by winning" (Albiston 1999) is one hazard of rights litigation.

Litigation in the name of rights can also set a movement back by casting an unfavorable light on the litigants. Smart (1989, 147) says that in the conservative political climate of the 1980s, the language of a "woman's right to choose" contributed to viewing abortions as a free choice and hid from view the often desperate circumstances surrounding that choice. As a result, she argues, women who needed abortions came to be seen as frivolous and selfish rather than distressed. Kristin Bumiller (1988) makes a parallel point, contending that civil rights claims for women and minorities do not end their subordination and in some ways reproduce their victimhood. Because enforcing civil rights laws requires individuals to come forward as victims, Bumiller argues, some people resist filing claims to preserve their sense of autonomy and dignity.

Critics also say that taking progressive causes to court as rights claims siphons protest away from other, more effective venues. This is what Rosenberg (2008, 420) means when he refers to the judicial arena in the United States as "the fly-paper court." Because our system of justice promises equality under the law, social movements are drawn to, but then stuck in, rights litigation. To use a different metaphor, at a time when formal rights have been extended to most groups and the forces of subordination are more likely to lie elsewhere, rights litigation may be a mirage that draws us away from the real sources of relief—such as unionization, mass protest, boycotts, and the like. In the end, Rosenberg (1991, 338) says, "Turning to the courts to produce significant social reform substitutes the myth of America for its reality." Occasional victories might be eked out through the courts, these critics say, but the larger struggle may be lost as a result.

An anecdote might help clarify these limitations of rights litigation. When I was a college student, I initially couldn't decide whether I wanted to major in psychology or sociology. Like so many others, in my youthful innocence I knew only that I was "interested in studying people" and having a positive impact. By happy coincidence, I attended a lecture where the speaker told this allegory. She said that a man was once sitting by a stream and suddenly noticed a body floating down the river, barely alive. Instantly, he rushed into the water to save the person, dragging her onto the shores to safety. As soon as he had saved her, another body appeared, gasping for air. He spent all morning doing this, saving many but unable to rescue everyone, until it dawned on him to go upstream to see who was throwing all the people into the river.

This, the lecturer said, is the difference between psychologists who study individual behavior in an effort to save some people from drowning and sociologists who study the social structures and processes that systematically propel people over the side of the bridge (needless to say, this sold me on sociology). Maybe we can recycle her allegory to apply to the limitations of adjudication as a life-saving vehicle. Like the good Samaritan on the riverbed, adjudication requires intense and focused attention on the individual case before it. In the process, we are distracted from the social conditions that throw whole categories of people overboard and that might be dealt with better through broad social activism.

All of this evidence that rights and legal reforms are limited as instruments of change—that they can even backfire—has dampened the hopes of many law and society scholars that their field can make a difference. Recall the Robert Taylor projects in Chicago where Sudhir Venkatesh (2008) became "gang leader for a day"? The fate of that public housing serves as an apt metaphor for this age of disillusionment. The Robert Taylor Homes were built in 1962, at a time when urban planners and sociolegal scholars alike believed that they could help bring about progressive social change. Planners in the early 1960s touted high-rise housing projects like Robert Taylor Homes as a way to clear the decrepit slums of urban America and provide decent, affordable housing to the poor. A scant thirty years later, the projects—by then squalid concentrations of crime, poverty, and police neglect and abuse—were slated for demolition. In 2007, the last of the Robert Taylor Homes was torn down. The demolition serves as a poignant symbol of dashed hopes for progressive change, whether through urban planning or through law.

BUT AS USUAL, things are not so simple. Rosenberg's (1991, 35) *The Hollow Hope*, first published in 1991, opened up a lively debate among law and society scholars over the merits of the book and the accuracy of its central thesis "that court decisions are neither necessary nor sufficient for producing significant social reform." Michael McCann (1992, 721) argued there was "slippage" in Rosenberg's analysis, and

Malcolm Feeley (1992, 745) called the book "both important and wrong." Feeley claimed that Rosenberg had slain a straw man, setting up an exaggerated version of the Court's goals and then showing it had not realized them. Using *Brown v. Board of Education* as an illustration, Feeley reasoned that the Court did not set out to integrate society but only to desegregate schools. It made no sense, Feeley continued, to proclaim its failure on the grounds that it did not achieve what it did not set out to do.

McCann, while praising aspects of *The Hollow Hope*, argued that Rosenberg focused all his attention on obvious direct impacts, ignoring indirect effects. Court decisions, he said, "express a whole range of norms, logics, and signals that cannot be reduced to clear commands or rules" (732). Citing a *Yale Law Review* article about decision making in divorce proceedings (Mnookin and Kornhauser 1979), McCann pointed out that disputants "bargain in the shadow of law" (734). That is, even divorcing parties who do not go to court make decisions in the negotiation process based on their predictions of what courts would do if they went to trial. Even more powerful indirect impacts can be found in the area of law and social change. According to McCann, *Brown* may not have produced racial integration, but it raised blacks' expectations and in a variety of other ways was key to black activists' "evolving leadership role" (736).

In a subsequent book on the pay equity and comparable worth movement, McCann (1994) demonstrates that while the movement did not secure legal decisions requiring that women be paid the same as men doing comparable jobs, it did succeed in politicizing its participants, mobilizing women, and building union strength. Francesca Polletta (2000) takes a similar tack in her analysis of the indirect political consequences of the civil rights movement. The civil rights movement, she argues, had multiple motivations and goals—only one of which was immediate sociolegal change. As she puts it, "Standing up for one's rights was the goal, not merely [the] means to it" (390). And "standing up for one's rights" can have dramatic indirect effects on participant politicalization and the shifting parameters of political discourse.

Even before "rights" became a household word in the 1950s and 1960s, there was evidence that mobilizing for one's rights had a positive effect, whatever the concrete outcome of that mobilization. George

Lovell (2012) analyzed hundreds of letters written to the U.S. Department of Justice by ordinary citizens from 1939 to 1941. The letters were complaints about perceived civil rights violations and covered a wide variety of issues, from due process problems, racial discrimination, police brutality, and denial of voting privileges to idiosyncratic matters involving "dead dogs" and "bad divorces" (70). While the vast majority of these appeals to the Justice Department were ignored or denied, the letter writers were not discouraged or dissuaded. Instead, the very act of letter writing seems to have strengthened their commitment to rights. Lovell writes, "There is . . . little to suggest that writers' sense of entitlement was dampened by their engagement with law. To the contrary, writers more often seemed emboldened by the choice of a legalized rhetoric of rights" (32), often persistently following up their denials with additional letters and demands.

My own coauthored work on grievance writing by California prisoners also suggests that legal mobilization, even when unsuccessful, may heighten the rights consciousness of those who engage in it (Calavita and Jenness 2013, 2015). As you may recall from chapter 3, prisoners across the United States are required to exhaust an internal grievance process before gaining access to federal courts to appeal their conditions of confinement. Congress mandated the grievance system in 1996 in order to limit access to court of the rapidly burgeoning prisoner population. It has now become an institutionalized feature of prison life, and tens of thousands of grievances are filed every year by prisoners across the United States. The institutionalization of the grievance system, its presence in every prison and jail, and its very physicality in the form of grievance boxes in every prison cell block, arguably stoke prisoners' rights consciousness. As one California prisoner told us, when they perceive that some prison policy has been violated, they "go get that book [the policy manual] and . . . write it up."

McCann's work on rights talk in the pay equity and comparable worth movement, Polletta's study of the politicizing effects of the civil rights movement, and our work on prisoner grievances all suggest that a focus on rights can have positive, indirect effects. Rights talk is even defended by some who are otherwise sympathetic to the tenets of critical legal studies. Some scholars of color (Matsuda 1987; Williams 1991) argue that the critique of rights is a luxury of white males in elite law schools whose own rights are secure. People of color, they say, may not be quite so ready to jettison a discourse they have depended on and have a continued need to deploy. Martha Minow (1987, 1910), noting an elitist bent to the critique of rights, warns, "I worry about criticizing rights and legal language just when they have become available to people who had previously lacked access to them. I worry about those who have, telling those who do not, 'you do not need it, you should not want it.'"

Lending even more credibility to this already-powerful critique of the critique of rights, there is evidence that under some conditions rights talk can help produce concrete and immediate change. Remember the stories of resistance I told in chapter 3. The child brides, Nujood and Arwa, escaped their domestic tyranny and fueled a social movement against forced child marriage, using the sturdy vehicle of human rights discourse. The global justice movement described by Boaventura de Sousa Santos and César Rodríguez-Garavito also harnesses the concept of human rights. So does the resistance movement against the damming of the Narmada River and the flooding of the valley.

Another story of resistance brings home not only the potential of rights talk and legal action but also the strategic savvy required to tap it. In "Public Interest Lawyers and Resistance Movements," Sameer Ashar (2007) describes a campaign for worker justice in the New York City restaurant industry. Restaurants in the United States employ more workers than any other industry in the private sector. In most major urban areas, the majority of restaurant workers are immigrants, and many are undocumented. Because of the concentration of undocumented workers, high worker turnover, and large numbers of workers scattered across many sites, the industry has a low unionization rate and low wages and benefits. Ashar links immigrants' meager wages and benefits to "neoliberal globalization." He argues that, as part of this neoliberalism, the World Bank and International Monetary Fund imposed austerity measures on developing countries, triggering mass migration, while the developed countries that were receiving many immigrants scaled back workplace enforcement and let minimum wages stagnate.

Ashar tell us that the upscale Windows on the World restaurant, perched on top of the World Trade Center in New York City, was one of the many restaurants that employed immigrants and one of the few that was unionized. After 9/11 destroyed the tower, the union set up a support network for families of the deceased workers and the few survivors. This group soon spawned a new workers' center for justice, the Restaurant Opportunities Center of New York (ROC-NY). At about this same time, the Windows on the World management opened a nonunion restaurant in the heart of Times Square. Determined to keep it nonunion, they initially refused to rehire their old (unionized) workers who had survived 9/11. ROC-NY took advantage of media attention to the new restaurant and used direct action tactics to shame management into taking them back. They then broadened their campaign to focus on upscale corporate chain restaurants throughout New York City. Drawing in public interest lawyers and the City University of New York Law School's Immigration and Refugee Rights Clinic, ROC-NY combined protests, media campaigns, and lawsuits to secure improvements for all restaurant workers. They chalked up a long list of victories in multiple venues, including negotiated settlements for improved wages and working conditions and damages for those who had been retaliated against for union activism. As impressive, they managed to resuscitate enforcement of the Fair Labor Standards Act as well as state labor laws.

Ashar attributes these successes to a number of things. First, of course, was the persistence and solidarity of the workers and their advocates. Beyond that, he argues that ironically the participants' cynicism about law as a vehicle of progressive change was key to their ability to use it effectively. Organizers and their lawyer-collaborators were versed in the critical legal studies critique of rights; they used the critique not to shun rights talk but to deploy it strategically and with eyes wide open. Taking their cue from the academic critique of rights and their own experiences, organizers crafted their tactics to avoid the predictable pitfalls. Rights talk and litigation were used with caution, but, as Ashar tells it, they were vital ingredients in these workers' successes.

Collaborations like these between lawyers and activists are the theme of a body of law and society scholarship that examines "cause lawyering." Much of this scholarship documents the moral and political motives of lawyers who become advocates for a cause and the tensions between concepts of professional neutrality and the explicitly political quality of cause lawyering. Some also focuses on the challenges of using law as a tool of social justice and the various strategies entailed in making it work (Sarat and Scheingold 1998, 2006; Scheingold and Sarat 2004; Heinz, Nelson, Sandefur, and Laumann 2005; Barclay and Chomsky 2014). As in Ashar's piece, this scholarship suggests that rather than jettisoning rights talk and adjudication, cause lawyers can capitalize on knowledge of their limitations.

OTHERS WHO DEFEND the utility of adjudication counter the critics of constitutional courts as antidemocratic institutions. For example, Maveety and Grosskopf (2004) argue that the new constitutional court in Estonia is an important vehicle of reform following the collapse of communism. The court has advanced the linguistic rights of minorities and has incorporated a number of other international human rights norms into its decisions. According to Maveety and Grosskopf, it has done so without sacrificing nationalist concerns and domestic priorities and in the process has accrued legitimacy and authority that position it well for future challenges. Far from the "constrained court" that many judicial analysts describe, the Estonian Supreme Court is a "conduit for democratic consolidation" (463).

In another case from Eastern Europe, Peter Solomon (2004) tells us of the many successes of citizens in post-Soviet Russia who take state actors to court in administrative cases. The citizen complaints cover a lot of territory, from contesting officials' actions having to do with civil rights (involving, for example, the processing of passports) to tax challenges, to cases involving the details of military careers such as moving expenses and housing. In 2000, the military courts alone heard 190,500 cases, with 90 percent being decided in the plaintiff's favor. While the citizens' success rate varies according to the matter being contested and the type of court, it is generally well over 50 percent. The caseload continued to rise throughout the 1990s, as ordinary people increasingly saw these courts as a way to get justice.

It is hard to think of a better example of one-shotters against repeat players than these ordinary Russians taking on government officials. Yet Solomon says the one-shotters are winning, time after time. He wonders if this high rate of success is the result of self-selection among plaintiffs. That is, since the public at large in Russia is generally still wary of courts in the post-Soviet era, maybe only people with dramatic and strong cases venture into court. But, he reasons, given the simultaneously increasing number of cases and increasing success rates since the early 1990s, self-selection cannot be the whole story. It is more likely that these successes reveal an independent judiciary that is willing to put even state officials on notice, at least with regard to administrative cases like these.

An independent judiciary has also forged change in the criminal justice arena in the United States, where court-mandated reforms from 1965 to 1986 changed the way prisons are run (Feeley and Rubin 1998). Prior to the 1960s, federal courts in the United States took a "hands-off" approach, using the logic that state prisons were under the jurisdiction of the states and that the principles of federalism precluded their encroachment. The laissez-faire period ended in 1964, when Muslim prisoners won *Cooper v. Pate*, giving them the right to challenge religious discrimination by prison officials. Supported by advocacy groups like the National Prison Project of the ACLU and a network of other local and national organizations, the prisoner rights movement went on to win many landmark cases.

In the course of two decades, prisoners in the United States won the right to be heard in federal court and enhanced their free speech and religious freedoms. Feeley and Rubin (1998) argue that these advances are more than illustrations of the emancipatory power of the judiciary as interpreters of the constitution; they are indications of judicial *policy making*, arguably the most extreme form of the "unconstrained court." Feeley and Rubin end their book with a discussion of what was not achieved by this judicial policy making. Most obviously, it didn't end overcrowding, which continued apace and accelerated, leaving prisoners in some states in worse conditions than when the reform era began.

And there's the rub. Courts can spearhead progressive change in some areas but fail entirely in others. There is no one-size-fits-all answer to the question of whether the courts can drive progressive reform. Solomon (2004, 575), in his otherwise-optimistic description of ordinary people's successes in Russian courts, concedes that these cases do not tell us anything about what happens in the constitutional court where decisions with broader impacts are made, in "high-stakes business disputes," or even in those administrative cases where the authorities being challenged have powerful political connections.

In the United States, prisoners have secured some additional rights through the courts over the past several decades, winning the right to attend a religious service of their choice, to receive mail, to read their favorite books, and even to file grievances against their captors. But the courts cannot or will not address the economic disparities and racial stereotypes that send a disproportionate number of poor people and people of color to prison in the first place. In Russia, the United States, and around the world, the evidence is clear but mixed. Adjudication and rights talk is good for some purposes, not so good for others, and fatal for a few. One of the tasks for law and society scholars and those who advocate for progressive change more generally is to sort out which is which, and why. Remember that Rosenberg (1991), after analyzing the disappointing aftermath of *Brown v. Board of Education*, did not conclude that courts are impotent. Instead, he said, "Courts can matter, but only sometimes, and only under limited conditions" (106).

The sorting is bound to be complicated. It is not just that some issues lend themselves to progressive adjudication and others do not, but that the surrounding conditions have to be ripe. And this is true whether the context is the contemporary United States or "fragile" states in war-torn regions of the world. As Mark Fathi Massoud (2013) reveals in his award-winning book about the law in Sudan, law can be put to use in all sorts of ways for all sorts of purposes, particularly in situations of instability. In Sudan, where the state is weak and has shifted chaotically from colonialism to socialism to authoritarianism and beyond, humanitarians attempting to use law to promote stability and human rights find a Pandora's box of challenges. In that context, the rule of law might be deployed to enhance human welfare, but the authoritarian state can also exploit it to release pressure, shore up legitimacy, and stabilize the regime. Massoud sums up the mixed lesson he learned from Sudan: "In erratic or threatening environments, a wider array of legal tools and concepts can be harnessed, manipulated, and discarded to build support for colonial administrators, authoritarian governments, and human rights groups seeking to reach the war-displaced poor" (6).

Rajagopal (2005) too explains that the use of law in the Narmada

Valley protests in India was not an either-or proposition. Instead, activists deployed law tactically, all too aware of its risks as well as its potential. Rajagopal's first sentences in this case study highlight the ambiguity of law's role: "Popular struggles have an ambivalent relationship with law. At one level, they tend to see law as a force for status quo and domination, which must either be contested as part of a larger political struggle or largely ignored as irrelevant. Yet, they can hardly avoid the law as it also provides them space for resistance" (183). As the Narmada Valley activists knew all too well, navigating this dilemma requires a quick eye for, and strategies for exploiting, the conditions that truly open up room for legal resistance versus those that will ensnare them. Among the most important of conducive conditions, according to Rajagopal, were international visibility and pressure from human rights and environmental groups. Parenthetically, it is worth noting that some scholars attribute formal legal gains for African Americans in the United States in the mid-twentieth century (like *Brown* and the Civil Rights Act) to Cold War pressure to compete internationally with the Soviet Union as the standard-bearer of equality and justice (Dudziak 2000). According to this argument, the fall of communism explains the stagnation of those gains by the late 1980s. If accurate, this attests once again to the powerful impact of political, legal, and normative pluralism, or its absence.

Micropolitics matter too. The child brides of Yemen, Nujood and Arwa, were fortunate to find sympathetic judges when they fled their violent marriages. Nujood's lawyer told a *New York Times* reporter that in a place where child marriage is common and girls have few civil rights, it was a stroke of luck that the judge assigned to them was shocked by Nujood's story (Worth 2008). "We were lucky with this judge," he said. "Another judge might not have accepted her in court, and would have asked her father or brother to come instead" (A8). In that case, Nujood would have been sent back to her abusive husband, and we would never have heard of her.

All the successes I have pointed to here, from the global justice movement to the New York restaurant workers' struggles, the achievements of the Estonian constitutional courts, the victories of Russians who challenge government officials, and prisoner litigation in the United States, have been wrested—sometimes tentatively and not always permanently—from specific conditions that were ripe for the wresting. The authors in all of these studies take pains to delineate the precise constellation of conditions that made these advances possible. For example, in the restaurant workers' struggles, Ashar tells us it was the organizers' cynicism and savvy about which conditions were more favorable to litigation and which required direct action that allowed them to achieve their fragile victories.

Where does this leave us? Courts and rights talk are sometimes essential for social change but sometimes fatal. This is a scary proposition. The only way to proceed is to carefully calculate which is which in a particular situation. It might be useful to conjure up one more time the story of the psychologist or good Samaritan saving a few lives on the riverbed while ignoring the social conditions that drowned so many more. I implied that sociology was the nobler discipline for going to the roots of social problems. And I likened psychology to adjudication, which can siphon activists away from social mobilization and trap them in narrow legal solutions that leave murderous social conditions intact. But maybe I was too hard on the psychologists. After all, they do save people, which is better than watching passively as the bodies float by. And maybe dragging people out of the water can put a human face on the larger tragedy and hasten social reform. In other words, maybe activists need not choose between adjudication or social activism but instead focus on when and how to use the former, which conditions are conducive to success, and how to avoid getting stuck on the deadly flypaper.

Kim Scheppele (2004) opens a special issue of *Law & Society Review* on constitutional courts by talking about paleontologist Stephen Jay Gould's struggle with cancer. He had an unusual kind of cancer, and his doctor told him that, on the basis of the statistics, he did not have long to live. But as Scheppele put it, "What he cared about, being human, was not aggregate rates of mortality but what was going to happen to him" (389). As it turned out, Gould lived for twenty years after his cancer diagnosis and eventually died of something else.

Scheppele turns Gould's (sort of) happy ending to creative use: "Gould's lesson also applies to constitutional regimes. The scholar, the citizen, and the politician typically care about constitutional orders one at a time, as individuals care about their own life trajectories. And sometimes the unexpected and the contingent matter more than the broad patterns in determining what occurs in individual cases" (390).

That is why, she says, we need "constitutional ethnography," where we can examine under a microscope individual specimens in all their complexity. Only then will we be able to talk about how a particular constitutional regime will fare, as opposed to making statistical generalizations that, like Gould's prognosis, might be completely off the mark. And only then will we be able to piece together more sophisticated theories about the economic, political, and cultural factors that singly and in combination affect the progressive potential of courts.

IF COURTS are unreliable agents of social change, maybe the legislative arena has more potential. Remember that Rosenberg said it was only after the Civil Rights Act and Voting Rights Act were passed in the 1960s that we began to see some of the changes expected after *Brown v. Board of Education*. In fact, for a decade after the Civil Rights Act, African Americans were hired in sectors and companies where they had never been employed before. The textile industry in South Carolina employed *no* black women from 1910 to 1964, and black men accounted for only 5 percent of the workforce, and exclusively in janitorial and yard work. This hiring pattern was transformed in 1965, the year after the Civil Rights Act was passed, when blacks were suddenly well represented throughout the workforce. A Nobel Prize–winning economist, James Heckman, coauthored a study of this change and concluded through economic modeling and statistical analysis that it could be attributed only to the civil rights laws of the era (Heckman and Payner 1989).

This hopeful picture of the potential of civil rights legislation began to fade in the 1980s for a number of reasons. First, as we know, what happens to law-on-the-books depends on enforcement agents on the ground. Like judicial reform, legislative reform goes nowhere without the cooperation and proactivity of those responsible for its enforcement. After an initial period of relatively rigorous enforcement of the Civil Rights Act, it leveled off and then waned. In 1999, the U.S. Justice Department's Civil Rights Division under President Clinton initiated 159 criminal prosecutions for civil rights violations—a paltry number given that official complaints to the division reached five digits. During the George W. Bush administration, the retreat was even more dramatic. By 2004, four years into the Bush administration, there were only eighty-four prosecutions, and complaints were holding steady at twelve thousand annually. In this context of nonenforcement, whatever compliance there is has to be considered voluntary. While the law-on-the-books made it illegal to discriminate, the law-in-action turned it into an advisory.

The picture at the U.S. Equal Employment Opportunity Commission (EEOC) is no brighter. U.S. workers who want to launch lawsuits of workplace discrimination have to file charges with the EEOC, the federal administrative agency established by the Civil Rights Act of 1964 to investigate and resolve discrimination complaints. If the EEOC finds a claim has sufficient merit and alleges a serious enough offense, it may forward the case to the Justice Department's Civil Rights Division for criminal prosecution. Approximately seventy-five thousand complaints of discrimination were filed with the EEOC in 2007, and there was an additional backlog of almost fifty thousand cases. By 2014, more than ninety thousand discrimination complaints had been filed. As we saw already, very few of these are actually prosecuted by the Civil Rights Division. The vast majority of EEOC cases are resolved administratively and favor the employer. Hirsh (2008, 239) did a statistical analysis of the outcomes of these EEOC complaints, finding that "fewer than one in five charges results in outcomes favorable to the complainant." Consistent with Galanter's repeat-player scenario and Edelman's ideas on the endogeneity of legal meaning making, Hirsh finds that the reasons for this pattern of employer-friendly outcomes include employers' judicial expertise and resources and their ability to claim compliance by virtue of having compliance structures in place.

These obstacles to aggressive enforcement of civil rights laws are compounded by the high standards courts sometimes require to prove discrimination. Despite the established principle that laws and practices with discriminatory outcomes for racial minorities are subject to "strict scrutiny," courts have increasingly put the burden of proof on the complainant to prove intent. And proving subjective intent, especially now that we are all well schooled in denying any prejudicial attitudes or intentions, is usually impossible.

In his book *And We Are Not Saved*, Bell (1987) tells the "Chronicle of the Amber Cloud" to show how pernicious this intent standard is. He is discussing with his mythological heroine, Geneva, whether a common crisis in the United States could bring whites and blacks together. A skeptical Geneva tells the allegory of an amber cloud descending on the homes of affluent white teenagers, overnight making them apathetic, insecure, and sometimes violent. Suffering from what comes to be called the "Amber Cloud Disease," the children's grades plummet, they can't focus, and they are alienated from the rest of society.

Geneva notes that many minority adolescent boys already suffer from these same symptoms, which social scientists associate with urban poverty and racial discrimination. A national emergency is declared and a cure for Amber Cloud Disease is found, at the price of $100,000 a piece, to be paid for by the government. But poor minority children are denied the cure. Geneva argues that this practice would hold up in court, on the grounds that no intent to discriminate could be proved. The government would argue that while the children's symptoms were similar, only the suburban teens contracted them from the Amber Cloud, and so only they are eligible for the Amber Cloud cure.

The first time I read this allegory was right after the disastrous Northridge, California, earthquake of 1994. Tens of thousands were left homeless by the devastating quake and were given coupons by the government to receive temporary shelter. I was reading about this tragedy in the newspaper, and my attention was caught by a report about a creative advocate for the homeless who advised his constituents to get in line for the shelter. Predictably, they were turned away. The shelter program was meant for those the earthquake had made homeless, not those who were already homeless for other reasons. As in the Amber Cloud story, the policy discriminated, but without provable intent.

Of course neither the fictional Amber Cloud incident nor the real-life Northridge earthquake case made it to court. But we don't have to look far for actual judicial decisions based on this narrow intent standard. In McKleskey v. Kemp (1987), an African American man in Georgia who was convicted of murder and sentenced to death, challenged his sentence on the grounds that the death penalty is imposed in a racially discriminatory manner. When the case came before the U.S. Supreme Court, his lawyer presented dramatic statistical evidence to substantiate the claim. The evidence showed that from the mid-1970s to the mid-1980s, an African American convicted of murder in Georgia was twenty-two times more likely to get the death penalty for killing a white person than for killing another black person. Nationwide, the statistics showed that a black person who killed a white person was five times more likely to get a death sentence than a white person who killed a white person. Overall, 90 percent of the executions in the United States from 1930 to 1980 were carried out against blacks. Faced with these overwhelming data, the Supreme Court conceded blandly, "A discrepancy that correlates with race appears to exist." But they did not overturn McKleskey's death sentence. Because, the Court explained, McKleskey's lawyer had not proved there was any intent to discriminate against him.

A case from the U.S. war on drugs provides another example of the immunizing power of the intent standard. In *United States v. Armstrong* (1996), the enforcement of crack cocaine laws in Los Angeles was challenged as racially discriminatory. It seems that the U.S. attorney in Los Angeles had been prosecuting blacks charged with violating crack cocaine laws in federal court while diverting whites charged under the same laws to state court where the sentences are shorter. The plaintiffs cited evidence that of the 2,400 crack cases in Los Angeles prosecuted in federal court over four years, not a single one involved a white defendant. The U.S. Supreme Court ruled that the plaintiffs had not proved racial discrimination, since no concrete evidence was presented that the reason for the discrepancy was intent to discriminate.

An article in the *Los Angeles Times* called "A Force for Civil Rights Now Fights Them" reports a startling statistic (Schwartz 2000). From 1992 to 2000, minorities won only nine of the twenty-six race-related cases heard by the U.S. Supreme Court. The trend continued in 2001 and extended beyond race-based discrimination. In the first four months of 2001, the Supreme Court issued seven rulings (all by the same 5–4 vote) involving charges of discrimination against African Americans, Latinos, women, gay men, the elderly, and the disabled. In every case, the Court majority rebuffed the plaintiffs. In *Alexander v. Sandoval* (2001), Scalia's majority opinion declared that states, schools, and colleges cannot be sued by individual members of minority groups for policies that negatively affect them, absent proof of intentional discrimination. He went on to argue provocatively that the courts had been mistaken for the previous thirty-five years in allowing private lawsuits for the purpose of enforcing the Civil Rights Act. A reporter for the *Los Angeles Times* observed that the Supreme Court had "closed the courthouse doors to most claims of racial bias" (Savage 2001, A20).

I HAVE TALKED here about the potential and limits of law in ushering in real social change. Robin Stryker (2007), in her masterful survey of studies of law and social change in capitalist democracies, sums up this mixed record in her evocative title, "Half Empty, Half Full, or Neither." As we have seen, law and society scholars have done structural analyses of courts that explain their tendency to favor the haves (Galanter), investigations of law's dependence on prevailing ideology and public opinion (Rosenberg) and its manipulability for diverse purposes (Massoud), critiques of the strategic and ambivalent quality of courts' commitment to racial justice (Bell, Dudziak), documentation of the central role large organizations play in the creation of legal meaning (Edelman), exposés of the antidemocratic quality of some constitutional courts (Hirschl, Tushnet, Massoud), and critiques of rights talk (Kennedy, Scheingold, Smart). Others have spoken more optimistically about the potential of law, vindicating rights talk (Williams, Matsuda), doing case studies of the successful deployment of law by resistance movements (Santos and Rodríguez, Ashar), and conducting analyses of constitutional regimes that serve as vehicles of reform (Maveety and Grosskopf, Solomon, Scheppele).

But I have not mentioned what may be the most fundamental limit of law as an instrument of radical change. Remember Macaulay, Friedman, and Stookey's (1995, 7) observation that "sooner or later, [legal systems'] shape gets bent in the direction of their society. . . . *Medieval law looked, smelled, and acted medieval.*" By the same token, capitalist law looks, smells, and acts capitalist. Our late-modern societies are rife with inequality and structured by a capitalist economic system and nominally democratic politics. Following the logic of one of our field's foundational ideas, there is no reason to expect law to leap out ahead of the prevailing social reality. And there is every reason to expect that it won't. I am not talking here only about law not getting too far ahead of popular opinion (à la Rosenberg). I am referring instead to the fact that law and the web of economic and social processes it is embedded in are part of a seamless whole.

We saw in chapter 2 that law is tailored to the needs of the production system. This is partly because of the power of those who own and manage the means of production but also because economic systems have such an impact on how society is organized and therefore on the shape of social interaction and its ideological products. Workers claiming discrimination in employment are often rebuffed by the legal system, and I have delineated a number of reasons for this anemic enforcement. But there is another, more fundamental, dimension to this that rarely emerges in our studies. That is, in a capitalist economy the workplace is the private property of the employer, and employers make hiring and most other workplace decisions. Paraphrasing Reiman (1984) again, they own the sources of oxygen. While civil rights laws and labor standards (and union contracts, if any) may put limits on how employers can treat their workers, the logic of the economic system puts limits on how far such policies can intrude on employers' right to make decisions about their property. The former—civil rights laws, regulations, and unions—are more visible and sometimes railed against; the latter are so foundational to the socioeconomic system that they largely remain invisible and unchallenged.

Our economic and legal systems are linked through the organizing principles of the marketplace, private property, contracts, and competitive individualism. Economic inequalities are both prerequisites for and products of this ensemble. Redistributive policies that eliminate or substantially reduce inequality are unlikely in part because inequality is an intrinsic input and output of the economy and in part because such redistributive strategies are apt to violate the market principles and private property rights that undergird that economy.

An example of the power of market principles to veto even relatively modest redistributive policies can be drawn from the field of urban planning in the United States. Land-use policies that pursue some public good (like preserving wetlands or developing a community center) but reduce a property owner's land value may be designated an illegal "taking" by the courts—a legal term that connotes theft and captures perfectly the centrality of the ownership model the economy is built on. In determining whether a government action that negatively affects property value constitutes an illegal taking, the courts weigh how severe the property loss is against the importance of the state interest involved. This would suggest that property rights are malleable and that the public good can override them. But I do not know of any instance of such government action that is solely for redistributive purposes. Maybe this is because it would be hard to make the claim that equality as a public good trumps private property in an economic system where inequality is intrinsic. I do not want to be reductionist here. The degree to which governments are willing to pursue redistributive policies varies across capitalist democracies—with the United States at one extreme and Northern European welfare states at the other. But even in those nations pressed by popular opinion, unions, opposition parties, and/or cultural mores into more redistributive policies, the legal system imposes limits on how far these policies can go and how much they are allowed to violate the organizing principles of property and the market.

Social change of course is not only possible; it is guaranteed. Sometimes change is progressive, and occasionally law is its midwife. A movement to ban child marriage builds in Yemen, restaurant workers wrangle settlements and raise consciousness in New York City, and a global justice coalition gains ground against unsustainable development in India. What these victories have in common is that they are meticulously strategized and that law is used tactically and with precision. The lesson is that if law is to bring about progressive social change, it will be partnered with a social movement that challenges and transforms the social realities on the ground at the same time that it presses the legal system to accommodate the shifting realities.

Maybe this is not as unlikely as I have made it seem. A lot of law and society scholarship is discouraging to those of us interested in using law for social change, but we can draw some hope from our field as well. Our studies of legal pluralism suggest there are many types of law; and studies of the books-action gap tell us that the trajectory of law is indeterminate, and its destination is more often than not decided en route. Tactical social actors can exploit law's plural and fluid nature under the right conditions and at the right moment, tweaking and nudging it toward progressive outcomes. It is true that ultimately law is contoured to the surrounding social form ("Sooner or later, [a legal system's] shape gets bent in the direction of [the] society"). But *law and social form move in tandem, bending together.* Remember Tigar and Levy's (1977) account of the alliances between the English bourgeoisie, monarchs, and lawyers that hastened the transformation from feudalism to capitalism, with the help of law. As we see clearly in that case, law not only is "bent" to the shape of society's structures, institutions, and logics but also can sometimes be a powerful force in its own right, bending and shaping those same social realities.

Finally, remember in the previous chapter when I talked about critical legal studies scholars and others who argue that the progressive promises of law-on-the-books are not kept and that the promises themselves reinforce inequality by masking it with their lofty rhetoric. Isn't it possible that the ideological work of those promises may ultimately be *subversive*, inspiring change? High-sounding rhetoric about the right to free speech, equal opportunity, or racial justice may—as these critics contend—legitimate and shore up the status quo. But it might also be a double-edged sword. After all, inspiring rhetoric about freedom and equality broadcasts the nobility of those (unrealized) principles and cultivates the ideological ground for activists, under the right conditions, to call the bluff and sow the seeds of change. *Brown v. Board of Education* and the Civil Rights Act did not end racial inequality in the United States. But if we ever get there, my bet is that the principles those legal actions proclaimed will be part of the reason.

In his presidential address at the annual Law and Society Association conference, Michael McCann (2014) presented an overview of the myriad paradoxes of rights. He concluded, "We study rights because, whatever their limits, their lightness, and their paradoxical heaviness, they can and often do matter in struggles for social justice, especially given the limited availability of alternative normative discourses" (267).

CHAPTER EIGHT Reflecting on Law's Image: An Inward Turn?

Gordon Gekko, fictional villain of the 1987 movie *Wall Street*, was famously contemptuous of anyone "naive enough" to believe in democracy:

> The richest one percent of this country owns half our country's wealth, five trillion dollars.... You got ninety percent of the American public out there with little or no net worth. I create nothing. I own. We make the rules, pal.... Now you're not naive enough to think we're living in a democracy, are you buddy?... Greed, for lack of a better word, is good.

Gekko's "greed is good" motto captured the essence of his era and that of the decades to come, as the figures on the concentration of wealth in the U.S. continued to climb. As the twenty-first century got under way, the winner-take-all economy and its political-ideological wrappings were well entrenched in the United States and had spread to much of the world. A new Oxfam report estimates that if current trends continue, by 2016 the richest 1 percent will own more wealth than the other 99 percent of the world's population, and that the wealthiest eighty people in the world (whose wealth doubled from 2009 to 2014 alone) currently own more than all the 3.5 billion people in the lower half of the world's income scale. The Gekko character has been so closely associated with this new political-economic order that former Australian prime minister Kevin Rudd said in a 2008 speech that the financial collapse of that year was brought on by the "21st-century children of Gordon Gekko."

This political-economic order—what some call "neoliberalism"—is in large part the result of specific laws and policies. In the United States regulations on banks and other financial institutions were loosened in the 1980s and 1990s, laws prohibiting anti-union activity were effectively gutted, corporate and personal income taxes on top earners were slashed, the value of the minimum wage fell, affirmative action was limited by court orders, and punitive criminal justice policies sent millions of mostly poor people of color to prison. Clearly, law had not ushered in progressive social change in the United States, as some early law and society scholars envisioned it might; on the contrary, law itself was an aggressive usher into the present neoliberal era. It could be said that the financial collapse and its surrounding political-economic landscape were not so much the children of Gordon Gekko as they were the children of Law.

As we saw in the previous chapter, a scholarship of disillusionment emerged in this context. From Galanter's (1974) "Why the 'Haves' Come Out Ahead" and Scheingold's (1974) *Politics of Rights* to Rosenberg's (1991) *Hollow Hope*, Bell's (2004) *Silent Covenants*, and Edelman's (2005) "Law at Work," much of the law and society field has engaged in a post mortem for progressive legal change, carefully investigating the causes of death. At the same time, a rigorous debate ensued (profiled in the last chapter), with many law and society scholars pushing back against the critique of rights and insisting that law has a place in struggles for progressive change—albeit one that must be strategically managed.

Here I raise the question of whether the disillusionment of the current neoliberal era has caused some to go one step further, turning away altogether from structural and institutional analyses of law and the potential for, or limits to, reform. The "extreme ethnographies" I discussed in chapter 6 are a possible example of this turn. Gone from ethnographies such as those of Venkatesh (2008) and Goffman (2014) are the explicit aspirations for legal and social change that characterized so much sociolegal research in the past. Gone too is the kind of institutional, legal, or social-structural analysis often inspired by that reformist impulse. In their place are riveting and sometimes terrifying stories. This is reportage. Like journalists in a war zone, extreme ethnographers risk their lives to get the story and report back. Which is not to say that they don't take sides. Venkatesh writes that he "resented the fact that the standard tools of sociologists seemed powerless to prevent the hardships [he] was seeing" (176). And, like any good reporter, he hoped his story would "contribute to the national discussion on poverty" (277). But he was "not so foolish" (277) as to imagine his work would have any specific benefits.

These ethnographies arguably represent a turning away from both the optimism of the engaged research of the 1960s and early 1970s and the subsequent debates about the limits of and possible strategies for effective legal reform. But they are relatively rare, which is not surprising, given the personal risks involved and the long-term nature of this kind of ethnography. More significant for our purposes may be what is sometimes called the "cultural turn" in the field. This cultural turn entails a focus on the subjective experience of law and culture, and on their deep interpenetration. More radically, it's about how law is actually found *within* cultural images and practices. Much as the "legal consciousness" described in chapter 3 can be thought of as a form of "law," so too are the images of law produced in culture. As Austin Sarat (2000, 9) put it in his presidential speech to the Law and Society Association, "Today we have law *on the books*, law *in action*, and, now, law *in the image*." He explained, "Law lives in images that today saturate our culture and that have a power all their own" (39). As early as 1983 anthropologist Clifford Geertz (1983, 173) made a similar point, arguing that law does not simply entail legal rules but is "part of a distinctive manner of imagining the real."

Culture is a tricky concept, and many law and culture scholars have weighed in on how to define it. Lila Abu-Lughod (1991), Raymond Williams (1983), Rosemary Coombe (2003), Naomi Mezey (2003b) and others, note that historically the concept of culture (as in "superior" and "inferior" cultures) was used to justify racist and colonialist practices, and that cultural analysts today must "transcend and transform its initial categories" (Coombe 2003, 21) if it is to be analytically useful. Because of its sordid history as a legitimating instrument of colonial domination and land grabs, and because the term "culture" is so slippery and multidimensional, decades ago Raymond Williams (1983, 87) called it "one of the two or three most complicated words in the English language."

Colloquially, "culture" refers to a wide range of phenomena, from the human artifacts of past civilizations to highbrow art and music, the lifestyles of communities of color, and vague zeitgeists such as our "culture of violence," which are used to explain tragedies like the 1999 Columbine High School massacre. However, Naomi Mezey (2003b) offers a definition that most cultural studies scholars would probably be comfortable with. She writes, "I will provisionally call culture any set of shared, signifying practices—practices by which meaning is produced, performed, contested, or transformed" (42). According to this definition, Mezey notes it is not altogether accurate to talk about the study of "law and culture," since law is itself one of the signifying practices that "produce, perform, contest, and transform meaning" (45–46). It is in other words an integral part of culture. Conversely, as we saw earlier, cultural images of law can themselves be thought of as a form of law.

Mezey (2003b) suggests that the study of law and culture might follow three tracks. First, we could talk about the power of *law* over *culture*. As she notes, "Legal rules structure the very baseline from which we negotiate our lives and form our identities. Furthermore, these legal ground rules are all the more effective because they are not visible as law" (47). According to this insight, which Mezey calls the traditional "realist" position, the strictures of law are everywhere and shape our social practices and cultural meanings. For example, property laws structure class relationships and the distribution of wealth while simultaneously naturalizing those social forms as inevitable. This approach is similar to what we have seen periodically throughout this book, most obviously in chapter 3, where we examined the myriad ways law shapes how we live, talk, and think.

The second version of this relationship between law and culture focuses on the power of *culture* over *law*. Mezey (2003b) uses the example of speed limits. Those of us who drive know there is an official speed limit and an unofficial, de facto speed limit (from my experience as a white middle-class female, I figure it is usually five to eight miles per hour over the official limit). We also know that it is this de facto limit—arrived at by local customs, cultural conventions, and social identity—that actually counts, that largely determines whether or not we will be pulled over. Indeed, according to Mezey, this *customary* speed limit often affects the determination of the official, legal speed limit (rather than solely the other way around). Furthermore, whether or not you are stopped by the highway patrol while going this customary speed is shaped by the cultural practice of pulling over people of color disproportionately. This trumping power of local culture over formal law may sound familiar, as we talked about it extensively in chapter 4, "The Color of Law," and in chapter 6, "The Talk versus the Walk of Law."

But it is the third version of the relationship between law and culture that most current cultural studies scholars are interested in. This version, as described by Mezey, emphasizes "law as culture as law" (51). That is, it focuses on the dynamic and constitutive relationship between the two—or rather, the "slippage" (54) between them as distinct concepts. An example from my own research might be helpful here. In doing research for my recent book on the prisoner grievance system in California (Calavita and Jenness 2015), my coauthor and I were repeatedly told by prison officials that prisoners file grievances over trivial matters. In this context, one particular story kept surfacing. In interviews and conversations, the officials told us over and over again about a prisoner who filed a grievance over a broken cookie he had received at lunch. We were first told this story during a pre-study prison visit to secure endorsement for our research from a prison warden. Upon hearing that we intended to focus on the grievance process, the warden and his team of deputy wardens, appeals coordinators, and various assistants regaled us with details of the "broken cookie" grievance, including their claim that the appellant had won his case at the U.S. Supreme Court.

Although we searched and never found concrete evidence of this grievance—much less its court appearance—the truth of the story is less important than its prominence in prison-official folklore. Much as the McDonald's coffee case and other symbols of American litigiousness are so entrenched in American cultural knowledge that their names have become a familiar shorthand for legal excess (Haltom and McCann 2004 3), so the broken cookie has become cultural code among these prison staff for all that is wrong with the prison grievance system. Universally told with derision, the story has a mantric quality as a tale of rights gone wrong and of the personal and moral deficiencies of prisoners. Most relevant here, this culturally inscribed broken-cookie story is part and parcel of the meaning of "law" for these officials, and it shapes their practices vis-à-vis prisoner grievances (denying virtually all of them). Law as culture as law.

The key here is the understanding of culture as "any set of shared, signifying practices." Once culture is understood as a set of signs and practices that confer meaning, law and culture are seen as dialectically entangled, in fact virtually indistinguishable. What's more, according to this definition that emphasizes symbols and interpretation, subjectivity is analytically privileged over structural or institutional analysis or "objective reality" (e.g., whether there ever was a broken-cookie grievance).

This focus on the reality and power of shared subjective meaning reminds me of a dialogue sequence in the movie *Harry Potter and the Deathly Hallows: Part 2*. Harry Potter and Professor Dumbledore are dead and inhabiting what appears to be a train station. Harry asks, "Is this real? Or has this been happening inside my head?" Dumbledore replies, "Of course it's happening inside your head, Harry, but why on earth should that mean it's not real?" Just so, for these scholars who have taken the "cultural turn," shared signs and their subjective meaning are the real stuff of both law and culture. They are in fact the living tissue that binds them and makes them one.

In the introduction to their edited volume *Cultural Analysis, Cultural Studies, and the Law*, Austin Sarat and Jonathan Simon (2003, 6) suggest that this cultural turn is called for now because we live in a "postsocial environment." They argue that the 1960s and early 1970s were dominated by a *social* logic of governance, exemplified by expansions of the welfare state and public services and the participation of social scientists in policy making. In contrast, the contemporary era has witnessed a "crisis of the social" (3), in which the social safety net has been pulled away, public services privatized, social scientists discredited, and the legitimacy of all things "social" questioned (former British prime minister Margaret Thatcher is even reported to have said in a 1987 interview that "there is no such thing as society"). At the same time, Sarat and Simon say, "culture is in ascendance" (1), as cultural politics and identity emerge as governing logics, and images in the media and popular culture suffuse both public space and individual and collective subjectivity. Sarat and Simon welcome the shift in scholarship from the social to the cultural as "a self-conscious reflection" (6) on this altered environment.

In a somewhat more critical posture, Richard Abel (2010, 17) also argues that the cultural turn is a product of our times:

> Might our concern with images reflect a depoliticized culture? Having lost faith in the state's willingness or capacity to effect social

change, we look to individual agency and see consciousness as the obstacle. Americans who once defined themselves by political ideologies now do so by consumer preferences: How they look, what they wear, the foods they eat, the music they listen to, the soaps they watch, the sports they play, the teams they cheer.

In this high-tech age, he might have added, "the tweets they send, the blogs they follow, the Netflix they stream, the podcasts they listen to, the YouTube videos they watch . . ."

The cultural turn, then, can arguably be seen as a turn inward, away from institutional or structural analyses and toward the study of image, subjectivity, and consciousness. At a time when we have "lost all faith" in the possibility of meaningful structural or legal reforms, cultural studies not only changes the subject but also rejects the premise that power resides exclusively or even primarily in those realms. In this new context, Sarat and Simon (2003) propose "widening the moments of subjectivity" (9) in our scholarship, as they exhort us "to consider law as a world of images whose power . . . is found in the image itself" (10).

In a moment, I will question whether law and cultural studies can be said to have unilaterally turned inward or to have retreated from concerns for social change, as Abel (2010) argues, and as seems apparent in the focus on image and subjectivity. For now, though, let's flesh out what some of this scholarship on the interpenetration of law and culture tells us.

The work varies widely, but one dominant strain focuses on the images of law in film and other media, and the role these images play in our myths about law and in our collective hopes and anxieties. Take, for example, Austin Sarat's (2000) speech to the Law and Society Association on the complex images of law in the 1997 film *The Sweet Hereafter*. Sarat argues that images of fatherhood and images of law in that film are so intertwined that people's fantasies and anxieties about each are expressed through the other. The film reveals that both fathers and law are associated with dread, abuse, and loss. But Sarat suggests it also shows that these realities "are contingent and variable" (42), with some images of kind and empathetic fathers, and of law as it could be. Projecting images from the film onto a screen during his speech, Sarat demonstrated how the film exposes such contingencies and "shows law, like fatherhood, to be at once powerful and powerless, potent and yet vulnerable" (15).

The speech emphasized the entangled cultural meanings of law and fatherhood, but also the variability of those meanings. Illustrations of this variability abound. For, if *The Sweet Hereafter* projected an image of law as fatherlike, a contrasting image of law as an overly permissive, yet nitpicking nanny runs through many other popular movies. Think *Dirty Harry* (1971), or more recently, the *Taken* trilogy (2008, 2012, 2015). In contrast to the image of law as a strong (but vulnerable) father, these films portray law as soft and, arguably, feminine—to be countered, or more precisely ignored, by real men. In the first *Taken* movie, a former CIA agent rescues his daughter from sex traffickers in France (in this respect, the story line follows that of the "damsel in distress" discussed in chapter 3), blowing up cars, killing those in his way, and otherwise wreaking mayhem in his quest. The imagery is evident: law is embodied in the form of the French police, with the not-so-subtle implication that the effeminate French are no match for this manly, lawbreaking American.

While not limited to the vigilante genre, it is here that the image of law as soft (and the parallel image of the feminine as weak) is most glaring. In *Dirty Harry*, Harry Callahan (played by Clint Eastwood) is a San Francisco police officer determined to bring a serial killer and rapist to justice, whatever it takes. The law is represented by the district attorney, who repeatedly stymies Harry by throwing constitutional objections in his way. Legal finery such as due process and the presumption of innocence are presented as the permissive side of the nanny state—wimpy technicalities to be disdainfully snickered at by the bad-boy heroes who can be counted on to get the job done.

Stewart Macaulay (1987, 214) was one of the first law and society scholars to call for studying "the symbols related to law found in American culture." In his 1986 presidential address to the Law and Society Association, he illustrated with the film *Star Chamber*. This movie's legal imagery is much like that of *Dirty Harry* and *Taken*. As Macaulay tells it, images of law as permissive and fraught with hand-wringing technicalities pervade *Star Chamber*, while the he-man heroes deliver justice. Macaulay is eloquent:

In this film an evil creep is tried for killing little old ladies to steal their Social Security payments. He evades just punishment by asserting his constitutional rights. The Warren Court's rules about criminal prosecution force the judge to throw out the case. But . . . other judges . . . solved this problem by direct action: They hire hit men to kill the creeps. (197)

Macaulay adds that even the *Wall Street Journal*'s editorial page chimed in, applauding both the vigilante plot of *Star Chamber* and the audiences who relished it: "Even in our chic New York uptown theater," wrote the *Journal* editors, "the audiences cheered when the judges' hit man blew away the little-old-lady-killer" (quoted in Macauley 1987, 197).

Let me give you a few more timely examples of how a cultural lens might be applied to media analysis, before we get back to the course that this scholarly turn has taken. Recently, streamed series on Netflix, Amazon, and other sources seem to have displaced the movie as pop culture's must-see medium. People even talk about "addiction" to their favorites, "bingeing" on four or five episodes at a time. Think *Orange Is the New Black*, *The Wire*, *Damages*, *Breaking Bad*, *The Good Wife*, *The Killing*, *True Detective*, and countless other series (By the time you read this, you will be able to name scores more) that cast law as either a central player or a prominent subtext. In the Seattle-based *The Killing*, Detective Linden and her sidekick, Holder, often circumvent the law to catch the creepy bad guys, somewhat in the style of *Dirty Harry*. In the first season of *True Detective*—which I have just finished watching—detectives Marty and Rust are even more ruthless in their quest for justice.

This police-as-vigilante theme has given way in many popular series to an image of law as straight-out corrupt (rather than a well-intentioned but pesky obstacle to justice) and/or dysfunctional. As I write this, *Orange Is the New Black* is Netflix's most-watched series ever. Here, law, as embodied in the prison staff, is depicted alternately as authoritarian, greedy, double-handed, sadistic, and most of all bumbling—something to be manipulated and played by its prisoner counterparts. Given the structured relationship of power between the mostly young female prisoners and the mostly older male officials who are in charge of them, it is tempting to see images of law and (fallible, coercive, and sexually abusive) fatherhood once again intertwined. No doubt *Orange Is the New Black* will be fodder for cultural analyses for years to come—as it should be. For this show, originally expected by its producers to appeal to a narrow niche audience given the race and gender of most of its characters, has become a cultural icon. The law that is projected in these iconic shows and the cultural context they emerge from not only reproduce and enhance each other; they constitute a single, signifying network.

Returning to our main thread, since Stewart Macaulay called for this kind of analysis almost three decades ago, the cultural turn in legal studies has flourished. In 1989, the prestigious *Yale Law Journal* devoted a special issue to "popular legal culture," with the introductory essay by Stewart Macaulay (1989) himself. Starting from the premise that "culture is not a tangible thing [but instead] is both ideas in people's heads and the stock of symbols and stories recognized by at least some members of a group" (1547), most of the essays examined the relationship between popular culture and the twists and turns of what in earlier chapters we called legal consciousness. The field took off, and diversified in the process. By the late 1990s, the Association for Law, Culture, and the Humanities was formed, holding annual conferences, handing out awards, and mentoring graduate students. And, in 2005, the association launched its own journal.

Much of the work in this wide-ranging field continues to focus on the powerful imagery projected in films and similar media and the myriad ways they are entangled with and reverberate through the culture. One edited volume unpacks the concepts of justice, race, fatherhood, and law in the 1962 film version of Harper Lee's *To Kill a Mockingbird* (Sarat and Umphrey 2013). Among the major themes weaving through this volume is the importance of temporality or historical context. Harper Lee's book, set in the 1930s, was first published in 1960, between the landmark *Brown v. Board of Education* decision desegregating schools and the Civil Rights Act of 1964. The essays in the volume make it clear that the book—and the film—have become classics in part because of the powerful questions they elicit about authority figures (in this case, legal actors and, once again, fathers) and the fallibility and potential of law (and fathers), but also because of their resonance with the cultural and historical moment in which these questions were raised.

It is not only the story lines and characters of movies that parallel, embody, and evoke legal meaning. In fact, according to Carol Clover (2003), it is not primarily a film's *story* that is interesting in this context. Rather, it's the way the "narrative substructure" of many American movies "rhymes with the narrative substructure" (100) of that central element of the Anglo-American legal system—the trial. Clover uses the 1992 movie *Basic Instinct* to make her point. On the off chance you haven't seen *Basic Instinct*, the opening scene shows a naked man and woman (whose face is not visible) having passionate sex—until the woman grabs an ice pick from under the bed and stabs her lover to death. This opening scene, says Clover, is "the functional equivalent" (113) of a trial's opening statement. The murder is presented to the audience as the movie begins, breaking the usual cinematic convention of thrillers by providing up front what would usually be the culminating scene. It works, says Clover, because we are culturally attuned to the narrative structure of a trial, where the jury is asked to pay close attention to opening statements, with the assurance that gaps and facts will be filled in as the trial proceeds. Clover shows us how the presentation of these facts, the cinematography in which close-ups of key players are akin to lie detector tests, and the "reasonable doubt" we are left with at the end of the movie hew closely to the structure of a trial. Of the ambiguous final scene, Clover writes, "You are the jury; you decide." She concludes, "The kind of movie narrative at issue here—fragmented, evidence-examining, forensically visualized, backstory-driven, X-no-X-structured, polygraphically photographed, intricately plotted, doubt-cultivating, and jury-directed—is . . . culturally characteristic" (117). Its appeal and its power are drawn from its equivalence to the Anglo-American adversarial trial. What Clover might have added is that the power of the trial system is in turn enhanced by our familiarity with its cinematographic counterpart. Not only do the trial structure and film structure imbue each other with power; to borrow a word from Clover, they so closely "rhyme" that they're practically homonyms.

I recently listened to the first season of *Serial*, the podcast version of a crime thriller, based on a true story. *Serial* tells us in the first episode of the disappearance and murder of a high school senior and the arrest of her former boyfriend, who insists on his innocence. We are then led through a maze of events and evidence. The podcast is seriously "addictive," as all my friends say. The fact that it is entirely audio no doubt adds to its appeal, as we are called on to use our imaginations to fill in visual images. It dawned on me, as I was listening to the last episode after reading Clover's article on *Basic Instinct*, that the narrative structure of *Serial* also mimics the trial narrative structure, and this may help explain its seductive power.

The focus on law and culture as deeply embedded in each other has opened up whole new terrains of research, and as Macaulay (1989, 1558) put it long ago, "It promises to be fun." Soap operas, movies, podcasts, Netflix, reality TV, rap music—all are grist for cultural-legal research. And it's not just the media that are analyzed. Among a vast array of other topics, etiquette and its close sibling—hypocrisy—are compared to the rules of the American judicial process (Bybee 2005); the scientific method is analogized to the rule of law (Dimock 2003); food culture is tied to the sexism and racism of the powers that be, legal and otherwise, and to their resistance by African American women (Williams-Forson 2006); the English Channel tunnel is used to explore law and landscape as triggers for and markers of English identity in the new Europe (Darian-Smith 1999); and intellectual property laws are probed for their constitutive relationship with political, authorial, and consumer culture (Coombe 1998; Woodmansee 2003).

Even children's literature is a lens for investigating the relationship between, and functional equivalence of, law and culture. J. K. Rowling's Harry Potter novels are a particular favorite for cultural analysis (Barton 2006; Thomas and Snyder 2010), no doubt because of the cult-like following of these books, which have sold more than 450 million copies worldwide. If you are one of the millions of children and their parents who have savored Harry Potter over the years, you may be wondering what the books have to do with law. Ostensibly, nothing. But the despotic and incompetent nature of Rowling's Ministry of Magic arguably tells us a great deal not only about the author's libertarian attitude toward government, law, and bureaucrats but also about the cultural stereotypes of inept government that the books' images tap into and help reproduce (Barton 2006).

At first glance, this focus on mundane aspects of daily life and on what appears to be the fluff of popular culture, and the close attention to image and subjective meaning, do indeed seem to be a turning inward, a turning away from yesteryear's engaged discussions of law and social change. Some of these cultural analysis scholars reject as illegitimate the "instrumental" approach to research which is driven by a desire for legal change. In her analysis of the "trifles" within mystery novels, Ravit Reichman (2005, 15) writes: "My approach to law, which is cultural and literary in focus, reinforces Paul Kahn's insistence that theory and practice amount to different—and distinct—pursuits." Quoting Kahn (1999, 40), she continues, "A cultural study of law is precisely not a part of the practice of law. It should not, therefore, be asked to reform law. It has nothing to say in this respect. . . . We can know more about ourselves. This is all that a cultural study of law can promise."

Social scientists have long debated what the relationship should be between our research and theorizing on one hand and the policy-making audience on the other. Although the field of law and society was born in part from a desire to be engaged and relevant, we have been reluctant to hitch our wagons to that of specific policy makers, whose agendas are often circumscribed and politically expedient. Our engagement as law and society scholars has generally been with the more far-reaching ideal of social justice, which policy makers and bureaucrats do not always have the luxury of entertaining. Austin Sarat and Susan Silbey (1988) warned us decades ago against succumbing to "the pull of the policy audience," arguing that doing so can jeopardize the integrity of our research by allowing others to shape the questions we ask as well as the range of acceptable answers. This is a very real risk, but I for one have come to respect enormously those who attempt to finesse this potential pull problem and use evidence-based research to try to push the policy audience in progressive directions.

Now, having for the most part rejected the pull of the policy audience, we find ourselves in the audience of *Basic Instinct*, *Dirty Harry*, and *Orange Is the New Black*, deciphering their cultural codes and reimagining their images. Clearly, some in our field have not only resisted the siren song of the policy audience; they appear to have shunned political engagement altogether. But the cultural study of law is almost as wide and diverse as law and society itself. Its merit lies in its untethering us from our conventional ways of viewing both culture and law, as well as our traditional methods of studying the law and society relationship. This unboundedness is one of the defining characteristics of the law and culture movement, and it is what defies any effort to pigeonhole it as depoliticized or isolationist.

We do not have to look far to find scholars of law and cultural studies who are doing engaged scholarship and who are committed to giving voice to the oppressed and opening up spaces of resistance. After all, the roots of this movement go back to Antonio Gramsci (1971), with his synthesis of material conditions and ideology, and to Raymond Williams's (1958, 1961) studies of the dynamic interplay of culture, power, and political economy. Given this heritage, it might not be surprising that some who have identified with critical legal studies (discussed in previous chapters) have partially taken up the mantle of cultural studies.

Duncan Kennedy is one example, albeit a controversial one. In his much-debated 1993 book *Sexy Dressing Etc.: Essays on the Power and Politics of Cultural Identity*, Kennedy's focus is on the ways disempowered groups can contest and transform their positions through harnessing the counterhegemonic power of cultural images. A response to criticisms that critical legal studies had omitted the voices of minorities and women and had overlooked the power of identity politics, *Sexy Dressing* includes discussions of affirmative action and the power and contingency of identity. But it is Kennedy's analysis of the Madonna phenomenon that has drawn the most attention. Kennedy argues that in our culture men's sexual pleasure, sexual abuse of women, and women's oppressed sexual identities are linked together. Further, he suggests that the singer Madonna's explicit, in-your-face sexuality inverts this traditional power relationship. In place of the objectified female whose purpose is to please men, Madonna strategically dresses and poses to evoke an image of a woman with sexual autonomy who exercises power over men through her sexuality. In other words, according to Kennedy, Madonna exploits the objectified image of women as sexual pleasure givers to do work *against* that image, turning it on its head. And, he posits, Madonna's music videos have the potential to develop a woman's self-identity as a "sexually autonomous woman" with her own pleasures (203).

As a legal theorist, Kennedy's assumption is that acts of resistance such as this (and arguably of rap music and other similar forms of resistance in popular culture) affect not only cultural identities but also forms of victimization and, ultimately, law. In her review of Kennedy's book, Naomi Mezey (1994, 1858) writes, "The smallest, most private interpretive commitments help create and maintain the normative universe. This is why what we choose to wear and how we choose to wear it can influence our interpretations of the law governing sexual abuse."

Kennedy recognizes the inherent danger in these forms of resistance. In the absence of eradicating the social inequalities that structure gender and race relationships, they may backfire. For example, Madonna's sexually explicit videos signaling liberation—and presumably those of more recent artists who have followed her lead such as Miley Cyrus and others—may result in "something else, something bad, instead" (206), as young women without the fortress of celebrity and class to protect them remain vulnerable to abuse. Kennedy even suggests that, within the context of a society that remains structurally unequal and culturally permeated with images of objectified and victimized women, Madonna herself is open to danger.

Kennedy's book has been criticized by those who question his right as a heterosexual white man to speak on behalf of women and people of color, and at least one critic has suggested there is something lurid in his fascination with Madonna's wardrobe (Mezey 1994, 1850). Whatever the merits of these challenges, the book stands as an early example of cultural studies' engagement with issues of oppression, identity, and resistance. As Toby Miller (2003, 74) has put it, cultural studies has the potential to "see people not simply as consumers but as potential producers of new social values and cultural languages," as these scholars study the ways "the socially disadvantaged use culture to contest their subservient position."

In a different approach, Rosemary Coombe's (2003, 64) sweeping overview of and argument for "a critical cultural studies of law" urges us to focus "upon concrete fields of struggle." In her own work on intellectual property, Coombe shows "how relationships between law and culture have been established and maintained in the world, effecting new distributions of wealth and new inequalities of power, legitimating some identities and delegitimating others" (64). Addressing at once the dynamics of power and its resistance, Coombe's critical cultural studies is not "instrumental" or pitched to the policy audience, but by no means is it disengaged. Indeed, the potential of these new political struggles of identity and resistance is woven through and animates much of this new cultural studies scholarship.

Other examples abound, including many that you read about in chapter 3. Elaine Rapping's (2003) analysis of racialized images of crime in television, Dawn Cecil's (2007) critique of the sexualized representation of female prisoners, and Haltom and McCann's (2004) discussion of "pop torts" like the McDonald's coffee case—all are versions of an engaged critical cultural studies of law. So is queer theory, which includes a focus on diverse sexualities, identity, resistance, and law (Capers 2008; Mogul, Ritchie, and Whitlock 2012). A few of these scholars even engage directly in action and then use their experience as data. Toby Miller (2003, 88), for example, writes of his "applied research" in which he joined a fight by graduate students at New York University from 1999 to 2002 to be granted the right to unionize. In the essay about his experience, he describes the "circuit of culture"—borrowing a term from Stuart Hall (1997)—that links cultural discourse and representation with identity (in this case, the identity of graduate students as labor, or not-labor) and its "production, consumption, and regulation" (98).

In another take on the production and regulation of identity through a cultural lens, Leti Volpp (2000) examines the ways our public and legal discourse about "culture"—who has it and what its consequences are—racialize immigrants and set them apart from white Americans. Using real-life examples of both early voluntary marriage and forced marriage, Volpp shows that in cases in which an immigrant adolescent girl and her parents are involved, their behavior is talked about in the media and by law enforcement as indicative of their different cultural values; instead, in cases where white Americans are the subjects, a narrative of individual aberrant behavior is engaged and there is no mention of "white culture."

Volpp recounts the story of thirteen-year-old Tina Akers, who married her twenty-nine-year-old boyfriend in Maryland and had a baby with him. Her husband was investigated for sexual assault on a minor (but never prosecuted), and her parents were investigated for child abuse. In contrast, when fourteen-year-old Mexican immigrant Adela Quintana had a baby with her boyfriend in Texas, not only was the man charged with and prosecuted for aggravated sexual assault on a minor but also the media went on at length about how the incident "expos[ed] a cultural divide" and revealed "a clash between two cultures" (quoted in Volpp 2000, 92). The man's lawyer said about Adela that she was "buxom" and that "in rural Mexico, 'once a girl hits puberty she is fair game'" (93). *Dateline NBC* aired a program on the incident in which correspondents interviewed people from Adela's village in Mexico and concluded that the boyfriend was "an innocent player in a big cultural misunderstanding" (93).

Volpp points out that in cases like this (and forced marriage cases, which she also discusses), culture is ascribed to immigrant "others" and is made responsible for their behavior. But when white Americans engage in similar behavior, cultural explanations are not deployed (except, as Volpp suggests, when those involved are poor or working class, in which case cultural explanations may surface). The result is threefold. First, there is "an exaggerated perception of ethnic difference that equates it with moral difference from 'us'" (89); second, an implied identity construction takes places such that "white people are individual actors; people of color are members of groups" (90); and third, "an irreconcilable tension" (90) is thus assumed to exist between ourselves and racialized immigrants. Volpp is concerned because these narratives exaggerate our differences, but also because they obscure the gendered, classed, and raced dynamics of power in other cultures as well as our own, and lead to dysfunctional and unjust policies, most obviously justifying restrictive immigration laws.

So, the question of whether law and cultural studies represents an inward turn is an open one. Or rather, the question is problematic, as it falsely assumes this movement is monolithic. Instead, it is as diverse as the field of law and society itself. Austin Sarat (2004b, 8) writes about law and society, and "postrealist" studies such as law and culture as an emerging movement within it: "With growth has come a greater inclusiveness, but also fragmentation. . . . One measure of the progress of this field is uneasiness about what its boundaries are, what is orthodox and what is heresy." This openness, this diversity, is one of the field's greatest strengths. Our methods range widely too. Some are ethnographers, some pore over historical documents, some conduct surveys, some do film analysis, and some collect statistical and other quantitative data. This is not usually just a matter of expediency, skill set, or personal preference (do I want to sit in a room reading archives, or do I prefer to talk to people?). Instead, there are deep divisions within the field about what constitutes objective "data" (are demographic statistics more valid data than film images?), and whether there is any such thing as objectivity anyway.

Physicist and Nobel laureate Percy Bridgman (1950, 370) once said, "There is no scientific method as such, but . . . merely [doing the] utmost with [one's] mind, *no holds barred*." Whether we identify primarily with the social sciences (as I do) or with the humanities (as many scholars of law and cultural studies do), our understanding of law and its relationship to society is most likely to be advanced by a plural community of scholars continuing to do the "utmost with their minds"—*no holds barred*.

One last thing. As I was writing this chapter, I came across an article in the *New Yorker* that told of a "Harry Potter Alliance" joining the protests in New York and elsewhere demanding an increase in the minimum wage (Wiedeman 2014). The alliance apparently brings together a hundred thousand enthusiasts of Harry Potter books who agitate for progressive social change. Its campaigns include "Not in Harry's Name," which pushes for Harry Potter–branded chocolates to be made with fair-trade cocoa, and a YouTube series entitled *Dark Lord Waldemart*, which contests Walmart's labor policies and has been viewed nearly three million times. Wiedeman (2014) quotes the founder of the alliance as saying that the Harry Potter books facilitate recruiting youth to social issues. Wiedeman points to the activist drawing power of "racism between Muggleborns and Wizards, slave labor in terms of house elves, Sirius Black having his habeas corpus suspended in a time of terror" (44). In light of the previously referenced analysis of the Harry Potter series (Barton 2006) as promoting conservative libertarianism, the Harry Potter Alliance just goes to show that you can't judge a book by its cover. Or, to put a less colloquial spin on it, it affirms what many law and culture scholars have told us: that cultural images contain within them multiple possible interpretations, some more obvious than others, and that resistance often comes from surprising places.

CHAPTER NINE Conclusion

The taxi driver who thought I said "lawn society" instead of "law and society" got me thinking about law and lawns. "Law," according to Webster's dictionary, can mean "theorem," and "lawn" can mean "an open space between woods." Maybe law and lawns are related after all, and the taxi driver gets the last laugh. A theorem can itself be an open space, not yet definitively confirmed or debunked; the "open spaces" of law—with its silences and ambiguities—are legion; and the gaps between the words of law and its actions are part of the law and society canon. Maybe our field is about both law and lawns, theorems and open spaces.

Some of our theorems are well established, and not so open to dispute. One, for example, is that law and society are nested, each within the other. This idea that law and society (and culture) are mutually embedded in each other is sometimes associated with what is called the "constitutive" perspective, but variations of it can be found in almost all law and society work. Remember that Marxist materialists like Rusche and Kirchheimer document the tight relationship between forms of punishment and economic systems. For Foucault, the emergence of the prison is traceable to modernity's disciplinarity, and the panopticon is not just a specific prison design but an emblem of modern society. Schwartz tells us about two different kinds of Israeli communities with their corresponding forms of law. Garland shows us the interlocking logics of contemporary punitiveness in the United States and England and the broader "culture of control" in these societies. And Sarat traces the convergent images of law and fatherhood in film. There are profound theoretical differences among these scholars, but they share the notion that law and society move together and coalesce around each other (so complete is this coalescence that some in our field argue that the term "law *and* society" is misleading in that it implies two distinct entities).

We also tend to agree that law shapes how we live on a daily basis, not just by its explicit mandates but through its language and categorizations and related legal consciousness. This hegemonic power of law is obvious in the long history of judicial race making in the United States, in the legal promotion of distinct gender roles, and in the many ways law-based words (think "mother-in-law" or "illegal immigrant") are part of our vernacular and so our thought processes. Law also suffuses our daily lives and consciousness in the form of the legal metaphors we routinely use. We "take the law into our own hands," "lay down the law," and "read someone the riot act." And it permeates social life in more mundane ways too. In small-town Nebraska, law moves in and through daily life as residents keep the police informed of yodeling incidents, squirrels in fireplaces, and boys mowing lawns—incidents that travel seamlessly from social life to police reports and back again as the local paper keeps people apprised of community activities. This ubiquity of law and its permeation of daily life is another law and society principle that we mostly agree about.

Our studies also consistently reveal a gap between formal law and real law, law-on-the-books and law-in-action. We see repeatedly that law as it is written gets selectively enforced, unrecognizably transformed, and even nullified as it is put into practice. Some scholars tell us this is because enforcement agencies face structural dilemmas; others point to racial or class biases; still others note that officials try to minimize hassles downstream, or that it has to do with the nature of capitalist democracies and their vacuous promises, or even that it is built into the logic of particular laws, with lawmakers sometimes counting on the perversion and/or violation of the statutes they pass (think of the tax on illegal drugs). The theoretical approaches of those of us who study this phenomenon vary, but the "open space" of law— its ambiguities and omissions, and the gaps these invite between formal law and law as it's practiced—is a law and society theorem with a certain degree of closure.

A lot of consensus exists too about the ways law racializes. As we saw, critical race theory emphasizes the contingent quality of racial categories and the part law plays in parsing those categories and shoring up their boundaries. The courts in the United States historically had trouble deciding who was white and who was nonwhite, with whole nations of people being flipped overnight from one category to another. The courts' inconsistency in divvying people up was matched only by their certainty that they were following natural, biological principles in doing so. This kind of explicit judicial race-making is mostly a thing of the past, but we have seen that law and legal processes still produce racialization. Segregation in California prisons and the subjective identification it calls on and reinforces, racial profiling in law enforcement, the thickening of Mexican ethnic identity in California after the passage of Proposition 187, and the othering of North African immigrants by Andalusian farmworkers after Spain's first immigration law was passed—these are among the many ways law contributes to racial construction today. These contemporary legal constructions are less transparent but arguably no less powerful than when courts in nineteenth-century America declared, "Persons half White and half Native American are not White." Few law and society scholars contest the broad outlines of this theoretical approach that focuses on the "color of law."

But if you were paying close attention, you might have noticed that law and society ideas are often in tension with each other. Let's start with the basics: we do not agree about how law should be defined. Many of us follow the lead of anthropologists like Malinowski who have an inclusive view of law as any set of norms that regulates conduct and provides for social control; some go even further and see "law" in the *image* of law and in consciousness; others insist on a narrower definition and, like Schwartz, argue that not all societies have "law," which, they say, occurs only when informal controls are weak.

We have seen too that types of law correspond to types of society— except when they don't. Tamanaha critiques the mirror image of law and society, showing us that the transplantation of law from powerful countries to peripheral ones often means that law is out of sync with the surrounding social order. Legal pluralism is a dominant theme in law and society research, especially as globalization advances and as colonial and postcolonial studies gain favor. But the well-accepted, legal pluralism notion that social systems contain within them multiple, sometimes conflicting forms of law can seem to have little affinity with the equally well-accepted constitutive approach, and at times threatens to unsettle it.

Other fault lines can be found in our debates about the utility of rights talk and more generally the power of law as a tool of progressive social change. Many studies document the failures of landmark judicial decisions like *Brown v. Board of Education* and legislation such as civil rights statutes to usher in meaningful racial justice. Some of our most innovative theoretical thinking has outlined the reasons for these limits of law, from law's endogeneity to the built-in advantages of resource-heavy repeat players and elitist pressures on constitutional courts. Maybe most provocatively, rights discourse—the presumed mother lode of social justice litigation—is indicted as politically fickle, useless in the fight against systemic injustices, and a distraction from more effective strategies. At the same time, though, we read hopeful studies of a workers' justice movement in the New York City restaurant industry that deploys law successfully against the backdrop of neoliberal globalization, constitutional courts in Eastern Europe that convey major reforms, and judicial policy making in the U.S. prison system that has brought relief to tens of thousands of inmates.

This "openness" of many law and society theorems is in part because there are lively disagreements in the field. The frequent appearance of seemingly mutually exclusive pairs of ideas is sometimes a reflection of this disagreement. Austin Sarat (2004a, xi) writes in his preface to *The Blackwell Companion to Law and Society* that disciplines are not bounded by theoretical agreement; rather, they have "a set of shared conversations. . . . The canon establishes the minimum grammar with which we must be familiar if we are to talk law and society and to have our talk recognized by others." Law and society scholars do not always agree on the answers, but they often converge around which questions are worth asking and which conversations are worth having.

But there is another reason for these unwieldy pairs of seemingly contradictory ideas. And that is that there is a dialectical quality to sociolegal reality itself. Law is both "hegemonic and oppositional," to quote Hirsch and Lazarus-Black (1994, 20) again, simultaneously contributing to the taken-for-grantedness of existing social arrangements and provoking people to contest that power. Law *can* be both fatal to reform efforts and reformers' best weapon. And law is both contoured to and infused in society and often imposed from afar or above. Some of our most profound truths appear to contradict each other, not because we cannot decide but because they are both right—and it is in this inclusivity of warring halves that law and society incorporates the complexity of social reality itself.

Have you ever noticed that the wisdom of proverbs comes in contradictory pairs? "Good things come to those who wait," but "He who hesitates is lost." "Out of sight, out of mind," but "Absence makes the heart grow fonder." "Actions speak louder than words," but "The pen is mightier than the sword." "Nothing ventured, nothing gained," but "It's better to be safe than sorry." Or think of the famous French dictum *plus ça change, plus c'est la même chose* (roughly, "The more things change, the more they stay the same"). Or Albert Einstein's cryptic wisdom, "There are only two ways to live your life. One is as though nothing is a miracle. The other is as though everything is a miracle." These apparently conflicting sayings do not represent competing philosophies or lapses in logic; rather, they embody the complexities of life and the dialectical quality of truth, and therein lies their wisdom. Just so, the tensions within and between some law and society propositions speak not of disagreements but of the contingent and essentially dialectical nature of the reality we study.

As this conversation comes to an end, I want to revisit a couple of things I said in the introduction. First, I must reiterate the disclaimer that I have by no means covered the whole field of law and society or touched on all the conversations we have. Mostly, I have mentioned those I know best—the ones closest to my discipline of sociology and conducted in English. Dozens of topics are not included here, and vast terrains remain unexplored. I have barely touched on legal anthropology and its rich ethnographies of formal and informal legal systems. I have shortchanged globalization studies that foreground the tectonic shifts in sociolegal forces as a new global order takes shape. While I have discussed at some length materialist analyses of law that highlight the impact of economic forces, I have neglected the "law and economics" approach that applies the methods and assumptions of the discipline of economics to the study of law. I have slighted important work in psychology and law as well, including studies of jury behavior, false confessions, and repressed memory.

Likewise, I have not mentioned important contemporary movements by name, although I have included some of their work. For
example, I have not referred specifically to postmodernism and the
epistemological relativity it espouses. And I have not explicitly ad-
dressed what is called the empirical legal studies movement, with its
renewed focus on empirical research that counters the more cultural,
humanities-oriented approaches discussed in chapter 8, although I
have cited some work by scholars in that movement.

While these may be limitations to a book like this, they are deliberate. My goal has not been to describe every bit of our terrain—even
were I capable of doing so—but to invite you for a brief visit to part of
it. I have wanted to describe for you some of our ways of seeing and
some of the discussions we have. My greatest hope is that you will be
enticed to join the law and society conversation. And because it is the
substance of the conversation that is important for now, wherever
possible I have avoided unnecessary labels.

And this brings me to my second disclaimer. I said I would keep
this brief invitation to the field accessible and jargon-free. I know
there were some rough patches along the way when you probably
thought I had forgotten or reneged on my promise. This may be due
to a failure on my part to communicate clearly, but I like to think it is
an inevitable by-product of the field's variety and complexity, which I
have not wanted to sacrifice. As a flummoxed Louise said in the 1991
movie *Thelma and Louise*, "God, law is some tricky s——, isn't it?" It is
the tricky part that is interesting, and I have tried to share it here in as
straightforward a way as possible.

Peter Berger (1963, 162) warned that "sociological understanding
leads to a considerable measure of disenchantment." This is perhaps
all the more true of law and society scholarship, in which we upend
the conventional mythology of law as magisterial, or at least as bound
by majestic rules and logics, that to one degree or another secures
the very legitimacy of the sociolegal order. But, as Berger counseled,
disenchantment need not lead to abject cynicism. In the case of law
and society, disenchantment can turn instead to awe, no longer at the
alleged purity of law, but on the contrary, at the intricacies of legal processes, the spectacularity of their contingencies, and the fluidity but
no less patterned quality of their trajectories. This awesome complex-

ity of law as it actually exists provides us with intellectual challenges equaled only by the beauty of their rewards.

To borrow from Berger (1963, 18–19) one more time, "We could say that the sociologist, but for the grace of his academic title, is the man who must listen to gossip despite himself, who is tempted to look through keyholes, to read other people's mail, to open closed cabinets." As we look behind the closed door of law's room and into its filing cabinets, we find secrets that unmask the public persona of the room's occupant. It's not simple or straightforward, though. Along the way, we find conflicting records, indecipherable notes, bits and pieces of nuance, and other enigmatic evidence of the true character of our subject—who appears to be alternately compulsive, tyrannical, helpful, dismissive, and indifferent, depending on the circumstances. What emerges from our search, if we are lucky and can piece it together, is at one level a subversive exposé of law's self-presentation. What makes it all the more compelling, though, is that we find a figure whose reality in all its complexities is as seductive and engaging as the myth.

References

Abel, Richard L. 1989. *American Lawyers*. New York: Oxford University Press.

———. 1995. *Politics by Other Means: Law in the Struggle against Apartheid, 1980–1994*. New York: Routledge.

———. 2010. "Law and Society: Project and Practice." *Annual Review of Law and Social Science* 6: 1–23.

Abel, Richard L., and Philip S. C. Lewis, eds. 1988–89. *Lawyers in Society*. 3 vols. Berkeley: University of California Press.

Abu-Lughod, Lila. 1991. "Writing against Culture." Pp. 137–54 in *Recapturing Anthropology: Working in the Present*, ed. Richard G. Fox. Santa Fe, NM: School of American Research Press.

Agrela, Belén. 2002. "La política de inmigración en España: Reflexiones sobre la emergencia del discurso cultural." *Migraciones Internacionales* 1: 93–121.

AHRC News Services. 2003. "Judge Compares Homeowner Association to 'Banana Republic' and 'Spanish Inquisition.'" *CCFJ Foundation*, http://www.ccfj.net/HOACArecall.html.

Albiston, Catherine. 1999. "The Rule of Law and the Litigation Process: The Paradox of Losing by Winning." *Law & Society Review* 33: 869–910.

Alexander, Michelle. 2010. *The New Jim Crow: Mass Incarceration in the Age of Colorblindness*. New York: New Press.

Alvarez, Lizette, and Frances Robles. 2014. "Florida Finds Tricky Balance over Feeding of the Homeless." *New York Times*, November 13, A17–A18.

Amnesty International USA. 2004. *Threat and Humiliation: Racial Profiling, Domestic Security, and Human Rights in the United States*. New York: Amnesty International USA.

Andall, Jacqueline. 2002. "Second-Generation Attitude? African-Italians in Milan." *Journal of Ethnic and Migration Studies* 28: 389–407.

Apuzzo, Matt. 2014. "Guards Guilty in '07 Killings in Iraq Square." *New York Times*, October 23, A1, A19.

———. 2015. "Blackwater Crew Given Long Prison Terms for Killing Iraqis." *New York Times*, April 14, A1, A14.

Ashar, Sameer M. 2007. "Public Interest Lawyers and Resistance Movements." *California Law Review* 95: 1879–1926.

Baptist, Edward E. 2014. *The Half Has Never Been Told: Slavery and the Making of American Capitalism.* New York: Basic Books.

Barclay, Scott, and Daniel Chomsky. 2014. "How Do Cause Lawyers Decide When and Where to Litigate on Behalf of Their Cause?" *Law & Society Review* 48: 595–620.

Barker, Vanessa. 2009. *The Politics of Imprisonment: How the Democratic Process Shapes the Way America Punishes Offenders.* New York: Oxford University Press.

Barnard, Anne. 2008. "Drug-Spiked Rice Krispies, and Other Goodies New York Could Tax." *New York Times,* January 24, A19.

Barry, Dan. 2007. "A Rough Script of Life, If Ever There Was One." *New York Times,* September 2, 112.

———. 2008. "A Violation of Both the Law and the Spirit." *New York Times,* January 28, A12.

Barton, Benjamin H. 2006. "Harry Potter and the Half-Crazed Bureaucracy." *Michigan Law Review* 104: 1523–38.

Beck, Allen J. and Marcus Berzofsky. 2013. *Sexual Victimization in Prisons and Jails Reported by Inmates, 2011–12.* NCJ 241399, May, Bureau of Justice Statistics, Washington, DC.

Beckett, Katherine. 1997. *Making Crime Pay: Law and Order in Contemporary American Politics.* New York: Oxford University Press.

Beckett, Katherine, and Steve Herbert. 2010. *Banished: The New Social Control in American Cities.* New York: Oxford University Press.

Beckett, Katherine, Kris Nyrop, Lori Pfingst, and Melissa Bowen. 2005. "Drug Use, Drug Possession Arrests, and the Question of Race: Lessons from Seattle." *Social Problems* 52: 419–41.

Bell, Derrick. 1987. *And We Are Not Saved: The Elusive Quest for Racial Justice.* New York: Basic Books.

———. 2004. *Silent Covenants: Brown v. Board of Education and the Unfulfilled Hopes for Racial Reform.* Oxford: Oxford University Press.

Berger, Peter L. 1963. *Invitation to Sociology: A Humanistic Perspective.* New York: Anchor Books, Random House.

Berman, Harold J. 2006. "Translating Western Law into Chinese." Interview with Reporter Meredith Hobbs. *Fulton County (GA) Daily Report,* June 1, 2006, 1.

Berrey, Ellen. 2015. *The Enigma of Diversity: The Language of Race and the Limits of Racial Justice.* Chicago: University of Chicago Press.

Blackmon, Douglas A. 2008. *Slavery by Another Name: The Re-enslavement of Black Americans from the Civil War to World War II.* New York: Doubleday.

Blumberg, Abraham. 1967. "The Practice of Law as a Confidence Game:

Organizational Cooptation of a Profession." *Law & Society Review* 1 (2): 15–39.

Borland, John. 2004. "Judges Rule File-Sharing Software Legal." *CNET*, http://news.cnet.com/Judges-rule-file-sharing-software-legal/2100 -1032_3-5316570.html.

Botelo, Nelson Arteaga, and Adrián López Rivera. 2000. "'Everything in This Job Is Money': Inside the Mexican Police." *World Policy Journal* 17: 61–70.

Boyle, Elizabeth Heger. 2002. *Female Genital Cutting: Cultural Conflict in the Global Community.* Baltimore, MD: Johns Hopkins University Press.

Bridgman, Percy. 1950. *Reflections of a Physicist.* New York: Philosophical Library.

Brigham, John. 1987. *The Cult of the Court.* Philadelphia: Temple University Press.

Brooks, David. 2015. "The Devotion Leap." *New York Times*, January 23, A25.

Bumiller, Kristin. 1988. *The Civil Rights Society.* Baltimore, MD: Johns Hopkins University Press.

Butler, Judith. 1990. *Gender Trouble: Feminism and the Subversion of Identity.* New York: Routledge.

Bybee, Keith J. 2005. "Legal Realism, Common Courtesy, and Hypocrisy." *Law, Culture and the Humanities* 1: 75–102.

Cain, Maureen. 1993. "Some Go Backward, Some Go Forward: Police Work in Comparative Perspective." *Contemporary Sociology* 22: 319–24.

Calavita, Kitty. 1992. *Inside the State: The Bracero Program, Immigration, and the INS.* New York: Routledge.

———. 1996. "The New Politics of Immigration: 'Balanced-Budget Conservatism' and the Symbolism of Proposition 187." *Social Problems* 43 (3): 284–305.

———. 2001. "Blue Jeans, Rape, and the 'De-Constitutive' Power of Law." *Law & Society Review* 35: 89–115.

Calavita, Kitty, and Valerie Jenness. 2013. "Inside the Pyramid of Disputes: Naming Problems and Filing Grievances in California Prisons." *Social Problems* 60: 50–80.

———. 2015. *Appealing to Justice: Prisoner Grievances, Rights, and Carceral Logic.* Oakland: University of California Press.

Campbell, Michael C. 2014. "The Emergence of Penal Extremism in California: A Dynamic View of Institutional Structures and Political Processes." *Law & Society Review* 48: 377–409.

Campbell, Michael C., and Heather Schoenfeld. 2013. "The Transformation of America's Penal Order: A Historicized Political Sociology of Punishment." *American Journal of Sociology* 119: 1375–1423.

Capers, I. Bennett. 2008. "Cross Dressing and the Criminal." *Yale Law Journal* 20: 1–30.

Carlin, Jerome E. 1962. *Lawyers on Their Own: A Study of Individual Practitioners in Chicago.* New Brunswick, NJ: Rutgers University Press.

Cecil, Dawn K. 2007. "Looking beyond Caged Heat: Media Images of Women in Prison." *Feminist Criminology* 2 (4): 304–26.

Chambliss, Elizabeth. 2004. *Miles to Go: Progress of Minorities in the Legal Profession.* Chicago: American Bar Association Commission on Racial and Ethnic Diversity in the Profession.

Chambliss, William J. 1964. "A Sociological Analysis of the Law of Vagrancy." *Social Problems* 12: 46–67.

Chevigny, Paul M. 1999. "Defining the Role of the Police in Latin America." Pp. 49–70 in *The (Un)rule of Law and the Underprivileged in Latin America,* ed. J. E. Mendez, Guillermo O'Donnell, and Paulo Sérgio Pinheiro. Notre Dame, IN: University of Notre Dame Press.

Chicago Defender. 1954. "End of Dual Society." May 18.

Chua, Lynette J. 2014. *Mobilizing Gay Singapore: Rights and Resistance in an Authoritarian State.* Philadelphia, PA: Temple University Press.

Clover, Carol J. 2003. "Law and the Order of Popular Culture." Pp. 97–119 in *Law in the Domains of Culture,* ed. Austin Sarat and Thomas R. Kearns. 1998. Ann Arbor: University of Michigan Press.

Coben, Harlan. 2008. "The Undercover Parent." Week in Review, *New York Times,* March 16, 14.

Comaroff, Jean, and John L. Comaroff. 1991. *Of Revelation and Revolution.* Vol. 1, *Christianity, Colonialism, and Consciousness in South Africa.* Chicago: University of Chicago Press.

Comaroff, John L., and Jean Comaroff. 1997. *Of Revelation and Revolution.* Vol. 2, *The Dialectics of Modernity on a South African Frontier.* Chicago: University of Chicago Press.

Congressional Record. 1882. 47th Congress, 1st Session.

Conley, John M., and William M. O'Barr. 1998. *Just Words: Law, Language, and Power.* Chicago: University of Chicago Press.

Conti, Joseph A. 2008. "The Good Case: Decisions to Litigate at the World Trade Organization." *Law & Society Review* 42: 145–82.

Coombe, Rosemary J. 1998. *The Cultural Life of Intellectual Properties: Authorship, Appropriation, and the Law.* Durham, NC: Duke University Press.

———. 2003. "Contingent Articulations: A Critical Cultural Studies of Law." Pp. 21–64 in *Law in the Domains of Culture,* ed. Austin Sarat and Thomas R. Kearns. 1998. Ann Arbor: University of Michigan Press.

Coutin, Susan Bibler. 1994. "Enacting Law through Social Practice: Sanctuary as a Form of Resistance." Pp. 282–303 in *Contested States: Law, Hegemony and Resistance,* ed. Mindie Lazarus-Black and Susan F. Hirsch. New York: Routledge.

Crenshaw, Kimberlé. 1998. "A Black Feminist Critique of Antidiscrimination Law and Politics." Pp. 356–80 in *The Politics of Law: A Progressive Critique*, ed. D. Kairys. 3rd ed. New York: Basic Books.

Crewdson, John. 1983. *The Tarnished Door: The New Immigrants and the Transformation of America*. New York: Times Books.

Darian-Smith, Eve. 1999. *Bridging Divides: The Channel Tunnel and English Legal Identity in the New Europe*. Berkeley: University of California Press.

———. 2013. *Law and Societies in Global Contexts: Contemporary Approaches*. Cambridge: Cambridge University Press.

DeLand, Michael. 2013. "Basketball in the Key of Law: The Significance of Disputing in Pick-Up Basketball." *Law & Society Review* 47: 653–85.

Delgado, Richard, and Jean Stefancic. 2001. *Critical Race Theory: An Introduction*. New York: New York University Press.

Dezalay, Yves, and Bryant G. Garth. 1996. *Dealing in Virtue: International Commercial Arbitration and the Construction of a Transnational Legal Order*. Chicago: University of Chicago Press.

———. 2002. *The Internationalization of Palace Wars: Lawyers, Economists, and the Contest to Transform Latin American States*. Chicago: University of Chicago Press.

Dimock, Wai Chee. 2003. "Rules of Law, Laws of Science." Pp. 220–44 in *Cultural Analysis, Cultural Studies, and the Law*, ed. Austin Sarat and Jonathan Simon. Durham, NC: Duke University Press.

Dudziak, Mary. 2000. *Cold War Civil Rights: Race and the Image of American Democracy*. Princeton, NJ: Princeton University Press.

Durkheim, Émile. 1964. *The Division of Labor in Society*. Trans. George Simpson. Glencoe, IL: Free Press.

Edelman, Lauren B. 2005. "Law at Work: The Endogenous Construction of Civil Rights." Pp. 337–52 in *Handbook of Employment Discrimination Research*, ed. Laura Beth Nielsen and Robert L. Nelson. Dordrecht, Germany: Springer.

Edelman, Murray. 1964. *The Symbolic Uses of Politics*. Urbana: University of Illinois Press.

Emerson, Robert M. 1969. *Judging Delinquents: Context and Process in Juvenile Court*. Chicago: Aldine.

———. 1991. "Case Processing and Interorganizational Knowledge: Detecting the 'Real Reasons' for Referrals." *Social Problems* 38 (2): 198–212.

Epp, Charles R., Steven Maynard-Moody, and Donald Haider-Markel. 2014. *Pulled Over: How Police Stops Define Race and Citizenship*. Chicago: University of Chicago Press.

Epstein, Cynthia Fuchs, Robert Sauté, Bonnie Oglensky, and Martha Gever. 1995. "Glass Ceilings and Open Doors: Women's Advancement in the Legal Profession." *Fordham Law Review* 64: 291–449.

Eschholz, Sarah, Ted Chiricos, and Mark Gertz. 2003. "Television and Fear of Crime: Program Types, Audience Traits, and the Mediating Effect of Perceived Racial Composition." *Social Problems* 50: 395–415.

Evans, Thayer. 2008. "160 Arrested in Immigration Raid at a Houston Plant." *New York Times*, June 26, A15.

Ewick, Patricia, and Susan S. Silbey. 1998. *The Common Place of Law: Studies from Everyday Life*. Chicago: University of Chicago Press.

Feeley, Malcolm M. 1992. "Hollow Hopes, Flypaper, and Metaphors." *Law & Social Inquiry* 17: 745–60.

Feeley, Malcolm M., and Edward L. Rubin. 1998. *Judicial Policy Making and the Modern State: How the Courts Reformed America's Prisons*. Cambridge: Cambridge University Press.

Felstiner, William L. F., Richard L. Abel, and Austin Sarat. 1980–81. "The Emergence and Transformation of Disputes: Naming, Blaming, and Claiming . . ." *Law & Society Review* 15: 631–54.

Fields, Gary, and John R. Emshwiller. 2014. "For More Teens, Arrests by Police Replace School Discipline." *Wall Street Journal*, October 20. http://on.wsj.com/1sOeWIM.

Finkelman, Paul, ed. 1997. *Slavery and the Law*. Madison, WI: Madison House.

Foucault, Michel. 1977. *Discipline and Punish: The Birth of the Prison*. Trans. Alan Sheridan. New York: Random House.

Frankenberg, Ruth. 1996. "Whiteness and Americanness: Examining Constructions of Race, Culture, and Nation in White Women's Life Narratives." Pp. 62–77 in *Race*, ed. Steven Gregory and Roger Sanjek. Rutgers, NJ: Rutgers University Press.

Freeman, David. 2014. "Video Games Promote Racist Thoughts & Behavior, Study of White Gamers Shows." *Huffington Post*, March 25. http://www.huffingtonpost.com/2014/03/25/video-games-racise-linked-white-gamers_n_5023453.html.

Friedman, Lawrence M., Robert W. Gordon, Sophie Pirie, and Edwin Whatley. 1989. "Law, Lawyers, and Legal Practice in Silicon Valley: A Preliminary Report." *Indiana Law Journal* 64: 555–67.

Friedrichs, David O. 2001. *Law in Our Lives: An Introduction*. Los Angeles: Roxbury Publishing.

Frontline. 2013. "The Untouchables." January 22. http://www.pbs.org/wgbh/pages/frontline/untouchables/.

Galanter, Marc. 1974. "Why the 'Haves' Come Out Ahead: Speculations on the Limits of Legal Change." *Law & Society Review* 9: 95–160.

Garland, David. 2001. *The Culture of Control: Crime and Social Order in Contemporary Society*. Chicago: University of Chicago Press.

Gavigan, Shelley A. M. 2012. *Hunger, Horses, and Government Men: Criminal Law on the Aboriginal Plains, 1870–1905*. Vancouver: University of British Columbia Press.

Gawande, Atul. 2002. *Complications: A Surgeon's Notes on an Imperfect Science.* New York: Henry Holt.

Geertz, Clifford. 1983. "Local Knowledge: Fact and Law in Comparative Perspective." Pp. 167–217 in *Local Knowledge: Further Essays on Interpretive Anthropology.* New York: Basic Books.

Geismar, Haidy. 2013. *Treasured Possessions: Indigenous Interventions into Cultural and Intellectual Property.* Durham, NC: Duke University Press.

Gerber, Theodore P., and Sarah E. Mendelson. 2008. "Public Experiences of Police Violence and Corruption in Contemporary Russia: A Case of Predatory Policing?" *Law & Society Review* 42 (1): 1–44.

Gibson, James L., and Amanda Gouws. 1997. "Support for the Rule of Law in the Emerging South African Democracy." *International Social Science Journal* 152: 153–93.

Gilboy, Janet A. 1992. "Penetrability of Administrative Systems: Political 'Casework' and Immigration Inspections." *Law & Society Review* 26 (2): 273–314.

Gilmore, Ruth Wilson. 2007. *Golden Gulag: Prisons, Surplus, Crisis, and Opposition in Globalizing California.* Berkeley: University of California Press.

Goddard, Henry H. 1917. "Mental Tests and the Immigrant." *Journal of Delinquency* 2: 243–77.

Goehner, Amy Lennard, Lina Lofaro, and Kate Novak. 2004. "Ripple Effect: Where CSI Meets Real Law and Order." *Time,* November 1, 69.

Goffman, Alice. 2014. *On the Run: Fugitive Life in an American City.* Chicago: University of Chicago Press.

Goffman, Erving. 1974. *Frame Analysis: An Essay on the Organization of Experience.* Boston: Northeastern University Press.

Goodman, Brenda. 2007. "Day of Split Outcomes in Teenage Sex Case." *New York Times,* June 12, A12.

Goodman, Philip. 2008. "'It's Just Black, White, or Hispanic': An Observational Study of Racializing Moves in California's Segregated Prison Reception Centers." *Law & Society Review* 42: 735–70.

Gould, Stephen Jay. 1985. *The Flamingo's Smile: Reflections in Natural History.* New York: W. W. Norton.

Gramsci, Antonio. 1971. *Selections from the Prison Notebooks.* New York: International Publishers.

Grattet, Ryken, and Valerie Jenness. 2005. "The Reconstitution of Law in Local Settings: Agency Discretion, Ambiguity, and a Surplus of Law in the Policing of Hate Crime." *Law & Society Review* 39 (4): 893–942.

Grynbaum, Michael M. 2014. "Liberals Growing Frustrated with Mayor." *New York Times,* November 13, A24.

Gyory, Andrew. 1998. *Closing the Gate: Race, Politics, and the Chinese Exclusion Act.* Chapel Hill: University of North Carolina Press.

Hage, Ghassan. 2000. *White Nation: Fantasies of White Supremacy in a Multicultural Society*. New York: Pluto Press, Routledge.

Hall, Stuart. 1997. "Introduction." Pp. 1–11 in *Representation: Cultural Representations and Signifying Practices*, ed. Stuart Hall. New York: Sage Publications.

Halliday, Terence C. 1986. "Six Score Years and Ten: Demographic Transitions in the American Legal Profession, 1850–1980." *Law & Society Review* 20: 53–78.

Halliday, Terence C., and Gregory Shaffer, eds. 2015. *Transnational Legal Orders*. Cambridge: Cambridge University Press.

Haltom, William, and Michael McCann. 2004. *Distorting the Law: Politics, Media, and the Litigation Crisis*. Chicago: University of Chicago Press.

Hamill, Sean D. 2008. "A Goth Bonnie and Clyde, and Capture and Derision." *New York Times*, January 24, A12.

Haney López, Ian F. 1996. *White by Law: The Legal Construction of Race*. New York: New York University Press.

Harris, Angela P. 2000. "Equality Trouble: Sameness and Difference in Twentieth-Century Race Law." *California Law Review* 88 (6): 1923–2015.

Heckman, James J., and Brook S. Payner. 1989. "Determining the Impact of Federal Antidiscrimination Policy on the Economic Status of Blacks: A Study of South Carolina." *American Economic Review* 78: 138–77.

Heinz, John P., and Edward O. Laumann. 1982. *Chicago Lawyers: The Social Structure of the Bar*. New York: Russell Sage Foundation; Chicago: American Bar Foundation.

Heinz, John P., Robert L. Nelson, Rebecca L. Sandefur, and Edward O. Laumann. 2005. *Urban Lawyers: The New Social Structure of the Bar*. Chicago: University of Chicago Press.

Herbert, Bob. 2007a. "School to Prison Pipeline." *New York Times*, June 9, A29.

———. 2007b. "6-Year-Olds under Arrest." *New York Times*, April 9, A19.

Hier, Sean P. 2010. *Panoptic Dreams: Streetscape Video Surveillance in Canada*. Vancouver: University of British Columbia Press.

Hinton, Mercedes. 2005. "A Distant Reality: Democratic Policing in Argentina and Brazil." *Criminal Justice* 5: 75–100.

Hirsch, Susan F., and Mindie Lazarus-Black. 1994. "Introduction/Performance and Paradox: Exploring Law's Role in Hegemony and Resistance." Pp. 1–31 in *Contested States: Law, Hegemony and Resistance*, ed. Mindie Lazarus-Black and Susan F. Hirsch. New York: Routledge.

Hirschl, Ran. 2004. *Towards Juristocracy: The Origins and Consequences of the New Constitutionalism*. Cambridge, MA: Harvard University Press.

Hirsh, C. Elizabeth. 2008. "Settling for Less? Organizational Determinants of Discrimination-Charge Outcomes." *Law & Society Review* 42: 239–74.

Hoebel, E. Adamson, and Karl Llewellyn. 1941. *The Cheyenne Way: Conflict and Case Law in Primitive Jurisprudence.* Norman: University of Oklahoma Press.

Holmes, Oliver Wendell. 1881. *The Common Law.* Scanned and proofread by Stuart E. Thiel. Chicago, January 2000. http://www.constitution.org/cmt /owh/commonlaw.

Horsman, Reginald. 1981. *Race and Manifest Destiny.* Cambridge, MA: Harvard University Press.

Hund, John, and Malebo Kotu-Rammopo. 1983. "Justice in a South African Township: The Sociology of Makgotla." *Comparative and International Law Journal of South Africa* 16: 179–208.

Hurst, James Willard. 1964. *Law and Economic Growth: The Legal History of the Lumber Industry in Wisconsin, 1836–1915.* Cambridge, MA: Harvard University Press.

Jackson (MS) Daily News. 1954. "Bloodstains on White Marble Steps." May 18, 1.

Jenness, Valerie, and Ryken Grattet. 2005. "The Law-in-Between: The Effects of Organizational Perviousness on the Policing of Hate Crime." *Social Problems* 52: 337–59.

Jenness, Valerie, Cheryl L. Maxson, Jennifer Macy Sumner, and Kristy N. Matsuda. 2010. "Accomplishing the Difficult, but Not Impossible: Collecting Self-Report Data on Inmate-on-Inmate Sexual Assault in Prison." *Criminal Justice Policy Review* 21: 3–30.

Johnson, David T., and Franklin E. Zimring. 2009. *The Next Frontier: National Development, Political Change, and the Death Penalty in Asia.* Oxford: Oxford University Press.

Kahn, Paul W. 1999. *The Cultural Study of Law: Reconstructing Legal Scholarship.* Chicago: University of Chicago Press.

Kairys, David, ed. 1982. "Legal Reasoning." Pp. 11–17 in *The Politics of Law: A Progressive Critique,* ed. David Kairys. New York: Basic Books.

———. 1998. "Freedom of Speech." Pp. 190–215 in *The Politics of Law: A Progressive Critique,* ed. David Kairys. 3rd ed. New York: Basic Books.

Kennedy, Duncan. 1993. *Sexy Dressing Etc.: Essays on the Power and Politics of Cultural Identity.* Cambridge, MA: Harvard University Press.

———. 2002. "The Critique of Rights in Critical Legal Studies." Pp. 169–228 in *Left Liberalism/Left Critique,* ed. Wendy Brown and Janet Halley. Durham, NC: Duke University Press.

Klug, Heinz. 2000. *Constituting Democracy: Law, Globalism, and South Africa's Political Reconstruction.* Cambridge: Cambridge University Press.

Kohler-Hausmann, Issa. 2014. "Managerial Justice and Mass Misdemeanors." *Stanford Law Review* 66: 611–93.

Labaton, Stephen. 2007. "OSHA Leaves Worker Safety in Hands of Industry." *New York Times,* April 25, A1.

Lazarus-Black, Mindie. 1994. "Slaves, Masters, and Magistrates: Law and the Politics of Resistance in the British Caribbean, 1736–1834." Pp. 252–81 in *Contested States: Law, Hegemony and Resistance*, ed. Mindie Lazarus-Black and Susan F. Hirsch. New York: Routledge.

Lazarus-Black, Mindie, and Susan F. Hirsch, eds. 1994. *Contested States: Law, Hegemony and Resistance*. New York: Routledge.

Levine, Harry G., and Deborah Peterson Small. 2008. *Marijuana Arrest Crusade: Racial Bias and Police Policy in New York City, 1997–2007*. New York: New York Civil Liberties Union.

Lipsky, Michael. 1980. *Street-Level Bureaucracy: Dilemmas of the Individual in Public Services*. New York: Russell Sage Foundation.

Liptak, Adam. 2007. "Carefully Plotted Course Propels Gun Case to Top." *New York Times*, December 3, A16.

Los Angeles Times. 1994. "The Times Poll: Why They Voted." November 9, A22.

Lovell, George I. 2012. *This Is Not Civil Rights: Discovering Rights Talk in 1939 America*. Chicago: University of Chicago Press.

Lynch, Mona. 2010. *Sunbelt Justice: Arizona and the Transformation of American Punishment*. Stanford, CA: Stanford University Press.

Macaulay, Stewart. 1987. "Images of Law in Everyday Life: The Lessons of School, Entertainment, and Spectator Sports." *Law & Society Review* 21: 185–218.

———. 1989. "Popular Legal Culture: An Introduction." *Yale Law Journal* 98: 1545–58.

Macaulay, Stewart, Lawrence M. Friedman, and John Stookey. 1995. "Introduction." Pp. 1–18 in *Law & Society: Readings on the Social Study of Law*, ed. Stewart Macauley, Lawrence M. Friedman, and John Stookey. New York: W. W. Norton.

Maine, Henry Sumner. 2008. *Ancient Law*. 1861. Amazon Digital Services. Kindle ed.

Malinowski, Bronisław. 1982. *Crime and Custom in Savage Society*. 1926. Totowa, NJ: Littlefield, Adams.

Manza, Jeff, and Christopher Uggen. 2006. *Locked Out: Felon Disenfranchisement and American Democracy*. New York: Oxford University Press.

Martinez, Ruben. 1994. "Perspective on Prop. 187: The Nightmare Is Coming True." *Los Angeles Times*, November 28, B7.

Marx, Karl. 1906. *Capital: A Critique of Political Economy*. Vol. 1. Trans. Samuel Moore and Edward Aveling. Chicago: Charles H. Kerr and Company.

Mashaw, Jerry L. 1983. *Bureaucratic Justice: Managing Social Security Disability Claims*. New Haven, CT: Yale University Press.

Massoud, Mark Fathi. 2013. *Law's Fragile State: Colonial, Authoritarian, and Humanitarian Legacies in Sudan*. New York: Cambridge University Press.

Mather, Lynn, Craig A. McEwen, and Richard J. Maiman. 2001. *Divorce Lawyers at Work: Varieties of Professionalism in Practice.* New York: Oxford University Press.

Matsuda, Mari. 1987. "Looking to the Bottom: Critical Legal Studies and Reparation." *Harvard Civil Rights–Civil Liberties Law Review* 22: 323–400.

Maveety, Nancy, and Anke Grosskopf. 2004. "'Constrained' Constitutional Courts as Conduits for Democratic Consolidation." *Law & Society Review* 38: 463–88.

McCann, Michael W. 1992. "Reform Litigation on Trial." *Law & Social Inquiry* 17: 715–43.

———. 1994. *Rights at Work: Pay Equity Reform and the Politics of Legal Mobilization.* Chicago: University of Chicago Press.

———. 2014. "The Unbearable Lightness of Rights: On Sociolegal Inquiry in the Global Era." *Law & Society Review* 48: 245–74.

McKinley, Jesse. 2008. "Challenges to Bans on Handguns Begin." *New York Times*, June 28, A9.

Merry, Sally Engle. 2006. *Human Rights and Gender Violence: Translating International Law into Local Justice.* Chicago: University of Chicago Press.

Mertz, Elizabeth. 1988. "The Uses of History: Language, Ideology, and Law in the United States and South Africa." *Law & Society Review* 22: 661–85.

Mezey, Naomi. 1994. "Legal Radicals in Madonna's Closet: The Influence of Identity Politics, Popular Culture, and a New Generation on Critical Legal Studies." *Stanford Law Review* 46: 1835–61.

———. 2003a. "Erasure and Recognition: The Census, Race and the National Imagination." *Northwestern University Law Review* 97 (4): 1701–67.

———. 2003b. "Law as Culture." Pp. 37–72 in *Cultural Analysis, Cultural Studies, and the Law*, ed. Austin Sarat and Jonathan Simon. Durham, NC: Duke University Press.

Miller, Toby. 2003. "What It Is and What It Isn't: Cultural Studies Meets Graduate Student Labor." Pp. 73–104 in *Cultural Analysis, Cultural Studies, and the Law*, ed. Austin Sarat and Jonathan Simon. Durham, NC: Duke University Press.

Minow, Martha. 1987. "Interpreting Rights: An Essay for Robert Cover." *Yale Law Journal* 96: 1860–1915.

Mnookin, Robert, and Louis Kornhauser. 1979. "Bargaining in the Shadow of Law: The Case of Divorce." *Yale Law Journal* 88: 950–97.

Mogul, Joey L., Andrea J. Ritchie, and Kay Whitlock. 2012. *Queer (In)justice: The Criminalization of LGBT People in the United States.* Boston: Beacon Press.

Moore, Erin P. 1994. "Law's Patriarchy in India." Pp. 89–117 in *Contested States: Law, Hegemony and Resistance*, ed. Mindie Lazarus-Black and Susan F. Hirsch. New York: Routledge.

Moore, Sally Falk. 1973. "Law and Social Change: The Semi-Autonomous

Social Field as an Appropriate Subject of Study." *Law & Society Review* 7: 719–46.

Morsy, Soheir A. 1996. "Beyond the Honorary 'White' Classification of Egyptians: Societal Identity in Historical Context." Pp. 175–98 in *Race*, ed. Steven Gregory and Roger Sanjek. Rutgers, NJ: Rutgers University Press.

Munoz, Cecilia. 1994. "Harassment in the Wake of Proposition 187." *Christian Science Monitor*, December 27, 19.

Murakawa, Naomi. 2006. "The Racial Antecedents to Federal Sentencing Guidelines." *Roger Williams University Law Review* 11: 473–94.

Nader, Laura. 1990. *Harmony Ideology: Justice and Control in a Zapotec Mountain Village.* Stanford, CA: Stanford University Press.

New York Times. 1951. "Southwest Winks at 'Wetback' Jobs." March 28, 34.

———. 2008. "A Supreme Court on the Brink." July 3, A22.

———. 2009a. "Arpaio's America." February 9, A26.

———. 2009b. "Who's Running Immigration?" March 4, A20.

Nina, Daniel. 1993. "Community Justice in a Volatile South Africa: Containing Community Conflict, Clermont, Natal." *Social Justice* 20: 129–42.

Obasogie, Osagie K. 2010. "Do Blind People See Race? Social, Legal, and Theoretical Considerations." *Law & Society Review* 44: 585–616.

———. 2014. *Blinded by Sight: Seeing Race through the Lens of the Blind.* Stanford, CA: Stanford University Press.

Orfield, Gary, and Chungmei Lee. 2007. *Historic Reversals, Accelerating Resegregation, and the Need for New Integration Strategies.* Los Angeles: Civil Rights Project–Proyecto Derechos Civiles, UCLA.

Page, Joshua. 2011. *The Toughest Beat: Politics, Punishment, and the Prison Officers Union in California.* New York: Oxford University Press.

Pager, Devah. 2007. *Marked: Race, Crime, and Finding Work in an Era of Mass Incarceration.* Chicago: University of Chicago Press.

Parenti, Christian. 1999. *Lockdown America: Police and Prisons in the Age of Crisis.* New York: Verso.

Penner, Andrew M., and Aliya Saperstein. 2008. "How Social Status Shapes Race." *Proceedings of the National Academy of Sciences* 105: 19628–30.

Pérez-Perdomo, Rogelio. 2011. "Legal Education in Late Twentieth-Century Latin America." Pp. 56–64 in *Law in Many Societies*, ed. Lawrence M. Friedman, Rogelio Pérez Perdomo, and Manuel A. Gómez. Stanford, CA: Stanford University Press.

Perry-Kessaris, Amanda. 2008. *Global Business, Local Law: The Indian Legal System as a Communal Resource in Foreign Investment Relations.* Burlington, VT: Ashgate.

Polletta, Francesca. 2000. "The Structural Context of Novel Rights Claims: Southern Civil Rights Organizing, 1961–1966." *Law & Society Review* 34: 367–406.

Portes, Alejandro, and Rubén Rumbaut. 2001. *Legacies: The Story of the Immigrant Second Generation*. Berkeley: University of California Press.

Provine, Doris Marie. 2007. *Unequal under Law: Race in the War on Drugs*. Chicago: University of Chicago Press.

Rafter, Nicole Hahn. 1997. *Creating Born Criminals*. Champaign: University of Illinois Press.

Rajagopal, Balakrishnan. 2005. "Limits of Law in Counter-Hegemonic Globalization: The Indian Supreme Court and the Narmada Valley Struggle." Pp. 183–217 in *Law and Globalization from Below: Towards a Cosmopolitan Legality*, ed. Boaventura de Sousa Santos and César A. Rodríguez-Garavito. Cambridge: Cambridge University Press.

Ramji-Nogales, Jaya, Andrew I. Schoenholtz, and Philip G. Schrag. 2007. "Refugee Roulette: Disparities in Asylum Adjudication." *Stanford Law Review* 60: 295–412.

Rapping, Elayne. 2003. *Law and Justice as Seen on TV*. New York: New York University Press.

Reichman, Ravit. 2005. "Making a Mess of Things: The Trifles of Legal Pleasure." *Law, Culture and the Humanities* 1: 14–34.

Reiman, Jeffrey H. 1984. *The Rich Get Richer and the Poor Get Prison: Ideology, Class, and Criminal Justice*. 2nd ed. New York: Macmillan.

Rios, Victor M. 2011. *Punished: Policing the Lives of Black and Latino Boys*. New York: New York University Press.

Roberts, John G. 2005. "Opening Statement before the U.S. Senate Committee on the Judiciary." Reprinted in "Judges Are Like Umpires." *Los Angeles Times*, September 13, A10.

Robinson, Eugene. 2008. "A Whitewash for Blackwater?" *Washington Post*, December 9, A19.

Roediger, David R. 1999. *The Wages of Whiteness: Race and the Making of the American Working Class*. London: Verso.

Romney, Lee, and Julie Marquis. 1994. "Youth Dies as Medical Treatment Is Delayed." *Los Angeles Times*, November 23, A3.

Rosenberg, Gerald N. 1991. *The Hollow Hope: Can Courts Bring about Social Change?* Chicago: University of Chicago Press. (2nd ed. published in 2008.)

Rudd, Kevin. 2008. "The Children of Gordon Gekko." Speech given in Sydney, Australia. *The Australian*, October 6. http://www.theaustralian.com.au/archive/news/the-children-of-gordon-gekko/story-e6frg7b6-1111117670209.

Rusche, Georg, and Otto Kirchheimer. 1939. *Punishment and Social Structure*. Trans. Moishe Finkelstein and Otto Kirchheimer. New York: Columbia University Press.

Salyer, Lucy E. 1995. *Laws Harsh as Tigers: Chinese Immigrants and the Shaping of Modern Immigration Law*. Chapel Hill: University of North Carolina Press.

Santos, Boaventura de Sousa. 1995. *Toward a New Common Sense: Law, Science and Politics in Paradigmatic Transition*. New York: Routledge.

Sarat, Austin. 2000. "Imagining the Loss of the Father: Loss, Dread, and Mourning in *The Sweet Hereafter*." *Law & Society Review* 34 (1): 3–46.

———. 2004a. "Preface." Pp. x–xii in *The Blackwell Companion to Law and Society*, ed. A. Sarat. Malden, MA: Blackwell Publishing.

———. 2004b. "Vitality amidst Fragmentation: On the Emergence of Post-realist Law and Society Scholarship." Pp. 1–11 in *The Blackwell Companion to Law and Society*, ed. Austin Sarat. Malden, MA: Blackwell Publishing.

Sarat, Austin, and Stuart Scheingold. 1998. *Cause Lawyering: Political Commitments and Professional Responsibilities*. Oxford: Oxford University Press.

———. 2006. *Cause Lawyers and Social Movements*. Stanford, CA: Stanford University Press.

Sarat, Austin, and Susan Silbey. 1988. "The Pull of the Policy Audience." *Law & Policy* 10: 97–166.

Sarat, Austin, and Jonathan Simon, eds. 2003. *Cultural Analysis, Cultural Studies, and the Law*. Durham, NC: Duke University Press.

Sarat, Austin, and Martha Merrill Umphrey, eds. 2013. *Reimagining To Kill a Mockingbird: Family, Community, and the Possibility of Equal Justice under the Law*. Boston: University of Massachusetts Press.

Sarkeesian, Anita. 2014. "It's Game Over for 'Gamers.'" *New York Times*, October 29, A29.

Savage, David G. 2001. "High Court Sets High Bar as Term Begins." *Los Angeles Times*, October 2, A20.

Savelsberg, Joachim J. 1994. "Knowledge, Domination, and Criminal Punishment." *American Journal of Sociology* 99: 911–43.

Saxton, Alexander. 1971. *The Indispensable Enemy: Labor and the Anti-Chinese Movement in California*. Berkeley: University of California Press.

Scheingold, Stuart. 1974. *The Politics of Rights: Lawyers, Public Policy and Political Change*. New Haven, CT: Yale University Press.

Scheingold, Stuart, and Austin Sarat. 2004. *Something to Believe In: Politics, Professionalism and Cause Lawyers*. Stanford, CA: Stanford University Press.

Scheper-Hughes, Nancy. 1995. "Who's the Killer? Popular Justice and Human Rights in a South African Squatter Camp." *Social Justice* 22: 143–64.

Scheppele, Kim L. 2004. "Constitutional Ethnography: An Introduction." *Law & Society Review* 38: 389–406.

Schlanger, Margo. 2015. "Trends in Prisoner Litigation, as the PLRA Enters Adulthood." *UC Irvine Law Review* 5: 153–78.

Schoenfeld, Heather. 2009. *The Politics of Prison Growth: From Chain Gangs to Work Release Centers and Supermax Prisons, Florida, 1955–2000*. Evanston, IL: Northwestern University Press.

Schwartz, Herman. 2000. "A Force for Civil Rights Now Fights Them." *Los Angeles Times*, March 26, M2.

Schwartz, Richard D. 1954. "Social Factors in the Development of Legal Control: A Case Study of Two Israeli Settlements." *Yale Law Journal* 63: 471–91.

Scott, James C. 1985. *Weapons of the Weak: Everyday Forms of Peasant Resistance.* New Haven, CT: Yale University Press.

Selva, Andrea. 2003. "'Vagoni separati per gli immigrati.'" *La Repubblica*, January 18, 2003, 27.

Seng, Yvonne J. 1994. "Standing at the Gates of Justice: Women in the Law Courts of Early Sixteenth-Century Üsküdar, Istanbul." Pp. 184–206 in *Contested States: Law, Hegemony and Resistance*, ed. Mindie Lazarus-Black and Susan F. Hirsch. New York: Routledge.

Seron, Carroll. 1996. *The Business of Practicing Law: The Work Lives of Solo and Small Firm Attorneys.* Philadelphia: Temple University Press.

———. 2007. "The Status of Legal Professionalism at the Close of the Twentieth Century: *Chicago Lawyers* and *Urban Lawyers*." *Law & Social Inquiry* 32: 581–607.

Seron, Carroll, Joseph Pereira, and Jean Kovath. 2004. "Judging Police Misconduct: 'Street-Level' versus Professional Policing." *Law & Society Review* 38 (4): 665–710.

Sheleff, Leon S. 1975. "From Restitutive Law to Repressive Law: Durkheim's *The Division of Labor in Society* Revisited." *Archives Européennes de Sociologie* 16: 15–45.

Sillen, Robert. 2006. "Cruel and Unusual Prison Health Care." *Sacramento (CA) Bee*, October 8, E1, E5.

Simon, Jonathan. 2007. *Governing through Crime.* New York: Oxford University Press.

Smart, Carol. 1989. *Feminism and the Power of Law.* London: Routledge.

Smigel, Erwin O. 1960. *The Wall Street Lawyer: Professional Organization Man.* Glencoe, IL: Free Press of Glencoe.

Solomon, Peter H., Jr. 2004. "Judicial Power in Russia: Through the Prism of Administrative Justice." *Law & Society Review* 38: 549–82.

Sorial, Sarah. 2013. "Free Speech, Hate Speech, and the Problem of (Manufactured) Authority." *Canadian Journal of Law and Society/Revue Canadienne Droit et Société* 29: 59–75.

Sousa Santos, Boaventura de, and César A. Rodríguez-Garavito. 2005. *Law and Globalization from Below: Towards a Cosmopolitan Legality.* Cambridge: Cambridge University Press.

Stoddard, Lothrop. 1922. *Revolt against Civilization; The Menace of the Under-Man.* New York: Charles Scribner's Sons.

Stryker, Robin. 2007. "Half Empty, Half Full, or Neither: Law, Inequality, and Social Change in Capitalist Democracies." *Annual Review of Law and Social Science* 3: 69–97.

Suárez-Navaz, Liliana. 2006. *Rebordering the Mediterranean: Boundaries and Citizenship in Southern Europe*. New York: Berghahn Books.

Suellentrop, Chris. 2013. "In the Footsteps of Lara Croft." *New York Times*, December 15, AR9.

Sutton, John R. 2001. *Law/Society: Origins, Interactions, and Change*. Thousand Oaks, CA: Pine Forge Press.

Tamanaha, Brian Z. 2001. *A General Jurisprudence of Law and Society*. Oxford: Oxford University Press.

Tatlow, Didi Kirsten. 2014. "China Executed 2,400 in Last Year, Group Says." *New York Times*, October 23, A8.

Taub, Nadine, and Elizabeth M. Schneider. 1998. "Women's Subordination and the Role of Law." Pp. 328–55 in *The Politics of Law: A Progressive Critique*, ed. D. Kairys. 3rd ed. New York: Basic Books.

Taylor, Margaret H. 2008. "Refugee Roulette in an Administrative Law Context: The Déjà Vu of Decisional Disparities in Agency Adjudication." *Stanford Law Review* 60: 475–502.

Thomas, Jeffrey E., and Franklin G. Snyder, eds. 2010. *The Law and Harry Potter*. Durham, NC: Carolina Academic Press.

Thompson, Ginger. 2009. "Report Faults Homeland Security's Efforts on Immigration." *New York Times*, February 12, A19.

Tichenor, Daniel J. 2002. *Dividing Lines: The Politics of Immigration Control in America*. Princeton, NJ: Princeton University Press.

Tigar, Michael E., and Madeleine R. Levy. 1977. *Law and the Rise of Capitalism*. New York: Monthly Review Press.

Tushnet, Mark. 1999. *Taking the Constitution Away from the Courts*. Princeton, NJ: Princeton University Press.

Tyler, Tom R. 1990. *Why People Obey the Law*. New Haven, CT: Yale University Press.

U.S. Congress. House Committee on Agriculture. 1947. "Farm Labor Supply Program." Hearings before the Committee. 80th Congress, 1st Session.

U.S. Congress. House Committee on Immigration and Naturalization. 1920. "Biological Aspects of Immigration." Hearings before the Committee. 66th Congress, 2nd Session.

———. 1923. "Restriction of Immigration." Hearings before the Committee. 68th Congress, 1st Session.

U.S. Congress. Senate. 1877. *Report of the Joint Special Committee to Investigate Chinese Immigration*. Senate Report No. 689. 44th Congress, 2nd Session.

U.S. Congress. Senate Committee on the Judiciary. 1980. "Department of Justice Authorization and Oversight for Fiscal Year 1981." Hearing before the Committee. 96th Congress, 2nd Session.

U.S. Congress. Senate Immigration Commission. 1911. *Immigration Commission (Dillingham Commission) Report*. Volume 1. Senate Document 747. 61st Congress, 3rd Session.

U.S. Government Accountability Office. 2008. "Case Studies from Ongoing Work Show Examples in Which Wage and Hour Division Did Not Adequately Pursue Labor Violations." GAO-08-973T. Testimony before the Committee on Education and Labor, House of Representatives.

Valverde, Mariana. 2012. *Everyday Law on the Street: City Governance in an Age of Diversity*. Chicago: University of Chicago Press.

Van Asselt, Harro, Francesco Sindico, and Michael A. Mehling. 2008. "Global Climate Change and the Fragmentation of International Law." *Law & Policy* 30 (4): 423–49.

Venkatesh, Sudhir. 2008. *Gang Leader for a Day: A Rogue Sociologist Takes to the Streets*. New York: Penguin Books.

Volpp, Leti. 2000. "Blaming Culture for Bad Behavior." *Yale Journal of Law & Humanities* 12: 89–116.

Wacquant, Loïc. 2010. "Class, Race & Hyperincarceration in Revanchist America." *Daedalus* 139: 74–90.

Waldron, Mary Anne. 2013. *Free to Believe: Rethinking Freedom of Conscience and Religion in Canada*. Toronto: University of Toronto Press.

Ward, Geoff. 2012. *The Black Child-Savers: Racial Democracy and American Juvenile Justice*. Chicago: University of Chicago Press.

Washington Post and Times Herald. 1954. "A 'Healing' Decision." May 18.

Weaver, Vesla M. 2007. "Frontlash: Race and the Development of Punitive Crime Policy." *Studies in American Political Development* 21: 230–65.

Weber, Max. 1954. *Max Weber on Law in Economy and Society*. Ed. Max Rheinstein. Boston: Harvard University Press.

———. 1958. *The Protestant Ethic and the Spirit of Capitalism*. Trans. Talcott Parsons. New York: Scribner's.

Western, Bruce. 2006. *Punishment and Inequality in America*. New York: Russell Sage Foundation.

Wiedeman, Reeves. 2014. "#ACTIVISM." *New Yorker*, December 22 and 29, 44, 46.

Williams, Patricia J. 1991. *The Alchemy of Race and Rights: Diary of a Law Professor*. Cambridge, MA: Harvard University Press.

Williams, Raymond. 1958. *Culture and Society, 1780–1950*. London: Chatto and Windus.

———. 1961. *The Long Revolution*. London: Chatto and Windus.

———. 1983. *Keywords: A Vocabulary of Culture and Society*. New York: Oxford University Press.

Williams, Timothy, and Jason Grant. 2008. "In a Doll's Head, Some in Harlem See a Setback." *New York Times*, July 26, A16.

Williams-Forson, Psyche. 2006. *Building Houses out of Chicken Legs: Black Women, Food, and Power*. Chapel Hill: University of North Carolina Press.

Winn, Jane Kaufman, and Tang-chi Yeh. 2011. "Advocating Democracy: The Role of Lawyers in Taiwan's Political Transformation." Pp. 45–55 in *Law in Many Societies*, ed. Lawrence M. Friedman, Rogelio Pérez Perdomo, and Manuel A. Gómez. Stanford, CA: Stanford University Press.

Woodmansee, Martha. 2003. "The Cultural Work of Copyright: Legislating Authorship in Britain, 1837–1842." Pp. 65–96 in *Law in the Domains of Culture*, ed. Austin Sarat and Thomas R. Kearns. 1998. Ann Arbor: University of Michigan Press.

Worth, Robert F. 2008. "Tiny Voices Defy Fate of Girls in Yemen." *New York Times*, June 29, A8.

Zackin, Emily. 2008. "Popular Constitutionalism's Hard When You're Not Very Popular: Why the ACLU Turned to Courts." *Law & Society Review* 42: 367–96.

Zimring, Frank E. 2003. *The Contradictions of American Capital Punishment*. Oxford: Oxford University Press.

Index

Ashar, Sameer, 156, 157, 158, 162, 167

Asian Americans, U.S. Census Bureau and the creation of legal category, 67

Association for Law, Culture, and the Humanities, 180

asylum decisions, U.S.: disparate outcomes in, 92–93; examples of legal pluralism in, 91–92. *See also* administrative law

Banished (Beckett and Herbert), 27

Banking Act (1933), repeal of, 20

Baptist, Edward, 62

Basic Instinct (film), trial narrative structure of, 181, 182

Beckett, Katherine, 27

Bell, Derrick, 135, 136, 137, 164, 167, 172

Bengaluru (previously Bangalore), law and global capitalism study, 21

Bentham, Jeremy, 23

Berger, Peter, 1, 2, 10, 129, 194, 195

Berman, Harold J., 55

Berrey, Ellen, 137

Black Child Savers, The (Ward), 62

Blackmon, Douglas A., 111

Blackwater Worldwide, 93–94, 108

Blackwell Companion to Law and Society, The, 192

Blumberg, Abraham, 140

Border Patrol, U.S., 117, 118

Boyle, Elizabeth Heger, 97, 98

Bridgman, Percy, 188

Brigham, John, 7

broken-cookie grievance, "law as culture as law" (Mezey) and, 175, 176

"broken windows" policing, 27

Brown, Michael, 27, 73

Brown v. Board of Education (1954), 180; Cold War pressure and, 161; as example of law-on-the-books and law-in-action, 137; failures of, 136, 137, 170, 192; hopes for, 135–36, 163; incarceration surge, 78; indirect impacts of, 139, 144; narrow goals of, 160; potential of, 154; public opinion and, 135–36; Thurgood Marshall and, 148

Buck v. Bell (1927), 60–61. *See also* Holmes, U.S. Supreme Court Justice Oliver Wendell

Bumiller, Kristin, 152

Bureaucratic Justice (Mashaw), 91

Butler, Judith, 44

California Civil Rights Initiative (1996). *See* affirmative action: opposition to

California Department of Corrections and Rehabilitation (CDCR): racial sorting by, 67–68; rape of transgender prisoner, 44, 46

California gold rush, anti-Chinese racism, 63

Calvinism, 12. *See also* Weber, Max

Campbell v. Chaves, 48

Canada: closed-circuit surveillance in, 26; indigenous people and "low law" opposed to "high law" in, 102–3

capitalism and law, 12, 18–20, 100, 104–5, 167–70

Carlin, Jerome, 32

Cassidy v. Chertoff, 142, 143. *See also* "repeat–players" versus "one–shotters" (Galanter)

cause lawyering, 157–58

Cecil, Dawn, 40, 186

critique of rights, 147–57, 167;
critique of the critique of rights,
156–58, 172, 192
*Cultural Analysis, Cultural Studies, and
the Law* (Sarat and Simon), 176
cultural images, counterhegemonic
power of, 184. *See also* film,
images of law in; media, images
of law in
cultural turn: focus of, 173; in legal
studies, 180; as product of our
times, 176–77; shared subjective
meaning and, 176; variegated
reality of, 9
culture, difficulty in defining, 173–
74. *See also* law and culture
Culture of Control, The (Garland), 25
culture war: Durkheim's theory and,
17–18
customary law. *See* indigenous law,
examples of legal pluralism
and

Darian-Smith, Eve, 103, 104
Dealing in Virtue (Dezalay and Garth),
34
death penalty, U.S., 29, 37, 89–90,
106–7, 165–66
debtor's prison redux, and culture
of control, 28
DeGraffenreid v. General Motors (1983),
71. *See also* intersectionality
DeLand, Michael, 55
Delgado, Richard, 61, 70
deregulation movement, 20
de Sousa Santos, Boaventura, 51,
98–99, 104, 156, 167
Dezalay, Yves, 34, 35
dialectical materialism. *See* Marx,
Karl
Dillingham Immigration Commission Report (1911), 67

Dirty Harry (film), image of law and,
178, 179, 183
disability laws, legal pluralism and,
91
Discipline and Punish (Foucault), 23
disenfranchisement of felons in
U.S., 79–80. *See also* incarceration rates
Distorting the Law (Haltom and Mc-
Cann), 39
District of Columbia Home Rule Act
(1973), 89
District of Columbia v. Heller (2008),
148, 149; and gun control, 89
division of labor in society. *See*
Durkheim, Émile
divorce lawyers, local, 35
domestic law, within Santos's six
"clusters" of law in capitalist
societies, 104
drug laws: intent standard, 166;
kind-of-people targeting, 114–
15; medical marijuana and legal
pluralism, 88; racial discrimination in, 114–16, 134
dual legal systems, European and
indigenous law in colonial and
postcolonial contexts, 101–2
Dudziak, Mary, 167
Durkheim, Émile, 13; collective
conscience, 15–16, 18; division
of labor in society, 15–16, 18;
mechanical solidarity, 14–15, 18;
organic solidarity, 14–15, 16, 17,
18; repressive versus restitutive
law, 15–16, 18

economic interests and racial categories, 62–67
economics and the law, 19–23,
62–67, 140–44, 167–69. *See also*
capitalism and law

economic status and race, 65–67

Edelman, Lauren, 144, 145, 146, 164, 167

Edelman, Murray, 120

elective affinity. *See* Weber, Max

Elementary and Secondary Education Act (1965), 138

Emergency Quota Act (1921), 60

Emerson, Robert, 123, 124

employer sanctions, as example of symbolic law, 120–21

"endogeneity of law" (Lauren Edelman), 145, 164, 192

Enigma of Diversity, The (Berrey), 137

Epp, Charles, 76

Equal Employment Opportunity Commission (EEOC), U.S., 164

eugenics, 60–61, 64

European Union (EU), 99; supranational jurisdiction and, 96

Everyday Law on the Street (Valverde), 95

Ewick, Patricia, 54, 55

"extreme ethnographies," 131, 172–73

Fair Labor Standards Act, 157

Fair Sentencing Act of 2010, 114

Farmer v. Brennan, 146–47

fatherhood, law and, 177–78, 179–80, 189

Federal Death Penalty Abolition Act, 29

feeblemindedness theory, 59–62, 64, 66

Feeley, Malcolm M., 154, 159

Felstiner, William L. F., 57

Ferguson, Missouri: arrest warrants issued in, 27–28; police shooting of Michael Brown in, 27; police violence, 73

feudal law, transformation into capitalist law, 19–20, 169–70

film, images of law in, 177–81, 182, 183

finance capitalism, unfettered, 20

financial market collapse (2008), 14, 20, 171, 172

Finkelman, Paul, 62

Firearms Control Regulations Act, 86. See also *District of Columbia v. Heller* (2008)

Foucault, Michel, 23–24, 53, 189

Fountain Valley Chateau Blanc Homeowners' Association v. Department of Veteran Affairs (1998), 95. See also homeowners' associations; legal pluralism

Frankenberg, Ruth, 83–84

free speech: hate speech and, 151; Kairys on, 4–5, 127–28

Free to Believe (Waldron), 17, 18

free trade agreements, legal pluralism and jurisdictional conflict in, 99

Friedman, Lawrence M., 18, 35, 167

Furman v. Georgia (1972), 89. See also death penalty, U.S.

Galanter, Marc, 140, 141, 142, 143, 144, 146, 164, 167, 171, 172

Gang Leader for a Day (Venkatesh), 131, 132

Garland, David, 25, 26, 28, 29, 75, 78, 189

Garth, Bryant, 34, 35

Gavigan, Shelley, 102

Gawande, Dr. Atul, 5–7

gay rights, "pragmatic resistance" and, 52–53

Geertz, Clifford, 173

Geismar, Haidy, 103

Hurst, James Willard, on legal history of lumber industry in Wisconsin, 20–21
hybrid legal systems, in colonial contexts, 100–103

immigration: Bracero Program, 118–19; in California, 68; Chinese exclusion, 63–65; employer sanctions, 119–20; feeblemindedness theory and, 59–62; identity of Andalusians as Europeans, 69; IRCA, 119; local laws and ordinances, 87; nonenforcement of laws, 118–19; Proposition 187 in California, 121–22; and racial categorization, 66, 191; structural dilemmas associated with, 117–22; symbolic law, 120–22; undocumented immigrants, 121–22, 156; U.S. Quota Law of 1921, 60
immigration agency, U.S.: bad reputation of, 117–18; budget, 119; discretion of officials, 118–19; Immigration and Customs Enforcement (ICE), 117, 120; Immigration and Naturalization Service (INS), 68, 118, 119; structural dilemmas, 117–22. *See also* immigration
Immigration Reform and Control Act of 1986 (IRCA), U.S., 119
incarceration. *See* prison
incarceration rates: disenfranchisement and effect on U.S. elections, 79–80; job search experiences, 80–81; racial profiling and, 77–78
indigenous law, examples of legal pluralism and, 101, 102–3
industrial capitalist production, 23

informal law, Trobriand Islanders and, 30
intellectual property, indigenous law and legal pluralism and, 103
intent standard: immunizing power of, 166; perniciousness of, 164–66
"interest convergence" (Delgado and Stefancic), 61
internationalization of legal practice, 34–35
international law, legal pluralism and jurisdictional conflict in, 97, 99
Internet, and nonenforcement of copyright law, 110
intersectionality, 70–72
Invitation to Sociology (Berger), 1, 2
Israeli communities, social control in, 31
Italian Supreme Court, blue jeans rape decision, 139–40

Jenness, Valerie, 125
"Jim Crow juvenile justice," 62–63
Johnson, David, 106
Just Words (Conley and O'Barr), 44

Kairys, David, 4, 127
Kennedy, Duncan, 146, 167, 184, 185
Kimbrough v. United States (2007), 114. *See also* drug laws; kind-of-people targeting
kind-of-people targeting, 114–17; and drug tax law, 116, 117
King, Martin Luther, Jr., 113
Kirchheimer, Otto, 22–23, 25, 189
Klug, Heinz, 105
Kohler-Hausmann, Issa, 26–27, 131
Kotu-Rammopo, Malebo, 101
kvutza, informal controls and, 31, 32
Kyoto Protocol, 99

language, and legal construction of reality, 42–43

"late modernity," chronic insecurities tied to, 25

Laughlin, Harry, 60

Laumann, Edward O., 33

law: convergence between economy and, 19–23, 62; definitions of, 30, 36; fatherhood and, 177–78, 179–80, 189; informal controls and, 31; medicine and, 7–8; neoliberalism and, 172; as social construction, 7; socially constructed meanings of race, 70–72

law and culture, 174–88; children's literature, 182; "critical cultural studies of law" (Coombe) and, 185; Harry Potter Alliance and social issues, 188; images of law in film and other media, 177–82, 183; "law as culture as law" (Mezey), 175–76; "postsocial environment" (Sarat and Simon) and, 176; power of culture over law, 174–75; power of law over culture, 174; power of shared subjective meaning and, 176; production and regulation of identity through cultural lens, 186–87; scholarship on interpenetration of, 177–80

Law and Globalization from Below (de Sousa Santos and Rodríguez-Garavito), 51

Law and Societies in Global Contexts (Darian-Smith), 103

Law and the Rise of Capitalism (Tigar and Levy), 19–20

"law as culture as law" (Mezey), "broken cookie" grievance and, 175, 176

"Law at Work" (Edelman), 172

law in everyday life: concept of, 5; different views of, 3; hegemony of, 45–46, 49, 53, 190; language and law, 42–43, 44–45; legal consciousness, 54–57; legal metaphors, 190; media coverage of legal cases, 39–41; myth of American litigiousness, 57–58, 175; "semi-autonomous social fields," 41; speed limits and, 174

"law in the image," 173

law-on-the-books and law-in-action: in civil rights law compliance, 163–64; in employer sanctions, 119–20; "endogeneity of law" and, 145, 164, 192; gap between, administrative discretion, 109–10, 120, 123, 127, 129, 131; hate crime statutes, 125; in immigration, 117; "interorganizational knowledge," 124; legal pluralism and, 124; nonenforcement, 110–11, 113, 130–31; police, 115, 124–27; rhetoric of law, 127–28; selective enforcement of, 110, 111, 190; special-interest pressures, 123; structural dilemmas, 117–22, 127, 129, 190. See also Brown v. Board of Education (1954); critical legal studies (CLS); "Why the 'Haves' Come Out Ahead" (Galanter)

Lawyers in Society (Abel and Lewis), 32

Lazarus-Black, Mindie, 49, 50, 192

legal consciousness: among children, 55; in Chadron, Nebraska, 56; chameleon-like quality of, 54–55; concept of, 55–57; cultural turn and, 173; and myth of American litigiousness, 57–58; transformation in colonial societies, 100–102. See also hegemony legal education, social change and, 34–35

legal pluralism, 169, 191; in administrative law, 90–93, 124; in asylum decisions, 91–92; in colonial and postcolonial contexts, 100–104; critique of, 104; in death penalty cases, 89–90; definition of, 86; in disability claims, 91; federalism and jurisdictional levels in United States, 86–90; focus of, 8; in free trade agreements, 99; in gun control laws, 88–89; "hard" versus "soft" legal authority, 98; and hegemony, 103–4; in human rights, 97–98; medical marijuana, 88; minimum wage laws, 87; municipal regulations, 95–96; in public and private jurisdictions, 93–96; resistance by indigenous people within, 102–3; Santos's six "clusters" of types of law, 104–5; South African reconstitution, 105; supranational jurisdictions, 96–97; in tax law, 87; in worker safety rules, 87

legal profession, socioeconomic forces in, 32–36

legislation, social change and, 138–40

Levy, Madeline R., 19–20, 23, 169

Lewis, Philip, 32

Lipsky, Michael, 92

Llewellyn, Karl, 41, 42

Lloyd v. Tanner (1972), 128. *See also* free speech

local custom, and legal pluralism, 96–97

"localized globalisms" (de Sousa Santos), 98–99

Locke, John, 13

loitering laws: and gang injunctions, 114; selective enforcement of, 112–13. *See also* anticamping laws; kind-of-people targeting; vagrancy laws

"Looking beyond Caged Heat" (Cecil), 40

Louima, Abner, 72

Lovell, George, 154–55

Macaulay, Stewart, 18, 167, 178, 179, 180, 182

Maiman, Richard J., 35

Maine, Henry: criticisms of, 13–14, 18, 20; status to contract, theory of, 13–14

Malinowski, Bronislaw, 30, 31, 36, 41, 191

"manifest destiny," 63

Manza, Jeff, 79

Maritime Transportation Security Act, 142, 143

Marked (Pager), 80

Marx, Karl: dialectical materialism, 23; evolutionary theory, 13; Foucault and, 25; Reiman and, 19; Rusche and Kirchheimer and, 22–23, 189

Mashaw, Jerry L., 91

"mass misdemeanor" arrests, Kohler-Hausmann on, 26–27

Massoud, Mark Fathi, 160, 167

"masters of national space," white self-regard as, in Australia, 83

"material determinism," 61–62

Mather, Lynn, 35

Maveety, Nancy, 158, 167

Maynard-Moody, Steven, 76

McCann, Michael, 39, 57, 58, 153, 154, 155, 170, 186

McDonald's coffee burn case, 39, 175, 186

racial profiling: of African American men, 73, 74; of Arab men, 74–75; collective biases, 77; and fear of crime, 78–79; of Hispanics, 74; and incarceration rates, 77–78; of white men ("Bubba" profile), 75; Willie Horton, 79. *See also* kind-of-people targeting; racial discrimination; racism

racism: in Australia, 83; in Chinese exclusion, 63–65; convict lease system, 62–63; dispossession of Native Americans, 63; economic interests and, 62–67; employment obstacles and incarceration, 80–81; feeblemindedness theory and, 59, 61; and immigration, 59–62; in Italy, 69–70; "race law" (Harris), 61; romanticization of white "outlaws," 81–82; in Spain, 69; status biases, 14; white consciousness, 83–84. *See also* race; racial discrimination; racial profiling

Rajagopal, Balakrishnan, 52, 160, 161

Ramji-Nogales, Jaya, 92

Rapping, Elayne, 40, 186

rationalization, 11–12, 18, 25

"Refugee Roulette" (Ramji-Nogales et al.), 92

Reichman, Ravit, 183

Reiman, Jeffrey, 19

"repeat-players" versus "one-shotters" (Galanter), 140–42

repressive versus restitutive law. *See* Durkheim, Émile

resistance: by child brides in Yemen, 50–51, 156, 161, 169; concept of, 46–47; counterhegemonic potential of, 52, 53, 104; counterhegemonic power

of cultural images and, 184–85; cultural studies scholarship and, 185; Harry Potter Alliance and, 188; in Narmada Valley, India, 52, 156, 160–61; by opponents of apartheid in South Africa, 49; "pragmatic," 52; in prison, 47–49; by slaves in British Caribbean, 49; using law as tool of, 46–53, 102, 156; by women in sixteenth-century Istanbul, 50; by the Zapotec in Oaxaca, Mexico, 53

Revolt against Civilization (Stoddard), 60

rights, limits and potential of, 146–53, 170

Ríos, Victor, 75, 76

Roberts, U.S. Supreme Court Chief Justice John, 4

Rodríguez-Garavito, César, 51, 156, 167

Roediger, David, 83

Roe v. Wade (1973), 138. *See also* courts: and social change

Rosenberg, Gerald N., 137, 138, 143, 153, 154, 160, 163, 167, 172

Rowling, J. K., 182

Rubin, Edward L., 159

Rumbaut, Rubén, 68

Rusche, Georg, 22–23, 25, 189

same-sex marriage, 17, 18

sanctuary movement (1980s), 42

Sandefur, Rebecca L., 33

Saperstein, Aliya, 66

Sarat, Austin, 57, 176, 177, 183, 187, 189, 192

Sarkeesian, Anita, 40

Scheingold, Stuart, 146, 167, 172

Scheper-Hughes, Nancy, 101

Scheppele, Kim, 162, 167

The Chicago Series in Law and Society
Edited by John M. Conley and Lynn Mather

Dealing in Virtue: International Commercial Arbitration and the Construction of a Transnational Legal Order
by Yves Dezalay and Bryant G. Garth

Rights at Work: Pay Equity Reform and the Politics of Legal Mobilization
by Michael W. McCann

The Language of Judges
by Lawrence M. Solan

Reproducing Rape: Domination through Talk in the Courtroom
by Gregory M. Matoesian

Getting Justice and Getting Even: Legal Consciousness among Working-Class Americans
by Sally Engle Merry

Rules versus Relationships: The Ethnography of Legal Discourse
by John M. Conley and William M. O'Barr